Failing Teachers?

In an age of public accountability the issue of failing teachers is a highly topical one. This book describes the research undertaken during the Teaching Competence Project, a two-year research project which looked at five main areas surrounding this subject. The areas examined are:

- the views and experiences of head teachers who have dealt with cases of alleged incompetence
- a sample of teachers at both primary and secondary levels who have been labelled incompetent
- the observations and opinions of pupils aged between 6 and 16 on teacher incompetence
- the perspectives of union officials, LEA personnel officers and advisers, governors, parents and inspectors on those labelled poor teachers
- an analysis of incompetence procedures in various professions and in countries outside the UK.

The findings on such a sensitive subject make very interesting reading and this book provides an invaluable insight into what actually happens when a teacher is accused of failing.

Ted Wragg is Professor of Education in the School of Education at Exeter University where **Gill Haynes, Caroline Wragg** and **Rosemary Chamberlin** are all Research Fellows. They have between them a wealth of practical experience and are internationally recognised researchers in the field of education.

Failing Teachers?

E.C. Wragg, G.S. Haynes,
C.M. Wragg, R.P. Chamberlin

London and New York

First published 2000 by Routledge
11 New Fetter Lane, London EC4P 4EE

Simultaneously published in the USA and Canada
by Routledge
29 West 35th Street, New York, NY 10001

Routledge is an imprint of the Taylor & Francis Group

© 2000 E.C. Wragg., G.S. Haynes, C.M. Wragg, R.P. Chamberlin

Typeset in Goudy by
Keystroke, Jacaranda Lodge, Wolverhampton
Printed and bound in Great Britain by
Biddles Ltd, Guildford and King's Lynn

British Library Cataloguing in Publication Data
A catalogue record for this book is available from the British Library

Library of Congress Cataloging in Publication Data
Failing teachers? / E.C. Wragg . . . [et al.].
    p.   cm.
  Includes bibliographical references (p.) and index.
   1. Teacher effectiveness—Great Britain Case studies. I. Wragg,
E. C. (Edward Conrad)
LB1775.4.G7F35   2000
371.14′4′0941—dc21   99-37818
                               CIP

ISBN 0-415-22021-1 (hbk)
ISBN 0-415-22022-X (pbk)

Contents

List of tables

Preface

This book describes the research undertaken during the Teaching Competence Project, a two-year research project funded by the Gatsby Charitable Foundation. There were five interlinked studies in the research.

Study 1 was an analysis of the views and experiences of head teachers who had dealt with a case of alleged incompetence, based on 60 interviews and 684 case studies completed by a national sample of head teachers in primary and secondary schools.

Study 2 was based on a sample of 70 teachers in primary and secondary schools who have been labelled 'incompetent', and a second study of 57 teacher colleagues, not regarded as incompetent themselves, who have worked alongside them.

Study 3 analysed the views and experiences of 519 pupils aged six to sixteen, to elicit their constructs about teacher competence.

Study 4 investigated the views and experiences of 21 officials from the six major teacher and head teacher unions, 20 local education authority personnel officers and advisers and 74 chairs of school governing bodies, as well as a sample of 100 parents and 10 inspectors.

Study 5 was an analysis of incompetence procedures in various professions and countries other than the United Kingdom.

During the project we used mainly questionnaires and interviews, and these produced a substantial amount of data about a sensitive topic into which very little large-scale research has been conducted. There was a mixture of good news, in that many teachers were given support within and from outside the school and managed to improve their performance, and less happy news about the teachers who left the profession, or about the stresses and ill health that could sometimes ensue.

This book describes what actually happens during a rarely researched process, as seen through the eyes of three major constituencies:

1 **Professionals in the school** – heads and teachers, reported in Chapters 3, 4 and 5.

2 **Professionals outside the school** – teacher union and local education authority (LEA) officers, described in Chapters 6 and 7.
3 **The mainly lay people or 'clients'** – governors, parents and pupils, reported in Chapters 8, 9 and 10.

Acknowledgements

We should like to express our gratitude to the Gatsby Charitable Foundation for supporting the Teaching Competence Project. We should also like to thank the many heads, teachers, union and local authority officers, governors, parents and pupils who co-operated so fully with us, especially those heads and teachers who found the recall of events stressful.

Chapter 1

The need for skilful teaching

Why is there a question mark in the title of this book? For a book describing research into teachers alleged to be incompetent, the title *Failing Teachers?* appears to cast doubt on the issue. School inspection reports show that most teachers are regarded as professionally 'competent' or better, so who is failing whom? Are some teachers failing their pupils, or is society failing its teachers? Or when teachers have been identified as 'incompetent', is there some uncertainty about whether this label is accurate?

The answer is that we inserted the question mark deliberately, because the research project reported in this book was one of the most difficult we have ever undertaken. Although some teachers were agreed by all concerned to be failing to do their job properly, even in many instances by the accused teachers themselves, there were numerous other cases where the origins, causes, effects and responsibility were disputed. One person's 'incompetent teacher' can be another person's 'innocent victim'. The ambiguity of the title and its question mark, therefore, represent the uncertainty of the whole situation as we encountered it. It was the best (or the worst, depending on how one looks at it) example of what is often termed 'multiple perceptions of reality'. That is why we sometimes use the word 'alleged' in this account of our research findings.

Professional competence is not something detached from the rest of someone's life. For many people in a job, the expertise for which they are being paid constitutes a very important part of their whole life. If a practitioner is alleged to be lacking the necessary skills to carry out professional duties effectively, this can be a shattering blow. To attack someone's professional competence is to attack that person as a whole, not just one element, which is why a strong emotional aura sometimes cloaked the cases we studied. The following four quotes all come from people interviewed during the research:

I went to hell and back.

You're totally on your own. I was always frightened I was going to go off on long-term sick.

The whole affair has been like a sentence of death on me.

I was subjected to a barrage of criticism . . . and I was always on my own. . . .
The upshot was that I left in quite a state. I had no confidence when I left.

Who suffered anguish? Whose health was affected? Who felt alone? The first
and second of the quotes above are from head teachers and the third and fourth
are from teachers; whether you are the accuser or the accused, allegations of
incompetence tear at the very soul of those involved.

The fact that research into alleged incompetence is highly problematic,
however, is not a reason for walking away from it, and in reporting here the
findings of the Teaching Competence Project, a two-year research project funded
by the Gatsby Charitable Foundation, we were determined to shed light on what
had previously been largely ignored. Since it costs a great deal of money to train
and employ teachers, we were particularly interested in what were thought to be
successful practices in helping those regarded as incompetent to improve their
teaching. We did not undertake the research with any a priori intention either
to condemn or to excuse teachers said to be failing at their work, simply to
explore and explain what appeared to be happening. Like other human beings we
did, in some cases, form our own private opinions about the rights and wrongs of
particular cases, but we have tried to report what we encountered as objectively
as possible.

The failure of some teachers to do their job properly has been a taboo subject
in educational research. Very little systematic enquiry exists and what has been
done is often small in scale. As a research topic it is full of traps and pitfalls, for
how should terms like 'incompetence' or 'failure' be defined and who decides the
criteria? It is also extraordinarily difficult to carry out fieldwork, as the people
involved in a case of alleged incompetence are often in a highly emotional state.
It would not be easy to knock on someone's door and say 'We're carrying out a
study of incompetent teachers and we've been given your name . . .'.

The issue of competence and incompetence in the teaching profession is
not a new one, however. Teachers have always needed a wide range of subject
knowledge and a large repertoire of professional skills. Teaching children to read
and write, to understand the world around them, to grasp and be able to apply
fundamental mathematical and scientific principles, to use their developing
intelligence and imagination, to live and work harmoniously with others, all
these require considerable and varied skills and knowledge.

In the speedily moving society in which we now live, an effective teacher
needs to know and understand the ever-changing content of the subjects and
topics being taught, as well as be able to manage a class, explain clearly, ask intelligent and appropriate questions, and monitor and assess learning. Most of our
previous research has studied the thousands of practitioners who carry out these
duties skilfully, so it was with some sadness that we addressed the problems of the
minority who are judged to be falling short of what is expected.

WHAT IS PROFESSIONAL 'COMPETENCE'?

There has often been argument about what constitutes professional competence or its obverse, as indeed there has been debate about whether or not teaching can be called a 'profession'. Normally members of a profession are those that are paid to carry out the work of that profession, but in some definitions higher qualities are sought, to distinguish a profession from a mere 'job'. Usually these involve the profession having some say in who enters it and remains in it; about its conditions of employment, further training, evaluation and remuneration; as well as about the values and beliefs that underpin it and the practices it follows. With greater government intervention in such matters, however, this kind of definition has become less firm.

Teaching offers a certain degree of professional autonomy, but at the time we carried out the Teaching Competence Project there was no General Teaching Council in England to parallel the General Medical Council, and many of the usual determinants of a 'profession' had been assumed by central government, which laid down the curriculum for both schools and teacher training and effectively determined the structure and some of the detail of remuneration and conditions of service. Furthermore, the government had begun to prescribe some aspects of how teachers should teach, putting forward a detailed framework for daily literacy and numeracy hours in primary schools that teachers were expected to follow.

Two elements often found in a dictionary definition of 'competence' are relevant to teaching: (1) 'legally qualified' and (2) 'capable to do particular task or tasks'. Teachers in state schools are 'competent' in the sense that they are legally qualified to teach, and so, if they are said to be 'incompetent', it must be that they do not possess the necessary skill, ability, or will, to carry out their duties properly.

Being competent or incompetent in the classroom, however, is not as clear cut a distinction as being 'short' or 'tall', where fairly exact heights could be specified and then measured. The context is important. Since teaching is a multi-dimensional set of activities, it is possible that incompetent teachers may be capable in one aspect, but incapable in another. They might be competent to teach German to 16 year olds, but not to teach German to 13 year olds; to teach reading to the Reception class, but not mathematics to 11 year olds. They may know their subject matter, yet be unable to create the orderly environment needed to teach it effectively. That 'competence' is not an all-embracing quality is demonstrated by the frequent use, in educational writings, of the plurals 'competences' or 'competencies' for aspects of the job that teachers can do adequately or well. Although incompetent teachers are referred to almost daily in the news media, analysis of the concept of 'competence' does not feature prominently in academic writings.

One educational context in which 'competence' does arise is that of vocational education and training. In vocational training the teacher's job is nowadays seen as breaking down the subject matter into bite-sized chunks of skills and checking that the learner can carry them out adequately. Learners can then be judged competent to change a wheel, or give an injection. The same principle is sometimes employed in the initial and further training of teachers themselves in the practice known as Competency Based Teaching. Teaching is broken down into numerous discrete micro-skills, like 'asking higher order questions' or 'explaining a concept', for example.

A paper from the Unit for the Development of Adult Continuing Education (Assessment of Competence Steering Group, 1989) sounded a warning note about this atomised view of teaching, which saw education as 'a set of free-standing bricks from which individuals can build their own structures', rather than as a lengthy unified process:

> The critical question is how far it is possible to break up complex taught processes into smaller learned components without losing overall coherence. The clear danger is that the smaller units will concentrate on narrow objectives which are easily designed, achieved and measured [skills] at the expense of broader objectives [knowledge and understanding].
>
> (p. 4)

The paper emphasises that competence is concerned with what people can *do*, not what they *know*, and, therefore, requires clearly defined and measurable standards. It is more concerned with outcomes than with the learning process. As competence is a measure of what a person can do at a particular time, the writers also point out that there is no guarantee that the person will continue to be competent, saying:

> There is an assumption in all qualifications that the individual has demonstrated a certain level of ability and will continue to do so. However, the clear link between competence and doing, rather than understanding or knowing, calls this assumption into question very sharply.
>
> (p. 11)

Criticism of that particular concept of 'competence' tends to emphasise its narrowness. Like being said to be 'satisfactory', it sounds unexciting. There is a possible conflict, also, between the model of the good teacher as a 'reflective practitioner' and that of the 'competent teacher' able to carry out a set variety of tasks only to an adequate and measurable standard. We expect teachers to develop and adapt, to be able to respond to changing circumstances and select appropriate strategies. These are not qualities encompassed within a narrow notion of competence.

Broader definitions of competence were put forward by the Teacher Training Agency in its work on the competence of head teachers (1995). They include a variety of *tasks* such as assessing the quality of teaching and learning, or liaising with parents and the community, and *abilities* such as the ability to 'adapt to changing circumstances and new ideas', or 'negotiate, delegate, consult and co-ordinate the efforts of others'. The attempt has been made to list the skills, abilities and qualities required by successful head teachers. Similar work has been done for newly qualified teachers and for experienced teachers also.

The longer and broader the list, however, and the more it attempts to encompass important, but sometimes diffuse areas, such as values or interpersonal skills, the harder it is to measure how well people are performing. None the less, despite these difficulties of definition, measurement and identification, there are bound to be teachers who are not as skilled as their colleagues and who, in some cases, may seriously disadvantage the children they teach. It may be hard, but it is still worth the effort of addressing the issues and trying to improve current practice. We shall return to questions about definitions of competence in Chapter 2, when some of the research into professional incompetence is described.

Identifying and defining competence and incompetence in teaching

Even if the quality of teaching were to improve significantly, it may not happen fast and far enough to match the escalating demands on teachers. Unfortunately the accompanying public and press debate about teaching competence has too often been over-simplified and caricatured as 'traditional' versus 'progressive', 'formal' versus 'informal', 'phonics' versus 'real books', when the reality of classroom life is that many teachers prefer to use a mixture of methods rather than fill out a single stereotype.

In discussion between people outside the profession there is sometimes more agreement about the skills and qualities that make up competence, or are missing among those thought to be incompetent, than there is in the research and evaluation literature. Good teachers, it is commonly held, must be keen and enthusiastic, well organised, firm but fair, stimulating, know their stuff, and be interested in the welfare of their pupils. Few would attempt to defend the converse: that teachers should be unenthusiastic, boring, unfair, ignorant, and not care about their pupils. However, once the scrutiny of teaching is translated into the more precise terms demanded by the tenets of rigorous systematic enquiry, the easy agreement of casual conversation evaporates. Biddle and Ellena (1964), reporting the Kansas City role studies, found that there was not even clear agreement among teachers, parents and administrators about the role teachers should play. We shall be considering research addressing incompetence again in Chapter 2, so in this chapter we concentrate on the background to general issues of 'effectiveness' and 'competence'.

There have been attempts to seek consensus about 'effective' practice in research projects, especially by linking classroom processes to outcome. For example, Gage (1978), summarising research studies which had attempted to relate teaching style to children's learning, concluded that in the early years of schooling certain kinds of teacher behaviour did show some consistent relationship to children learning reading and arithmetic. From this he derived a set of prescriptive 'Teachers should' statements like 'Teachers should call on a child by name before asking the question', 'Teachers should keep to a minimum such activities as giving directions and organising the class for instruction', or 'During reading-group instruction, teachers should give a maximal amount of brief feedback and provide fast-paced activities of the "drill" type.' The Labour government introduced a daily literacy hour into primary schools in 1998, in which the hour was divided into four segments, each with prescribed types of activity, said to be based on research findings.

There has been some criticism of prescriptions based on summaries of research findings on competence and its obverse. Much American work on teacher effectiveness was based on short-term tests of memory. Formal didactic styles of teaching often show up better on short-term measures and could, therefore, easily be translated into long-term programmes on relatively flimsy evidence. The claims of the original pioneers of a new method or approach to teaching have sometimes proved difficult to replicate. Moreover, in experimental studies, the 'gains' of method A compared with method B have often been slight.

This last argument is skilfully countered by Gage (1985) in his book *Hard Gains in the Soft Sciences*. He shows how significant policy decisions, in fields such as medicine and public health, are often made on a degree of statistical 'superiority' that would receive little attention in educational research. He quotes examples of trials of beta-blockers and low cholesterol diets to reduce the incidence of heart attacks, which showed only 2.5 and 1.7 per cent differences respectively between the incidence of a second heart attack among members of 'experimental' compared with 'control' groups, but which none the less led to significant changes in public health policy and practice.

Doyle (1978) observed that reviewers of research into teacher effectiveness 'have concluded, with remarkable regularity, that few consistent relationships between teacher variables and effectiveness can be established'. Even reviewers of the same studies have sometimes reached different conclusions about them (Giaconia and Hedges 1985). Some investigations have used meta-analysis (Glass 1978) to aggregate studies and identify trends and effects, but the conclusions are often mixed. It is frequently the case, especially when pioneers of some new approach conduct research into their own practice, that a noticeable Hawthorne effect may occur. Later investigators find it difficult to replicate the impressive findings of the original pioneers, so prescribing in detail how all teachers should teach, on the basis of one or two studies, is not justifiable. That Kulik *et al.* (1979) found consistently higher learning gains in classes using the Keller Plan (a form of teaching which involves pupils completing individual assignments) compared with control groups, is not an argument for saying that all teachers should copy the approach. Teachers often aspire to achieve a mixture of shorter-term (complete a worksheet, learn a principle) and longer-term (develop a sustained interest in music, lead a healthy lifestyle) objectives.

The difficulty of identifying and evaluating teaching skills and their effectiveness is neatly illustrated by an old, but none the less interesting experiment at the University of Michigan. Guetzkow, Kelly and McKeachie (1954) divided first year students on a general psychology course into three groups. The first group was given a formal lecture course with regular tests, the second and third groups took part in tutorials and discussions. At the end of the course the lecture group not only outperformed the tutorial discussion groups on the final examination, but was also more favourably rated by the students. On the surface, therefore, this appears to represent a victory for lecturing and testing on two commonly used criteria: test performance and student appraisal.

The investigators discovered, however, that the students in the discussion groups scored significantly higher than the lecture groups on a measure of interest in psychology, the subject being studied. They hypothesised that, although the lecture group students gave a favourable rating of the teaching they had received, this may have been because they had less anxiety about grades for the course through their weekly feedback from test scores. It was decided to monitor the subsequent progress of all the groups. Three years later not one student in the lecture group had opted to study the subject further, but 14 members of the two discussion and tutorial groups had chosen to major in psychology. Thus, on short-term criteria the lecture method was superior, but taking a longer perspective, the discussion method appeared to motivate students more powerfully, and ultimately some must have learned a great deal more.

Defining teaching skill in such a way that all would agree, therefore, is not a simple matter. If we were to say that teaching skills are whatever strategies teachers use to enable children to learn, then most people would want to rule out intimidation, humiliation, the use of corporal punishment or other forms of teacher behaviour of which they personally happen to disapprove. It is perhaps easier when seeking a definition of teaching skill to describe some of the characteristics of skilful teaching which might win some degree of consensus, though not universal agreement.

The first might be that the behaviour concerned *facilitates pupils' learning of something worthwhile*, such as facts, skills, values, concepts, how to live harmoniously with one's fellows, attitudes, or some other outcome thought to be desirable. The notion of something being 'worthwhile' brings together both content and values in teaching. Skill is not a unidimensional concept. Teaching someone to steal might, in one sense, be 'skilfully' done, but it would attract odium from society, rather than admiration. A second quality therefore could be that it is acknowledged to be a skill by those competent to judge, and this might include teachers, teacher trainers, inspectors, advisers and learners themselves. We shall see in Chapter 10 that pupils can be shrewd in their appraisal of the teacher's craft, and that the ability to explain is often highly rated by them.

For it to be a recognised part of a teacher's professional competence *a skill should be capable of being repeated*, not perhaps in exactly the same form, but as a fairly frequent rather than a single chance occurrence. A chimpanzee might randomly produce an attractive colourful shape once in a while, given a brush and some paint, but an artist would produce a skilfully conceived painting on a more regular basis. Teachers who possess professional skills, therefore, should be capable of manifesting these consistently, not on a hit-or-miss basis.

A skill should *enable children both to learn and understand*. One frequently cited observation on skills is that of the philosopher Gilbert Ryle (1949) who distinguished, in his book *The Concept of Mind*, between being able to state a factual proposition and perform a skilful operation. The difference between 'knowing that' and 'knowing how', referred to in the field of vocational education at the beginning of this chapter, for example, is the difference between inert knowledge and intelligent action. Unfortunately, some competent teachers are not especially articulate about their skill, and it would be wrong to assert that skill may only be recognised as such if the person manifesting it is capable of explaining and analysing it in textbook language. The intelligence of an action may perfectly well be explained by another, and the behaviour is not necessarily unintelligent or shallow if its perpetrator is tongue-tied about it.

One problem encountered in defining teaching skills is that though in some contexts the term 'skill' has good connotations, attracts adulation, is a gift of the few, the result of years of practice or the mark of an expert, in other circumstances it is looked down upon, regarded as mechanical, the sign of a rude technician rather than an artist. We tend, for instance, to admire a surgeon's skill or that of a tennis player. Both may have had the same years of dedicated practice, but the intellectual nature of the knowledge and understanding required by the surgeon is vastly more exacting than that required by an elite sports performer.

Where the imagination is involved, even more fine distinctions exist. A sculptor would probably be disappointed to read a report that described his latest masterpiece as an example of 'skill'. Eulogies in the expressive arts are expected to contain words like 'imaginative' and 'creative', or even 'genius'. For those who liken teachers more to expressive artists than to surgeons, the very term 'skill' may be seen as belittling, reducing creative endeavour to mechanical crudity. It is difficult to dry-clean the term of these emotional associations with other kinds of human enterprise.

This uncertainty about the proper standing of the notion of skill when applied to teaching is partly explained by the varied nature of the teacher's job. Pressing the right button on a video recorder, or writing legibly on the blackboard require but modest competence, and are operations that most people could learn with only a little practice. Responding to a disruptive adolescent, or knowing how to explain a difficult concept to children of different ages and abilities by choosing the right language register, appropriate examples and analogies, and reading the many cues which signal understanding or bewilderment, require years of practice as well as considerable intelligence and insight. While the term 'interpersonal skills' is now quite widespread, there is still some reluctance to classify human relationships in this way.

There is not the space here to document the many forms of enquiry into teaching effectiveness which have been undertaken, nor the thousands of 'findings' of classroom observation and process analysis reported in the literature around the world. These are in any case to be found in several standard reference books such as that by Dunkin and Biddle (1974); Delamont (1976); Cohen and Manion (1981); Stallings and Mohlman (1985); Wragg (1984, 1999) and many others.

Since the hope of research into teaching has often been to establish a body of knowledge which would show some consistency about what successful teachers do, several writers have attempted to establish theories of teaching and learning based on systematic empirical enquiry. Techniques such as meta-analysis (Glass 1978) have been developed which aggregate quantitative studies based on correlation coefficients, chi-squares, or analysis of variance, and determine an overall effect size. Thus, it is possible to calculate from several studies the average relationship between, say, the teacher's use of praise and pupils' learning.

Although the apparent neatness of such aggregations may appeal to some administrators looking for guidance from research, the proposition that fairly exact relationships can be discovered between what teachers do or are, and what pupils learn, has been criticised by several writers. An early review by Jackson (1962) described the findings of half a century of study on the relationship between teachers' personalities and pupil learning as so low in intellectual food value that it is almost embarrassing to discuss them. Even in later research, small, if statistically significant, correlations of around 0.2 or 0.3 have been commonplace, leaving a great deal still unexplained.

The more carefully conducted quantitative analyses about teaching, as opposed to teacher effectiveness, have nevertheless yielded some useful and relevant information, even though much less has been delivered than was once hoped. For example, the extremely busy nature of the teacher's job is now well documented. Teachers may have up to 200 days a year with their classes, and an early survey by Jackson (1962) showed over 1,000 interpersonal exchanges in a day; teachers' use of praise seemed relatively infrequent and haphazard (Brophy 1981); some teachers in inner-city schools spent up to 75 per cent of their time trying to keep order (Deutsch 1960); teachers allowed on average one second between a pupil answer and their own statement (Rowe 1972).

It is quite clear that in the course of the millions of exchanges in which teachers may engage during a quite short phase of their career, they can find little time for a leisurely scrutiny of classroom processes. This is highly relevant to the present research, because when teachers are alleged to be incompetent, they are expected to improve, to change their behaviour for the better. Yet changing styles that have been shaped by thousands of hours of practice is not easy, even when being observed and tutored. Only half of a large sample of primary and secondary teachers said they had changed their classroom behaviour as a result of being formally appraised (Wragg et al. 1996).

With little time to think up fresh strategies during an actual lesson, many teachers develop fairly fixed patterns of teaching which may well be laid down at the training stage. These become *deeply embedded structures*. When new curricula, school reorganisation or other changes in circumstances come along, it is difficult to unlearn habits and strategies which have been rehearsed millions of times, even if they are no longer appropriate. Hence the criticism in some school inspection reports of teachers who have not looked critically at their own teaching styles, or the difficulties experienced by teachers trying to use a fresh curriculum with old teaching methods. Even highly skilled teachers found it difficult to change and adapt during the 1980s and 1990s. For those who were not especially competent, change and adaptation sometimes eluded them completely.

THE NEED FOR SKILFUL TEACHING

All professions have to be able to rely on their members' competence, for if they were generally incompetent, why should the public pay them for their services? Professionals, rather than amateurs, are paid because they are assumed to be the very best, and this applies in sports, as well as in professions like medicine, law and teaching. Furthermore, society needs to feel assured that professionals have been properly trained and monitored. Most of us are lay people in fields other than our own, so we have few ways of knowing, except by supposition and intuition, whether the professionals we meet and use from time to time are indeed masters of their field. If we do suspect them of incompetence there is often a feeling of impotence on our part. We are not ourselves experts, so will anyone believe us if we say that those who are regarded as such and paid for their professional expertise, are not, in our humble opinion, as competent as they should be? Dependency on expert advice and services increases when daily life becomes more complex.

During the last few years of the twentieth century there were many factors which combined to demand from teachers even higher levels of professional competence. They included the rapid growth in the acquisition of knowledge; the changing nature not only of adult employment, as millions of jobs disappeared from manufacturing industry, but also of recreation and leisure; greatly increased public pressure for accountability, accompanied by numerous additional demands and changes to curriculum, assessment and conditions of service; the development of new forms of educational, information and communication technologies, and the ever-broadening role of the teacher, with demands on skill spilling over into other professional fields, like 'administrator', 'social worker' and 'manager'.

Each single one of these individual issues could have justified a radical review of the teacher's professional role, and of the nature of professional competence required to accommodate change and improve practice. In combination they formed an overwhelming pressure for competence from all practitioners, even the many who already manifested a high degree of skill in the classroom. Since there were about 400,000 teachers in primary and secondary schools in the last few years of the twentieth century, it was not too surprising that many teachers struggled with the changing and increasing demands on them, while a few appeared to have great difficulty in coping at all.

Teaching in the twenty-first century is bound to be multi-faceted, as it had to be in the last years of the twentieth century, since teachers must possess many kinds of skill. This is in stark contrast with the nineteenth century, when teacher training institutions were known as 'normal schools', on the grounds that there was some single 'norm' endorsed by society. The function of a training establishment was to perpetuate this stereotype, and a 'Master of Method' was employed in the model school to ensure that each new generation of teachers was poured into the same approved mould (Rich 1933). Today the factors mentioned above combine to require levels of skill, understanding, imagination and resilience from novice and experienced teachers which demand considerably more professional competence than the rudimentary common sense and mechanical application fostered by the 'normal' schools of the nineteenth century.

The massive explosion of knowledge gathering during the last 50 years has produced colossal banks of data in such profusion that no human being is now capable of grasping more than the tiniest fraction of their contents. Computer-stored files of data offer speedy access to new research reports in numerous major and minor fields, and the largest stores, in subjects like chemistry and biology, contain millions of abstracts. There is an enormous difference between 'information', of which society possesses countless tons, and 'knowledge' which is inside children's heads. It would be wrong to assume that the mere existence of a society saturated in information will in itself ensure the successful transformation of this external information into internalised knowledge. Teachers increasingly become annotators of these extensive fields of information: shaping, fashioning, interpreting and explaining them.

It is not only in the pure and applied sciences that knowledge has burgeoned, but also in several other areas of human endeavour, including the humanities, with thousands of new books published and articles in many fields being added each year. In addition to this formidable advance in the discovery of new information there has been a considerable development of new skills. Transplant and bypass surgery, for example, unknown only a few years ago, have become a standard part of many surgeons' professional armoury.

The implications for teachers of this knowledge explosion are clear. First, if you cannot know everything, you must know something. Hence the many efforts made, either at regional or national level, to determine the *content* of education – what children of a particular age or level of ability ought to learn, or by teachers themselves at local level to shape and implement a coherent curriculum. Second, if you cannot know or learn everything, you must be able to find out for yourself, and that is why the *process* of learning, either autonomously or with others, has become important.

Mastery of learning processes is in addition to, not instead of, the learning of actual content. Since their pupils can acquire only a tiny fraction of the knowledge and skills currently available to humanity, teachers must develop teaching strategies which not only transmit information, but also encourage children to learn both independently and as a member of a group. Although no committee would ever have composed Beethoven's Fifth Symphony, it is also unlikely that any individual could have sent a rocket to the moon. A great deal of human achievement will in future be the result of both individualism and teamwork.

Alongside the demands placed on teachers by the expansion of knowledge and skills were those caused by the significant social changes in recent years which took place on a scale unparalleled in any period other than wartime. During the 1970s one million jobs disappeared from manufacturing industry in Britain, and millions more were obliterated during the following two decades. Most were unskilled and semi-skilled forms of employment which will probably never return. No employer is likely to get rid of a fork lift truck in order to provide employment for several unqualified workers with big biceps.

Faced with youth unemployment on a large scale, many teachers, especially in inner-city schools, found during the 1980s and 1990s that traditional forms of motivation, such as urging pupils to work hard at school so that they would obtain a good job, no longer had the appeal they once enjoyed. Disaffection over the apparent futility of learning was even experienced by quite young primary pupils. It offered another formidable challenge to the professional ingenuity of the teacher.

Employers, meanwhile, were able to erect artificial barriers when applicants for jobs vastly exceeded the actual vacancies, requiring public examination successes for posts previously taken by the less well qualified, or specifying that a degree would be needed for what had formerly been non-graduate professions. This spiralling demand for qualifications applied yet more pressure on teachers to use their skills effectively during the compulsory years of schooling. Parents of their pupils were all too well aware, from their own life experiences and that of others they knew, that in our increasingly technological and bureaucratic society those who leave school under-educated, for whatever reason, are at risk, likely to be unemployed, or fall victim to loan sharks and the other predators in society. Pressure on schools from parents and public increased as a result.

There are, of course, more optimistic predictions about the future: that labour will shift out of the factory and into the leisure industry, or into rewarding and fulfilling jobs working with people instead of machines; that we shall have more free time in future and be relieved of the tedium of monotonous and dangerous jobs; that early retirement will give a boost to community and life-long education. However, these are no less demanding on teachers' skills. To enjoy leisure adults must have learned how to use it fruitfully. Citizens in the twenty-first century may well live to be 90, 100 or more. They are more likely to be willing to learn throughout their very long lives if they have been fired and enthused, rather than rebuffed and demoralised in school.

The quality of personal relationships between teacher and taught can be a significant factor in successful teaching and learning. Any such quality is not a replacement for other kinds of proficiency, more a valuable adjunct to them. Positive social relationships in a classroom are a direct consequence of the interpersonal skill of teachers, or their lack of it, for they usually set the tone in a class, or have to take the initiative to improve relationships should they go awry. A notion of teaching skill that embraced only the transmission of knowledge would be a limited one in such a context. Teachers are now not only expected to pass on what has been learned over the centuries, but to achieve a great deal more as well.

As the twenty-first century progresses more and more people may commence or move to work in service industries, in fields such as care of the growing number of elderly citizens, in the many forms of communication, information and entertainment media, while others will run small businesses. This shift out of the factories and into closer contact with people, rather than machinery, requires a high degree of imagination, inventiveness, drive and interpersonal skills. Society expects such crucial personal qualities and skills to be established in primary and secondary schools, as well as in post-school education, so teachers who can nurture them are valuable, while those who cannot are seen as failures.

Public pressure for accountability increased considerably throughout the 1980s and 1990s, and it was an international phenomenon. Uncertainty over employment, scarcity of resources and demands for proper scrutiny of any enterprise receiving funding, public or private, combined to increase emphasis on a high degree of competence in the teaching profession. The pressure came in particular from parents, politicians, and the press. There is an inverse relationship between accountability and trust: the less trust there is, the more public accountability is required. The result of such intense public pressure on schools in the United Kingdom, as in many other countries, was a 'high accountability', but 'low trust' model of education. Teachers complained about increasing bureaucracy: having to tick boxes to show they had covered the national curriculum, or read numerous official documents.

One instrument of the high accountability model was the introduction of numerous Acts of Parliament, from 1980 to the end of the century. These introduced statutory requirements rather than relying on voluntary conventions, which had been the predominant style of government influence prior to 1980. By law schools had to publish information about themselves, carry out the appraisal of teachers and heads, teach a national curriculum, and apply national tests to children at different ages, the scores from which could then be published and compared with those of other schools. It was easy for teachers to fall foul of the law at any level of detail. Many schools found that their religious assembly, for example, was illegal, as it did not contain the right ingredients, or did not take place on a daily basis. In the first version of the national curriculum there were 17 different topics, or 'Attainment Targets' as they were known, in the science curriculum alone. Anyone not teaching just one of these 17 themes would have been breaking the law, as all of them were statutory requirements.

The new laws were accompanied, in 1992, by the establishment of the Office for Standards in Education (OFSTED), the school inspection agency which was to inspect all primary and secondary schools. Using a detailed written inspection framework, nearly 500 pages in length, and working initially on a four year cycle, though this was later lengthened, teams of inspectors, acting as private businesses, visited every school in the country. There were differences of opinion about the desirability or success of such legislation and the form of inspection that accompanied it, but irrespective of whether such developments were thought to be good or bad, they did apply further external pressure on schools.

New technological developments, such as the widespread introduction of the microcomputer in the 1980s and later of more highly interactive technology, offered a further challenge to teachers. Such novelties tested their flexibility and adaptability, as they needed to modify their teaching styles to accommodate at least some of the many developments which had a potential to improve learning. Indeed, broadcasting technology itself made teachers more vulnerable than ever before. The teacher attempting to teach the topic 'Insects' to a primary class 50 years ago would not have been compared with anyone other than a fellow teacher. Today he or she will be compared with the finest television presenters in the world, whose programmes on insects enjoy multi-million pound budgets and access to the very best of wildlife film available.

At the close of the twentieth century the role of the teacher broadened even more. The real or imagined ills of a society were often attributed, rightly or wrongly, to schooling. Teachers were expected to play many roles, such as social worker (dealing with children whose families experienced economic and social deprivation), jailer (coping with children reluctant to come to school), administrator (handling the increasing bureaucracy surrounding curriculum and assessment), public relations officer (meeting parents, members of the community, dealing with local meetings), and numerous others. Teaching was certainly not a job for those who were faltering, nor for the faint-hearted.

The average age of the teaching profession increased during that same period. A rapid expansion in the recruitment of teachers during the 1960s and early 1970s had been followed by a decline in the 1980s. Some teachers failed to find a job at all until the later years of the decade when schools expanded once again. The result of this roller coaster graph of teacher recruitment was that, by the 1990s, three out of every five teachers were aged over 40, leading to reduced promotion prospects and falling morale.

On the positive side, there was a great deal of professional experience available, which helped considerably when the first national curriculum was introduced in England and Wales in 1989. Many of the initiatives and reforms might have failed badly, had they been introduced to an inexperienced profession. The negative aspect, however, was that after years of experience of favoured teaching strategies, it was not always easy for older teachers in particular to make alterations to their teaching styles when they became necessary. Teachers aged over 40 had been laying down these deep structures, as described above, for 20 or more years, with thousands of questions, explanations, instructions, responses to pupils' work or behaviour every single week, and very little time, often a second or less, in which to make a decision. As this research was to show, it could be exceedingly difficult to unscramble deeply rooted habits.

In such dramatically changing circumstances it was not surprising that some teachers were, sadly, unable to cope with the demands on them as successfully as others. Although inspections of schools suggested that most teachers were regarded as competent or better, a small percentage were labelled 'incompetent'. Yet alleged 'incompetence', as we pointed out above, was an almost completely unstudied research field. Researchers tended to shy away from studying it, partly on the grounds that the methodological problems seemed intractable, and partly because of an understandable temptation to wish the whole issue out of existence. It was, therefore, in the near absence of evidence about those teachers who seemed to struggle with the exigencies of teaching in our complex and demanding society, that we began this research.

THE TEACHING COMPETENCE PROJECT

In the Teaching Competence Project we undertook a large-scale two year study of alleged incompetence as seen by both professional and lay people. It is relatively rare in educational research for several different constituencies to be investigated. For example, researchers may study teachers directly, but pupils only indirectly and their parents not at all. We wanted the voices of as many individuals and groups as possible to be heard, irrespective of their status, age, professional expertise, or the power they did or did not exercise.

It was not the purpose of this research to establish the overall number of 'incompetent' teachers currently working in our schools. This has sometimes been the subject of speculation in the press when the Chief Inspector of Schools, in his 1996 annual report, suggested there might be 15,000 incompetent teachers, based on an estimate of the number of teachers receiving the lowest grades on formal school inspections. We did undertake a large national survey of primary and secondary head teachers, reported in Chapter 3, but we could not draw conclusions about national numbers or percentages, as many of the teachers they described had left the profession. To estimate national numbers would have required a quite different kind of research.

Although we sometimes asked identical questions, we could not use exactly the same approach with every single group studied. Even when eliciting the views and experiences of a particular constituency, like children in school, we had to vary our research strategy, because they ranged in age from six up to sixteen. We conducted face to face interviews with the youngest, so their relative inability to express their views and experiences fully in writing would not disadvantage them, but gave questionnaires to the older pupils, so we could reach larger numbers.

Nor was it possible to adopt exactly the same methodology with all adult groups. Interviews were used in many cases, but questionnaires were also employed, especially in the national survey of head teachers' experiences. Much as we would have liked to observe lessons, it proved extraordinarily difficult. Everyone who took part in the research was guaranteed anonymity, so all the names of people or institutions in this book are fictitious. Classroom observation, an approach we have used frequently in other research projects, would have been too conspicuous and intrusive in this particularly sensitive research area, so we only undertook observations of one teacher, for special reasons.

What is described in much of this book, therefore, is a series of studies seeking the views and experiences of those closest to events. Several thousand people were involved in what turned out to be a much more substantial and far-reaching enquiry than we originally expected. In the absence of any significant research on the topic in the United Kingdom, and indeed in many other countries, we have tried to make our studies as comprehensive and wide-ranging as we could. When faced with a set of research questions that might provoke different types of response it is sometimes useful to seek a consensus of those thought to be competent to make a judgement. We decided, therefore, to consult, one way or another, the major constituencies formally or informally involved in allegations of incompetence. They included:

1   Head teachers
2   Teachers alleged to be incompetent
3   Fellow teachers of those alleged to be incompetent
4   Chairs of governing bodies
5   Pupils
6   Parents
7   Union officials who had dealt with cases from their members
8   Personnel officers and advisers working for local authorities
9   School inspectors
10 Organisations other than unions which had dealt with alleged incompetence

The significant research questions we drew up involved studying central concerns, such as:

• What constitutes 'incompetence' in the eyes of those making the judgement?
• How is the alleged incompetence identified?
• When teachers are regarded as incompetent, what steps, if any, are taken to address the issue?
• What are the views and reactions of those identified as incompetent?
• What are the views and reactions of others close to the events?
• What are the outcomes of action or inaction?
• Which seem to be successful and which unsuccessful solutions?

The Project was designed around five linked studies, in order to elicit the views of the different parties involved:

Study 1 A study of a national sample of head teachers in primary and secondary schools.

Study 2 A study of a sample of teachers in primary and secondary schools who have been labelled 'incompetent', and a second study of teacher colleagues, not regarded as incompetent themselves, who have worked alongside them.

Study 3 A study of primary and secondary pupils of different ages to elicit their constructs about teacher competence.

Study 4 A study of officers from teacher unions, local education authorities and those who chair or are involved in school governing bodies, as well as a sample of parents and inspectors.

Study 5 An analysis of incompetence procedures in other professions and other countries.

Despite some initial apprehensions about whether people would be willing to talk about such a sensitive issue, it soon became clear that many participants in the events were actually eager to share their experiences in confidence. This included a number of teachers who had themselves been subject to allegations of incompetence and who described graphically how stressful it was to revisit and relive what happened. As a result the samples were, in some cases, quite large. In the case of the smaller samples, such as the 21 union officers, these were key people in each of the six major teacher and head teacher unions, each of whom had substantial experience of incompetence cases, as did the 20 local authority personnel officers and advisers interviewed. Sample details are given below.

Head teachers

(a) Interviews with 60 primary and secondary head teachers.
(b) Analysis of 684 case studies of individual teachers alleged to be incompetent, reported on in detail by their head teacher.

Teacher unions

Interviews with 21 representatives from the six major teacher and head teacher unions.

Local Education Authorities (LEAs)

(a) Interviews with 20 LEA personnel and advisory officers.
(b) Document survey of capability/competence procedures.

Chairs of school governing bodies

Questionnaire survey of 74 chairs of school governing bodies.

Teachers

(a) Study of self-reports of 70 allegedly incompetent teachers.
(b) Study of accounts of 57 teachers, not alleged to be incompetent, who had worked alongside a colleague who was said to be incompetent.

Parents

Interviews with 100 parents.

Pupils

Questionnaire and interview survey of 519 pupils aged from six to sixteen.

Several ethical matters had to be addressed in the design of the research. We decided it would not be ethical to ask one individual about another named person we had studied. For example, we did not, as a general practice, interview an allegedly incompetent teacher and then ask that teacher's head, colleagues or pupils about the person concerned. First of all it would have breached confidentiality, and secondly it would have been unethical. In a very few cases we did interview a teacher and then interviewed the head teacher as well, but this was always done with the explicit agreement of both parties in advance.

The findings, therefore, come from a set of overlapping, but separate constituencies. Head teachers, parents, pupils, fellow teachers all talk about incompetence, but they are not referring specifically to the allegedly incompetent teachers described in Chapter 4 of this book. From a methodological point of view it might have been better to have focused on a particular teacher and then obtained the perceptions of fellow teachers, the head teacher, the chair of governors, pupils and their parents about this person. In research, however, paragon ideals are not always feasible when ethical and practical considerations are taken into account. Such was the emotional overlay in many of these cases that mayhem would have been caused in the school and community by such intrusive enquiry.

What we report, therefore, is the sometimes contrasting, sometimes complementary views and accounts of several different lay and professional constituencies. When interviewing children, for example, we did not ask them to describe a particular teacher. Instead they were asked to describe both good and bad teaching, as they had seen and experienced it. In practice many, especially the younger pupils, did have a particular teacher in mind when they responded, but they were never asked to name anyone, always to comment generally.

In the remaining chapters of this book we describe the findings of the Project through the eyes of the three major constituencies studied. There are the professional people working in the school: head teachers, teachers alleged to be incompetent, fellow teachers. Their experiences and views are described in Chapters 3, 4 and 5. The second major group consists of professional people working outside the school, like teacher and head teacher union officers, local authority personnel officers and advisers, and their story is told in Chapters 6 and 7, with brief reference to a small group of OFSTED inspectors and university teacher trainers in Chapter 11. The third constituency is the lay people involved, the 'clients' and their representatives, chairs of school governing bodies, parents and pupils. Their vantage point is described in Chapters 8, 9 and 10.

The order of reporting is not meant to be significant, though we are aware of the assumptions that can be implicit in *how* as well as *what* we report. For example, we open the account of fieldwork and, therefore, set the scene, in Chapter 3, with a description of the views and experiences of a large group of primary and secondary head teachers. This may appear to signal that their views are paramount, but that is not our intention. We have to start with something and whatever comes first may appear to have the authors' sympathy. Equally, since the views of lay groups, like children, parents and governors, are reported later in the book, this may appear to diminish their importance, as if their views must come second to those of professionals. This is certainly not our intention either, or we would not have sought their experiences in the first place.

In the final part of the book, Chapter 11, we try to bring together some of the major findings and issues, identifying those overarching precepts that occurred in many of the studies and considering what can be learned from what we have discovered and how practice can be improved in future. We begin, however, by looking at the whole question of competence and incompetence: what procedures operate for allegations of incompetence in professions other than teaching; what happens in countries other than the United Kingdom; what research has been done into incompetence.

Chapter 2

Professional incompetence

Teaching is not the only profession where there has been more public scrutiny of members' competence in recent years. Most professions have devised a set of procedures for looking at alleged incompetence and these have, from time to time, been subject to internal and external comment and scrutiny. Furthermore, procedures for looking at competence and incompetence in teaching are an issue in many countries, including those where there is no commonly agreed means of appraising teachers' skill, or lack of it. There is not a great deal of systematic research in the field, as was pointed out in Chapter 1, but it is worth considering such evidence and analysis as exists.

In the introductory chapter to this book we considered such matters as how skilful teaching might be defined and identified. Chapter 2 now reports what happens to those regarded as incompetent in professions other than teaching, as well as practices and procedures in different countries, particularly in the United States, when incompetent teaching has been alleged. Finally some of the relevant research in the field is reviewed.

COMPARISONS WITH OTHER PROFESSIONS AND ORGANISATIONS

There is an assumption, as common inside as outside the teaching profession, that incompetence is tolerated in teaching, but that in other walks of life those who do not meet required standards are dismissed easily and without compunction. It is not easy to compare in an exact way practices in different professions, with their varying histories, traditions and demands, but we were interested to investigate what differences and similarities there appeared to be between the way allegedly 'poor' performance was identified and dealt with in certain professions and in large organisations, and to see what might be gleaned from their custom and practice.

A comparison was made between the written procedures for dealing with poor performance in teaching and those found in the management manuals of several large national and multi-national companies and provided by the relevant bodies dealing with doctors, nurses, midwives, health visitors, barristers, solicitors and Local Authority employees. A small number of semi-structured interviews was carried out with lecturers in Business Studies and Human Resource Management and Human Resource Consultants (previously known as Personnel Managers) from local government and commercial firms dealing with the public. Procedures change in professional practice, so what is described below is the situation at the time of writing.

The problem of poor performance is something which needs to be addressed in every profession, organisation or company, and there has been a general movement away from an unquestioning belief in the infallibility of professionals and the impenetrability of businesses towards more accountability to those who use and pay for their services. This has resulted in a greater concern for dealing with complaints and for setting up procedures to maintain or raise standards of service.

There are differences in who is responsible for the maintenance of standards. In some professions the responsibility for combating poor performance lies with professional bodies. In commercial organisations it is supposed to be the management's job, while in some professions, including teaching, responsibility is shared between different parties. The major difference between the organisations we investigated, however, lay in the way poor performance was tackled. On one side was the proactive position of those who saw it as their responsibility to set up systems to *promote* improved performance and to monitor performance so that they could identify and deal with poor performance. On the other were those who *reacted* to individual complaints from clients or customers.

The division between 'performance-enhancing' and 'complaint-handling' practices largely follows the division between commercial organisations and self-employed professionals, with teachers falling somewhere in between. Even those which take the 'complaint-handling' view, however, are not immune from the general momentum of change, and several of the professional associations which investigated complaints have broadened their role in the 1990s. The General Medical Council (GMC), for example, extended its sphere of responsibility into promoting good practice and dealing more generally with poor performance, and the Solicitors Complaints Bureau was replaced by the Office for the Supervision of Solicitors which was given a wider remit. The intention was still to start from the investigation of individual complaints, but to use this process to maintain and raise standards, as the knowledge that complaints have been upheld and that certain practice was unacceptable percolated through to the rest of the profession.

Barristers

The Bar Council, the body which regulates the conduct of barristers, operates very much at the 'complaint-handling' end of the continuum. It has a compulsory Code of Practice, which sets out standards of service barristers should provide. It does not monitor performance, however, or take steps to discover bad practice unless there is a specific complaint, but it investigates complaints and takes action against those found to be in breach of its Code.

The first stage of the complaints process is consideration by a Complaints Commissioner, an official who is not a lawyer. The Complaints Commissioner may dismiss the complaint, suggest there is scope for conciliation, or decide that the matter should be investigated by the Professional Conduct and Complaints Committee which consists of barristers with two lay representatives. If this committee decides the complaint may be justified it goes to an Adjudication Panel, which is chaired by the Complaints Commissioner and usually made up of two barristers and one lay representative. As in teaching, a distinction is made between misconduct and incompetence. Professional misconduct is the more serious offence and the Bar Council can impose penalties of fines or even disbarment. Incompetence, or, as the Bar Council calls it, 'inadequate professional service', on the other hand, includes such offences as delay, serious rudeness and poor or inadequate work, but not the way that a barrister decides to conduct a case in court. If appropriate, the Panel may require the barrister to apologise, repay or reduce his or her fees or pay compensation up to £2,000.

There are very few similarities between the ways the poor performance of barristers and teachers are tackled. Barristers have clear guidelines in that they have a Code of Practice they are obliged to follow, but they are called to account only when a complaint has been made. In teaching, complaints about a teacher's performance are often important, in that they press the head teacher into action, but they are rarely complaints about a single incident which requires recompense. Thus, the process of examining a teacher's competence is not like a judicial hearing which attempts to find out the facts surrounding one case. It considers the teacher's performance in the round, and assessment of professional judgements is an integral part.

In an investigation of inadequate professional service, barristers' professional judgement, including, for example, how they conduct the case or which witnesses they choose to call or not call is not questioned. The process of dealing with complaints is retrospective, and though barristers may be called on to recompense a client for past poor practice, they are not set targets or given time scales in which to improve the service they give. Nor is their practice in other court cases observed or evaluated. It is assumed that barristers who frequently gave inadequate professional service would not bring much business to their chambers and might attract unfavourable comment or action from the Head of Chambers, but as long as they do not engage in serious professional misconduct they can continue to practise their profession.

Solicitors

Like barristers, solicitors react to complaints of specific incidences of poor practice, but they have recently changed the process by which they do this. Their supervisory body, the Office for the Supervision of Solicitors, came into being in 1996 replacing the Solicitors Complaints Bureau, and the change of name reflects a wider remit. The new body has two departments, the Office for Client Relations which deals with complaints, and the Office for Professional Regulation which regulates solicitors and investigates serious professional misconduct. As with the Bar Council, in dealing with complaints the Office for Client Relations can suggest conciliation, require compensation to be paid, reduce the solicitor's bill or direct the solicitor to correct the mistake. The Office for Professional Regulation deals with all matters relating to regulation and solicitors' conduct, and much of their work is concerned with malpractice. In addition to dealing with misconduct, however, it can also have an effect on the competence of solicitors, by directing them to go on a relevant training course, and it could prohibit them from practising in a certain type of law.

If solicitors disagree with the decision made by the Office, they can appeal to the Compliance and Supervision Committee, which is a Standing Committee of the Law Society and has 11 lay members out of the total of 28. This may impose sanctions which are kept on the solicitor's record, ranging from recording disapproval to a severe reprimand. The most serious cases involving criminal practices are dealt with by the Solicitors' Disciplinary Tribunal, which is independent from the Office for the Supervision of Solicitors, holds its hearings in public and has the power to strike a solicitor off the Roll of Solicitors.

Doctors

Doctors used to be in a similar position to that of barristers, being investigated only after specific complaints. The General Medical Council (GMC) set up a working party to investigate ways of dealing with poor performance by surgeons, following some high-profile cases of unacceptable practice being allowed to continue. Changes affecting General Practitioners (GPs) were introduced in July 1997, following the Medical (Professional Performance) Act 1995 giving the GMC powers to take action against doctors whose standard of professional performance is 'seriously deficient'. Before that the GMC was able to act only if GPs were considered unfit on health grounds or because of a criminal conviction. Now 'seriously deficient performance' is defined (GMC June 1998) as:

> a departure from good professional practice – whether or not it is covered by GMC guidance – sufficiently serious to call into question the doctor's registration

and this happens

> when there is repeated or persistent failure to comply with the professional standards appropriate to the work being done by the doctor, particularly where this places patients or members of the public in jeopardy.

(p. 2)

Like barristers, doctors are investigated by their professional body, rather than by management or employer, and the panel investigating their competence includes a doctor from the same specialism. In other words, they are judged partly by their peers. The procedures for dealing with alleged poor practice set out four stages:

1   Screening – to investigate complaints (not necessarily from patients) and decide whether there is no case to answer, or whether to proceed with the procedures or whether the matter should be dealt with under different procedures (e.g. health).
2   Assessment of performance.
3   Remedial training and reassessment.
4   Consideration by the Committee on Professional Performance.

These procedures bear some similarities to those used by LEAs; the procedures are distinguished from those for malpractice; they are intended to be as confidential as possible; and, there is the possibility for informal action to be taken early on, if that is all the 'screeners' consider necessary. The procedures are designed to be remedial. Although they arise from complaints, the GMC's interest is to improve future competence and not simply assess compensation for past shortcomings.

There are, however, some interesting differences. As has been mentioned, doctors are judged by other doctors, including one from the same medical specialism. Those whose competence is questioned are invited to co-operate in the proceedings, but if they choose not to, the process goes straight to Stage 4. They may choose to retire rather than go through the whole sequence but, unlike teachers, if they do this they cannot simply practise elsewhere. In order to practise again they would have to apply for restoration to the Register, and have their performance assessed as satisfactory – in effect to return to the procedures at Stage 2 or 3. Again, unlike teachers, doctors are expected to arrange to remedy their failings themselves. The panel may advise them, but it is the doctors' own responsibility to pay for the courses or undertake the necessary retraining themselves. An interesting difference, which might also be considered in the teaching profession, is that all doctors are assumed to have a professional duty to do something about colleagues who are not performing adequately.

To be judged as competent or not by one's peers, as happens in the legal and medical professions, must give the 'accused' person the confidence that those judging him or her understand the problems under which he or she operates. It is often, however, perceived by those outside the profession as too cosy an arrangement, which allows the profession to be a sympathetic judge and jury and does not take sufficient cognisance of the needs of the clients or the general public. The movement for greater accountability of professionals has seen the inclusion of more lay representatives on the bodies which assess competence, and teachers are unlikely to move in the opposite direction.

There had been discussions for many years about the benefits of having a General Teaching Council on the lines of the GMC, but, during the time our research took place, teachers did not have a professional body to set entry standards, produce a Code of Practice or judge them when they fell short of its requirements.

Nurses, midwives and health visitors

It is probably more profitable to compare teachers with nurses and other registered health practitioners, than with lawyers or doctors, as they have more in common in terms of their conditions of employment:

- Neither group is self-employed.
- Both are trained to nationally agreed standards and paid according to nationally set pay scales.
- They are subject to organisation by local bodies (LEAs or Health Trusts) and are supervised by their superiors in the smaller units in which they work.
- Written procedures exist for managers in both groups to enable them to take more serious incompetence to higher authorities.

The regulatory body for the nursing profession is the United Kingdom Central Council for Nursing, Midwifery and Health Visiting (UKCC) which states that its mission is: 'to establish and improve standards of nursing, midwifery and health visiting care in order to service and protect the public'. The UKCC does this partly by investigating complaints, either of professional misconduct or unfitness to practise for other reasons, but it deals only with serious issues which endanger the public. Complaints not only come from injured parties but can be made by fellow practitioners, employers and managers as well.

Registered practitioners have a *Code of Professional Practice* published by the UKCC which states that: 'As a registered nurse, midwife or health visitor, you are personally accountable for your practice'. It then specifies 16 requirements which the practitioner must meet. One of these is to 'maintain and improve your professional knowledge and competence' (June 1992), while others require collaborative and co-operative working and assisting colleagues to extend their own knowledge. The UKCC booklet, *Complaints about professional conduct*, explains that the Code sets out 'the standard which the public is entitled to expect from the average practitioner', but makes it clear that this is 'not . . . the highest possible standard of professional conduct' (March 1998, p. 4).

Having a Code of Practice is one aspect of the practices in the legal and medical professions which might be useful in the teaching profession as it sets out, albeit in general terms, the responsibilities of the professional. In particular, the duty placed on doctors and nurses to report inadequate performance might help with the early identification of problems with poorly performing teachers, while the requirement that nurses should work collaboratively and help their colleagues to develop their practice might also be beneficial in schools.

It is only the most serious complaints which are taken to the UKCC, if managers believe the practitioner is a danger to the public and should be removed from the register. Reasons for justifying removal from the register are conditions such as alcohol dependency, drug addiction, serious mental illness or personality disorders, rather than lack of professional knowledge or commitment.

In all other cases, the responsibility for dealing with performance on a day-to-day basis rests with the practitioner's line manager. In hospital nursing, for example, the process of dealing with poor performance is regulated according to the policy of the relevant NHS Trust. These policies also cover employees other than health practitioners, and they are far closer to those of LEAs than are those used by the professional bodies of the legal and medical professions. One states that the Trust aims to provide:

> A system whereby poor staff performance can be addressed in a positive manner, e.g. providing training, development opportunities and support without necessarily resorting to the Disciplinary Policy and Procedure.
>
> (a NHS Trust)

The policy identifies it as the manager's responsibility to recognise poor performance, to ensure that required standards and expectations are set out clearly in job descriptions and explained to staff, and to review the job description annually as part of an annual appraisal interview. Once a manager has identified poor performance, 'the gap between the manager's expectations of the job-holder in respect of their job role and the employee's actual performance in the their job', the procedures to be followed are in four official stages, preceded by an informal stage, at which the manager attempts to resolve the issue through supervision and regular discussions.

The formal stages start with a written invitation to a meeting at which the performance problems are clarified and a development programme is planned, with agreement on the required support and the time scale for improvement. If this improvement is not forthcoming, another action plan, time scale and review date are agreed and the consequences of not reaching the required standards are made clear. Stage 3 provides for redeployment, further time for improvement or dismissal on the grounds of capability. Stage 4 refers the matter to the next manager in line for an objective assessment of the case. As in teaching, there are arrangements for an appeal against a decision, and, also, as in teaching, the process is not a speedy one. A time scale of 'not normally less than 3 months' was specified by one Trust 'in order to provide staff the opportunity to address and improve on their performance'.

Local Authority employees

Local Authorities (LAs) employ thousands of people in many different occupations, and the responsibility for ensuring that standards of competence are met is delegated to the appropriate senior officers or heads of department, including the power to dismiss employees below a certain grade, or move a poorly performing employee to a more suitable post.

While a clear distinction is made, with doctors, nurses, lawyers and teachers, between misconduct and poor performance, this is not generally the case in Local Authorities. Instead, both are dealt with under the LA's disciplinary procedures, although it is acknowledged that they are not identical. One LA's *disciplinary* procedure states:

> If it is concluded that a minor breach has occurred the employee should be offered informal guidance as to the required standard of conduct and/or performance.
>
> (County Council Disciplinary Procedure)

It continues to set out different procedures to be followed in cases of poor performance, saying:

> In cases involving performance it will also be appropriate to indicate any time-scale over which the improvement must be attained and the method of guidance and support to be provided. In all such cases the employee must be informed of the consequences of not achieving the required standard.
>
> (County Council Disciplinary Procedure)

A Human Resources Manager from a County Council Social Services Department said in interview, however:

> It's very difficult sometimes to isolate whether it's an issue of competence or whether it's an issue of conduct. Can the person not do it, or is it that they can do it but can't be bothered? The cases, when you get into them, are often much more complex than somebody can't do the job, and I think you get into wrangles about 'Well, this should go down through the capability procedure' or 'This should go down through the disciplinary procedure'. And I just think you get yourself tied up in knots and, to be honest, the procedural steps are pretty much the same anyway.
>
> (Local Authority Human Resource Manager)

His Local Authority Disciplinary Procedure applied to employees with over six months' service, because of the practice of hiring personnel on probationary contracts for six months and removing poor performers at the end of that time without needing to go through the procedures. If the procedures were followed, employees had informal guidance, a formal written warning and a final written warning, against which they had the right of appeal. There was always the possibility of an industrial tribunal investigating unfair dismissal but he said:

> We would absolutely not shirk from dismissing someone because of an industrial tribunal. We're fairly confident of our way of handling it and to be honest, if it goes to an IT, the powers are all in the employer's hands anyway because, if it looks like you've got a dodgy case, you can always settle.

However, he acknowledged the importance of tackling the matter in the correct way because:

> Industrial tribunals place very high standards on big public organisations like us with the sort of resources we've got so they expect high standards. It is something which is important to us that we do well because actually, if you don't treat people properly through that process, other staff see it, and I think that you lead to a lack of trust.

The problem of *dealing* with poor performance, is, of course, closely connected with that of *identifying* it. One interviewee told us that there was no written definition of incompetence in his department, though there were some relevant ways of defining competence, such as NVQ and other qualifications. He said his department was trying to set out the various standards of competence it required, but that until this was completed a decision that someone was incompetent:

> would really arise out of a manager coming to a view that an individual isn't performing at the level which they would reasonably expect them to, so there's nothing concrete to measure it against really.

Commercial organisations

In industry, the assumption of easy hiring and firing proved inaccurate. People working for large organisations were not dismissed the moment complaints were made or management was dissatisfied with their work. As in teaching, misconduct was treated differently from incompetence, but when poor performance was identified people were not just sacked:

> People are given time to improve. They might be moved to another group, if the problem was to do with not getting on well with other people. If they were suffering from stress we might involve the occupational health. The line managers would set targets. They might have their unions to give them support, and the line managers are meant to support them as well.
>
> (Human Resource Consultant in international corporation)

There were, however several interesting differences and, we suggest, some lessons that might be learned. The most significant differences between the management of performance in large companies and those in most schools were:

- clarity of criteria on which performance is judged
- acceptance of frequent or continuous reviews of performance, and of management responsibility for staff development.

The ideal model of the performance management system adopted by many organisations is that objectives are set for the whole organisation, for the departments within it and then for the teams and individuals who make up the department. There is, therefore, clarity of expectations and standards, backed up by frequent or continuous reviews of performance. The capabilities required of staff are often set out in detail with descriptions of behaviour which represent each capability. Staff should, therefore, be in no doubt of what is expected of them, including the expectation that they should set and achieve definite targets. There is, as one of our interviewees put it, a 'cultural acceptance of being assessed', which is seen as having benefits and responsibilities for both management and managed.

Managers were responsible for the performance of those under them and once poor performance had been identified, it was the manager's job to provide the necessary support to bring about improvement. The statement in the procedures of one large corporation that 'poor performance should be identified and addressed without delay as part of day-to-day management' was typical, while the comment by one lecturer in Human Resource Management that 'it would be considered very poor practice for problems to be left to an annual appraisal meeting' was echoed by others.

In theory, dissatisfaction with any aspect of performance should not come as a surprise, even at briefer monthly reviews. Once problems had been identified, companies had procedures similar to those of many LEAs, with targets and time scales laid down for reviewing progress. If improvement was not sufficient, dismissal was a possibility, but there were other possibilities, some, such as moving to a different job within the organisation, which are rarely available in teaching.

One of the problems cited by teachers whose competence had been called into question was that they had often been teaching in a similar manner for some time, with no suggestion that they were unsatisfactory, or, indeed, with any comments, favourable or otherwise, having been made about their performance since had they passed their probationary year. They also often believed that they were being judged more harshly than others, and that any other teacher, subjected to the degree of supervision which exists once procedures have been initiated, would also be found to be wanting. These problems would be greatly diminished if there were greater clarity about what teachers should be doing.

This could be done on a broad front by having a Code of Practice and, more specifically, by adopting the good practices of commercial organisations in giving detailed job descriptions, setting clear targets and giving time for frequent reviews of performance for everyone. At these, teachers would also be free to bring up problems and suggest ways in which they could be helped to teach better. LEA officers and teacher association representatives have told us that there is a much greater chance of resolving a case satisfactorily if it is tackled promptly with the necessary support put in place. Thus all our evidence points to the crucial importance of early identification of problems.

Some companies' performance review procedures provide the opportunity for staff to appraise their managers as well as the other way round, something we did not find in schools. There was also scope, in some instances, for input from other interested parties such as clients. It would be naive, however, to assume that all goes smoothly in the business world. Despite a greater acceptance of continuous assessment, there are, apparently, still concerns about whether expectations are reasonable and targets are fair. One company's guidelines for management highlighted the fact that managers had been unwilling to tackle poor perform- ance in the past and that improvements in this area were necessary. It acknowledged that the process could be time-consuming, difficult and emotional. Clearly in any enterprise, whether private business or public service, confronting colleagues about their failings is not an easy thing to do.

POLICY AND PRACTICE IN THE OTHER COUNTRIES

In Study 5 of the Project we investigated how teaching performance is monitored in other countries, specifically France, Germany and the United States, and what happens if a teacher is identified as performing unsatisfactorily. Describing practice elsewhere is not a simple matter, as there is little evidence of formal procedures in many European countries and there can be substantial differences between school districts in the United States.

Some European practice

In several countries in mainland Europe there is far less rigorous and systematic appraisal of teachers' practice and performance compared with the United Kingdom. People from different countries told us that teachers' competence is rarely questioned. In both France and Germany the status of teachers is similar to that of civil servants, in that they are employed by the state and 'placed' in schools.

In Germany, on completion of the teacher training course at university, there is a probationary period of three years, after which time the teacher's head teacher has to write a report and, if this is satisfactory, tenure is awarded. In France a similar system is in operation but external inspectors are also involved in the evaluation of a probationary teacher. The teacher's lessons are observed and the teacher is interviewed. The inspector's report is considered in con- junction with that of the head teacher when the decision whether to grant tenure is made.

While gaining tenure is claimed to be a 'huge hurdle' in France, once tenure has been granted, it is rarely challenged. A similar situation was described by a

German professor involved in teacher training, who said that once a teacher has tenure 'that is the end of tests, of evaluation'. He went on to say that head teachers in German schools are required to monitor the performance of their teachers but, in practice, this rarely takes place: 'The headmaster is allowed to come in and he has to give you 24 hours' notice, but in reality they don't do it. It's a sleeping dog.'

Almost identical statements were made by officials from other countries, including a senior regional official in Austria and an experienced teacher trainer in Malta. A secondary school head teacher in Austria said:

> I am supposed to have a duty to monitor teachers, but in practice I would only talk to a teacher if parents had complained. It is highly unlikely that I would watch a lesson. Before I became a head I was a teacher for over 20 years and no one ever came into my classroom to check my teaching. Here a teacher has a job for life.

There is virtually no monitoring by external inspectors in Germany, we were informed, because staffing levels are so low.

Given that there is so little monitoring of tenured teachers' performance, it is not surprising to discover that the retraining or dismissal of incompetent teachers, in contrast with the evidence gathered of what occurs in England, is not an big issue in France or Germany. A French informant, an experienced teacher trainer, reported 'Nothing can really be done to sack an appointed teacher'. In both France and Germany it was reported that only teachers who had committed gross professional misconduct or had mental health problems were likely to be sacked or asked to leave the profession. There were no *national* capability procedures in place in the UK to deal with unsatisfactory performance at the time we did our research, though local authorities and schools did have their own conventions.

The United States

Generalising about the United States of America is rarely wise because the autonomy enjoyed by individual states means that for almost any practice or policy found in one state, the opposite may be found in another. On educational matters there is additional diversity because each state contains many school districts which largely form their own policies. There is, however, some common experience shared by the states and, consequently, some common factors in the methods used to identify and deal with poorly performing teachers.

Identifying poor performance

In 1983 a federal report entitled *A Nation at Risk: The imperative for the 21st Century* heightened public concern about the state of education in the United

States, and, consequently, about the quality of teachers. Tests to assess the ability of the teachers, usually at entry, sometimes at the point of acquiring tenure (permanent posts) and occasionally for tenured teachers, increased throughout the 1980s. Most of these tests, however, were criticised for not addressing the fundamental issue of identifying good teaching practice (Haertel 1991, p. 4). Instead they tested basic literacy and numeracy, factual knowledge of regulations and multiple choice questions for which the teacher has to select the correct teacher action for a given scenario.

Evaluation of existing teachers also increased, both as a method of identifying poorly performing teachers and as the basis for some individual pay awards. For these evaluations observation of lessons was used, and towards the end of the decade Bridges (1992), in his study of the way administrators deal with incompetent teachers, reported that lesson observation allied with supervisory ratings was the most frequently mentioned method of detecting poor performance reported by most school districts in California. Teachers were evaluated on a 1 to 5 scale, (1 = outstanding, 2 = good, 3 = satisfactory, 4 = needs to improve, 5 = unsatisfactory) but the rigour of this evaluation is questionable. In Baltimore, Philadelphia, in 1983, 44.6 per cent of teachers were rated 'outstanding' while 0.003 per cent received a rating of less than satisfactory (Digilio 1984). Similar figures are found in other states, and Bridges (1992) cites examples of many teachers, diagnosed as extremely poor performers, who had received satisfactory or even glowing evaluations for many years.

Lesson observations would seem to offer a better way of assessing teachers than tests with multiple-choice answers, but the way they were conducted and the criteria on which teaching was assessed have been as widely criticised as the inflated gradings (Haertel 1991, Darling-Hammond 1986). Darling-Hammond claims that:

> In many school districts it is a perfunctory bureaucratic requirement that yields little help for teachers and little information on which a school district can base decisions.
>
> (p. 531)

and that:

> The most important aspects of teaching are ignored in favor of measuring the measurable, no matter how trivial.
>
> (p. 535)

Nevertheless, as has been mentioned, teacher observations were reported as the most common method of detecting poor performance in school districts in California, most of which reported using at least three different methods. The methods were, in decreasing order of frequency:

1   supervisor ratings and observations
2   complaints from parents and students
3   complaints from other teachers
4   students' test results
5   follow-up surveys of former students
6   student ratings
7   exit interviews with parents
8   other – including number of times students referred for discipline problems,
    teacher's attendance

(Bridges 1992, p. 7)

As in England and Wales, complaints from parents were often the stimulus which prompted the principal to deal with the problem.

Dealing with poor performance

Improvement

When an American teacher is identified as performing poorly, the first step is to try to help the teacher to improve. Districts may have remediation staff who work with teachers referred to them by the schools' principal. Given, however, the minute percentage of teachers identified as failing, it is reasonable to assume that the ones who are so identified are at the extreme end of incompetence and so it is not surprising that efforts at improving their practice are rarely successful.

Principals have the same dual role as English heads of planning for improvement while also overseeing the evaluation and supervision which may result in dismissal. The fact that some may not sincerely wish the teacher to improve is common to both systems also, but US principals have the additional problem that if they are encouraging and supportive and praise the teacher for any improvement, this may be used against them if a case for dismissal ever comes to court. Their written observations of teachers' lessons, therefore, are given with at least one eye on the possibility of their being used as evidence, and principals who have tolerated poor performance and may have given praise and inflated ratings for years change. Bridges (1992) describes what he calls the salvage stage as:

> a period of unmuted criticism, defensive reaction, behavioral specification, limited assistance, restrained support, extensive documentation and little improvement.
>
> (p. 48)

The constraints on providing adequate support, together with the fact that many teachers are tackled about their failings after many years of being tolerated, are additional reasons why remediation is seldom a success.

Dismissal

When poorly performing teachers are identified, most states have policies which allow for their eventual dismissal, but the procedures for this are long and difficult to negotiate. A large majority of teachers in the US have 'tenure' which they are granted after two years teaching in the same District. Granting tenure is not supposed to be automatic, but, as with the supervisors' gradings of teachers, it is often criticised for not being sufficiently rigorous. Very few cases of poor performance ever come as far as dismissal, but of those that do the vast majority are of temporary staff, followed by probationers and a very few of tenured teachers. Bridges' (1992, p. 33) figures for California are: 69.8 per cent temporary staff, 25 per cent probationary staff and 5.2 per cent tenured staff, and these figures should be seen in the light of the fact that 80 per cent of California's teachers have tenure. Once gained, tenure is regarded as a property right which can only be taken away by action through the courts.

As the granting of tenure is taken to assume that the teacher is competent, the burden of proving, in court, that this is not the case lies with the District. Teachers with tenure have many rights, some similar to those found in LEA procedures (such as the right of appeal), but with an additional right to legal representation, access to the documents to be used, details of the charges against them, prior knowledge of the names of witnesses and an opportunity to cross-examine them in court. The legal procedures are expensive and, if it loses, the District pays the teacher's costs as well. Bridges (1992) found the cost (prior to 1986) was about $50,000 per case, sometimes more.

The District's job is made more difficult because there is no definitive definition of incompetence in teaching. Bridges (1992, p. 4) noted that, at the time, only in the states of Alaska and Tennessee had education administrators attempted a formal definition of the term, but even these did not supply any criteria for what incompetence in the classroom actually was. In addition, the Court of Appeals in Michigan listed five areas in which failure would show incompetence:

1   Knowledge of the subject
2   Ability to impart it
3   Manner and efficacy of discipline
4   Rapport with parents and other teachers
5   Physical and mental ability to withstand the strain of teaching

Any one of these could be taken to demonstrate incompetence, but, at the time of Bridges' research this was the only clear definition, and even that did not set any standards for judging whether a teacher had failed. The lack of clear criteria of incompetence makes it more difficult for a District to prove its case, but an additional result of this ambiguity is that standards of what counts as incompetence may vary from District to District as well as from State to State.

Before a teacher can be dismissed in California the District administration must issue the teacher with a notice of deficiency. This is a formal legal document which sets out the nature of the teacher's deficiencies, informs the teacher of 90 days allowed for improvement, and warns that dismissal will be enacted if there is none. If the teacher fails to improve, these 90 Day Notices are followed by a legal document stating the intention to dismiss, although sometimes the teacher will be informed that the District Education Board will not proceed with the dismissal if the teacher can suggest an alternative exit route.

Alternatives to dismissal

There are several alternatives to dismissal that may be negotiated, including resignation and retirement, often accompanied by financial inducements such as medical coverage, life insurance, additional years pension or even employment as a consultant. As in England and Wales, teachers are often assisted in these negotiations by their union. The unions attract some criticism from administrators for defending the indefensible, but they may be sued if they do not represent their members' interests adequately.

There are options open to administrators in the US which are not available to their English counterparts. In England, although teachers are paid by the LEA, they are recruited by the head and governors of each individual school while in the US, teachers are recruited and employed by the District. District administrators, therefore, are able to transfer teachers to other schools, place them as permanent supply teachers (the 'substitute pool'), make them tutors to individual children who are unable to attend school or find them other non-teacher positions, perhaps in school libraries, the museum, or even, as Bridges (1992) found, driving the school bus. US principals are able to recommend teachers for transfer, and this results, in some Districts, in poorly performing teachers being transferred from school to school in what has been called 'the turkey trot' or 'the dance of the lemons' (p. 36).

Further developments

The situation in the US is not static. Attempts are being made to find better ways of evaluating teachers and helping them to develop as well as of imposing stricter standards and overcoming the obstacles to dismissing incompetent staff. Darling-Hammond (1986, pp. 344–45) writes of the different policies being tried in different Districts, referring to one District in New York where teachers are involved in the drawing up of adverts for new teachers and in the selection process, which involves teaching demonstration lessons. Another, in Ohio, has an intensive and collaborative approach to the supervision of new teachers. If selection is more rigorous, evaluation has much less of a role of catching incompetents and more of helping individual professional development, and there are moves towards a less bureaucratic model of evaluation which recognises the diversity of a teacher's task.

Bridges (1992, p. 122) mentions one District where the relevant teachers' union has an agreement that unannounced observations may be made of teachers in the evaluation process, and that account may be taken of students' and parents' views. Principals in that District are required to spend 20–30 per cent of each day in classroom observing teachers (p. 126), and discretionary funds are available to pay for staff development specialists and also legal advice help from a counsellor for the head and teacher.

Some Districts are being tougher on principals who try to ignore the problem or evade their responsibilities. Bridges (1992, pp. 35–6) cites one District Superintendent who worked with heads on their evaluations to make them more specific and justify their positive comments, while another refused requests to transfer incompetent teachers but told the principals to confront the problem themselves. Innovations were also being introduced to help poorly performing teachers to improve, and Darling-Hammond (1986, p. 548) gives details of Districts in Toledo and Salt Lake which ran intensive remediation programmes, reporting that half of the teachers referred to them left teaching and the others improved. This is a far higher success rate than Bridges (1992) found in California.

As was stated above, the United States is a country of great diversity, and, therefore, the above report may have failed to do justice to the variety of policy and practice found in some states. There are, however, some national initiatives to improve the quality of teaching. The National Board for Professional Teaching Standards (NBPTS) was set up following a recommendation from the Carnegie Task Force on Teaching as a Profession's report, *A Nation Prepared: Teachers for the 21st Century* (1986). The NBPTS planned to set up a national, voluntary system of assessment and certifying teachers who meet its high standards, and their policy statement, *What teachers should know and be able to do*, aimed to provide a clear statement of what constituted the core of good teaching and thereby also define its opposite.

RESEARCH INTO INCOMPETENCE

We looked at some of the research into competent or effective teaching in Chapter 1 and to some extent what was described there is bound to overlap with the somewhat limited field of research into incompetence. Ramsay and Oliver (1995) claim that practical and ethical difficulties have inhibited the observation of teachers of poor quality. An example of the absence of substantial research is the lack of agreement in the research literature on the magnitude of the problem of incompetent teachers. Lavely (1992) claimed that, in the United States, approximately 10 per cent of teachers are incompetent. In England, the Chief Inspector of Schools proposed the figure of 15,000 which is nearer 4 per cent of the teaching force, based on the percentage of lessons judged to be unsatisfactory during formal school inspections.

Fidler and Atton (1999) point out that one unsatisfactory lesson does not identify an incompetent teacher and they claim that incompetent teachers are those who fail in a number of important areas, rather than performing unsatisfactorily in one aspect of the job. Nor should it be assumed, from the difference in the estimated extent of incompetence, that English teachers are more competent than their counterparts across the Atlantic. One of the problems of reviewing the research is the sheer diffuseness of the concept of 'incompetence': it can mean what people want it to mean. Different investigators use different definitions, which makes it difficult to make accurate comparisons or assessments.

According to Bridges (1992), who conducted a study of the way administrators deal with poorly performing teachers: 'Incompetence is a concept with no precise meaning' (p. 24).

This lack of clear criteria makes it harder to prove a case of incompetence, and Bridges also found it resulted in standards of what counted as incompetence varying from District to District, as well as from state to state. Similarly, a teacher may be considered incompetent in one school, but not in another, because of the standards reached by the other teachers. Potter and Smellie (1995) cite the case of an industrial tribunal which upheld the dismissal of a teacher from an independent school because his pupils did not get the high grades usually achieved at that school, even though they were adequate by average standards. The industrial tribunal found in favour of the school on the grounds that: 'The employer is entitled to rely on its own standards; it does not have to rely on any hypothetically reasonable standard' (p. 80).

Some of the work on incompetence is related to teacher evaluation. As early as 1915 Boyce reported that in 350 US cities teachers were judged according to a variety of criteria of which 'discipline', 'scholarship', 'instructional skill', 'co-operation' and 'planning' were the most frequently mentioned (Biddle and Ellena 1964, p. 51). In 1925, King reported that the US schools he studied rated teachers according to their teaching methods, personality, class management, pupils' achievement and their professional attitude, training and scholarship. These are not very different from the areas described in the Career Entry Profile for newly qualified teachers (Teacher Training Agency 1997, p. 18) which sets out the four main areas in which new teachers must be competent:

A   Knowledge and Understanding
B   Planning, Teaching and Class Management
C   Monitoring, Assessment, Recording and Accountability
D   Other professional requirements

Allowing for a difference in terminology, it has long been agreed that teachers should know their subject and be able to pass on their knowledge to each child in well-organised, orderly classes by means of carefully planned lessons. What is less clear, however, is exactly what a teacher has to do in these areas to count as incompetent. There is, as Cameron-Jones (1988) points out, a distinction between *criteria* (the areas in which teachers are expected to be competent) and *standards* which set out what they have to do in each area to be counted as competent:

> Criteria, therefore, are the characteristics that define competent teaching, for example, that it is well-planned, that its content is sequenced in a helpful way for learners etc., whereas standards are statements (judgements, scores, comments and the like) about the degree to which, for competence to be thought adequate, appropriate levels of each criterion should be or have been reached.
>
> (p. 67)

Until recently, there has, in the literature about ineffective teaching, been more about criteria than standards. Bridges (1992) says:

> There are no clear-cut standards or cut-off points which enable an administrator to say with certitude that a teacher is incompetent.
>
> (p. 24)

In his 1986 edition of *The Incompetent Teacher* he defines a 'fully' competent teacher as one who shows:

> more than satisfactory performance in terms of our criteria. Fully competent signifies that the teacher possesses at least one quality which sets him/her apart from most of the teachers on our teaching staff.
>
> (p. 132) (p. 152 in the 1992 edition)

This is a stiff definition, suggesting that a competent teacher is, to some extent, an exceptional teacher. In the 1992 edition Bridges admits to having modified his opinion and his new definition no longer implies that the teacher must be better than others, but includes the requirement that the teacher should have:

> demonstrated in multiple contexts his ability to satisfy the criteria which are used to evaluate teachers. These contexts should be differentiated primarily on the ability, ethnic status and socio-economic status of students.
>
> (p. 175)

Identifying incompetence

Fidler and Atton (1999) identify the causes of poor performance as rooted in either the management, the job or the individual and they claim that attempts to deal with poor performance should look at those three areas in that order. Only after eliminating the possibilities that management has not made clear its expectations, and that the job is not too onerous to be done satisfactorily by a teacher of average competence, should the decision be made that the problem lies with the individual.

Once the possibility that the problem is located within management or the job has been excluded, Fidler and Atton (1999) stress the importance of taking evidence of incompetence from a variety of sources over a period of time, in order to avoid bias. They claim that the most frequent methods of identifying incompetence are:

1   OFSTED inspections
2   complaints from parents or others
3   poor exam results or other performance criteria
4   perceived problems
5   staff appraisal

(p. 25)

They say, however, that before one of these methods identifies incompetence, there may have been other indications which had been overlooked. They found that a new head teacher or senior manager often takes action on poor performance which had been neglected previously, a feature which was to recur frequently in our own research.

Darling-Hammond (1986) notes the search for more effective ways to evaluate teachers, but claims that, although these changes have created more elaborate checklists, they have not changed the essential features of evaluation. Darling-Hammond criticises the forms of evaluation on the grounds that they cannot provide meaningful insight into teacher competence, apart from identifying the obviously extremely weak teachers. Administrators need to appear to treat all employees alike, so they have to evaluate everyone in the same way, which means they cannot allow for different contexts. She also points out that because nothing happens after evaluation, it does not seem important enough to do properly, and that principals may not have specialist subject knowledge to evaluate thoroughly.

Teachers teach in different ways in different contexts, and Darling-Hammond claims that 'ticklist' evaluation:

exacerbates the tendency to think of teaching as an unvarying didactic exercise that is unresponsive to the characteristics of students or the nature of learning tasks.

(p. 535)

For example, one state's evaluation lists context-free behaviours shown by research to be effective. An example is an evaluation list which contains items relating to 'starting class on time' and 'keeping a brisk pace of instruction'. Darling-Hammond says there is nothing to show which is more important, or to consider whether there are occasions when it would be more appropriate to introduce concepts slowly. It also has nothing in it about human relation skills or ability to relate to children or:

> whether a teacher has sufficient knowledge, skill, and judgement to make sound teaching decisions over a sustained period of time on behalf of many students of diverse needs.

(p. 533)

Darling-Hammond distinguishes between what she calls the 'bureaucratic' and 'professional' conceptions of teaching. In the bureaucratic model teachers do not plan or evaluate their work but merely perform it, while in the professional model teachers plan, conduct and evaluate their work both individually and with their colleagues. They also analyse the needs of their pupils and, taking account of the schools' policies and resources, select the appropriate teaching methods.

The evaluation schedules used in England by OFSTED inspectors would not satisfy all of Darling-Hammond's 'professional' standards, although they do take account of teachers' planning. At the time of our research the OFSTED schedule judged lessons on a 1 to 7 point scale, according to the quality of the teaching and the attitudes, attainment and progress of the pupils. Judgements made about pupils' attitudes and attainment were not related to the context of the school or the pupils but were either unequivocal, for example 'Do all pupils present show involvement, enjoyment and application?' or involved comparisons with national averages or national expectations. Inspectors assessed teachers' subject knowledge, planning, assessment and class management, and the teachers were then graded on a 1 to 3 scale, in which grade 3 was unsatisfactory.

Dealing with incompetence

The main problem which Bridges (1992) claims prevents managers in the US from dealing with poor performance is the job security of their teaching staff, as, once teachers have tenure, dismissal is difficult and the legal procedures are prohibitively expensive. He also reports principals' desire to avoid conflict which results in their withholding negative information from the teachers. The school district administrators he interviewed spoke of principals' desire to avoid conflict, gloss over problems, give good evaluations to encourage the teachers, and new principals said the same about the previous ones.

Bridges' data shows principals acting against all advice on managing poor performance. Potter and Smellie (1995) stress the importance of acting quickly, and of making clear the standards expected of teachers, saying:

> A member of staff cannot fairly be accused of underperforming if he or she has never been made aware of the standards of performance which are expected of him or her. The setting of those standards is something which

should be done in the initial contract of employment, in the job description, in day-to-day supervisions and in appraisals.

(p. 73)

Similarly critical of management, Fidler and Atton (1999) claim that much poor performance results from weak management at some time. They emphasise the importance of preventing poor performance and dealing with it as soon as it arises. They identify six criteria of good management practice for dealing with poorly performing staff in schools:

- the assessment of performance based on evidence not hearsay
- an approach combining support with a determination to secure acceptable improvement
- the seeking of innovative solutions, rather than an unbending obduracy which only seeks improved performance in an unchanged job
- giving consideration to the dignity of the poor performer, and honourable solutions are sought rather than punitive ones
- learning lessons about the prevention of future poor performance rather than accepting poor performance as inevitable
- ensuring the interests of children are paramount

(p. 6)

If poor performance is identified as soon as it arises, they claim, there appears to be more chance of helping teachers to overcome their weaknesses. The longer it is left unacknowledged, the less likely it is that improvement will be possible.

Bridges (1992) is dismissive of attempts to help teachers to improve, believing that it is very rare for ugly ducklings to be transformed into swans. The examples he cites, however, are largely of extremely poor teachers who have been unsatisfactory for a long time, usually without the problem being tackled. It is, therefore, unsurprising that they fail to improve. Another hurdle that Bridges' poor performers face is that principals and district administrators often want them to leave and, therefore, do not really help them to improve. For teachers to improve they need positive reinforcement of small improvements, but Bridges found that during what are supposed to be efforts to help teachers improve, principals tend to become more specific in their criticisms and less laudatory in their evaluations at this time. Their criticisms may be justified, but coming after years of neglect or praise, they diminish the teachers' confidence and lower their self-esteem. He claims:

The possibility of future legal action stimulates administrators to withhold the kind of support that might facilitate improvement. It also prompts them to take actions (for example, extensive documentation, criticism and behavioral specification) which are apt to intensify the teacher's anxiety and defensiveness.

(pp. 72–3)

Bridges quotes several administrators with views similar to those quoted below:

> 'Do we really want to spend a great deal of time and money on improving a teacher who will be at best just one cut above mediocre. The veteran teacher is near impossible to make a good teacher. I really question whether it's worth the grief and the aggravation.'
>
> (p. 72)

During the attempts at remediation, however half-hearted they may be, Bridges reports claims that poor performers tend to blame external factors for their failure, so are resistant to efforts to help them. This view is corroborated by Waintroob (1995) who found that teachers who failed to improve, despite being given help, were generally unhappy people who did not accept or understand that they had problems. Bridges (1992) notes examples of teachers fighting back (verbally) and denying the criticisms. The form the 'salvage attempts' take is usually that principals formulate behavioural directives setting out what the teacher must do. They may also send teachers on courses, and arrange visits to observe excellent teachers. Principals complain about the excessive paperwork that is generated by attempts to help teachers improve their practice, though much of this paperwork is written with possible dismissal proceedings in mind. It is there at least as much to prove that the principal did everything possible as to provide clarity for the teacher.

It appears from Bridges' findings that many principals and district administrators do not really want teachers to improve, believing that they will never become really good. He reports little success of these salvage attempts, even where there are remediation units really trying to help. The views expressed by principals and administrators were that these teachers rarely become good – just slightly less bad. Again, it must be remembered that Bridges was writing about teachers at the extreme end of the incompetence–competence continuum, whose failings had been ignored for years. He says:

> The seeds of failure are sown early in the teacher's career. Having been fed heavy doses of ceremonial congratulations and double-talk for years, the incompetent teacher becomes defensive in the face of unmuted criticism and resists the behavioral specification that accompanies it.
>
> (p. 72)

He notes, however, that programmes to aid improved performance have been successful with teachers with less than ten years' experience and argues for more research into differential treatment of incompetence according to the different causes, different degrees of severity and the different stages of a teacher's career at which it occurs.

When teachers fail to improve they may be made or persuaded to leave teaching. Bridges (1992) reports on 'the induced exit', when administrators sometimes apply pressure directly, by confronting teachers with every accusation the principal receives, or indirectly, by changing the teacher's working conditions. He quotes one new administrator:

> 'The first thing I did was talk to every teacher in the district so that I could find out what they were about including what positions they liked and didn't like. I knew that this teacher was not extremely fond of elementary school. I decided to move this staff member (a middle school teacher) to an elementary school in an effort to get rid of him.'
>
> (pp. 76–7)

This Machiavellian strategy not only goes against Fidler and Atton's (1999) advice that poor performers should be involved in attempts to make them improve, but also their belief that it is completely unethical to identify people as incompetent without telling them. Bridges (1992) also describes how some principals practised 'damage limitation', including the changing of teachers' timetables to avoid any one class being overexposed to them, or the assigning of non-teaching duties, such as looking after the school library.

Despite a few examples of indirect persuasion or underhand manipulation in the US, direct pressure is more common and ranges from gentle persuasion through inducements to threats of dismissal and unsatisfactory evaluation. Bridges (1992) reports that school district administrators offer many inducements to persuade an unsatisfactory teacher to resign or retire, including financial ones such as medical coverage, life insurance and additional years' pension or even employment as a consultant. In California the most common of 12 inducements mentioned was medical coverage (offered to 46 per cent of those induced to resign or retire), followed by employment as a consultant, cash settlement, and employment as a substitute teacher. Some administrators complained that teacher unions obstructed this process by pushing cases to the bitter end, though most thought that unions played a constructive role. Fidler and Atton (1999) argue that the unions have no interest in protecting incompetent teachers as:

> Quite apart from the principled views of members of a caring profession, the credibility of the teacher organisations and their case for improved pay and working conditions are enhanced when teaching is of high quality. They have nothing to gain from poor teaching standards.
>
> (p. 65)

They claim that the role of the teachers' unions is not to defend incompetent teachers to the last ditch, but to ensure that proper procedures are followed, giving their members the opportunity to overcome problems and, if they cannot continue in teaching, to preserve their dignity and to negotiate satisfactory terms.

In the absence of much published empirical research in the field, our decision in the Teaching Competence Project was to try to fill what seemed to be a world-wide gap: the near absence of any large-scale study based directly on an analysis of the views and experiences of those closely involved in allegations of incompetence. There was plenty of polemic, but little substance. In the rest of this book we describe our studies of the various constituencies.

Chapter 3

The views and experiences of head teachers

Anyone who believes that dealing with allegations of incompetence is easy for head teachers should think again. It may seem a simple matter – if the school has teachers who are not performing properly, just identify them, give them a chance to improve, and if they fail to improve, dismiss them – but it is not. Heads have several responsibilities: to their pupils, first and foremost, but also to their colleagues for whom they are the senior line manager. They must act within employment law, otherwise they could be liable for an unfair dismissal suit, which might cost the school a great deal of money. Furthermore, in order to be fair to all concerned and act within the law, they may have to expend a great deal of time and energy, the very elements normally in short supply for those in a busy job. Bridges (1992) describes one teacher in his study as being a 'three Morgan job'. A 'Morgan' is a box for holding legal papers which is about 12 inches wide, so the correspondence and paperwork for a single case was 36 inches in width.

In this and the following two chapters we investigate the views and experiences of the three most significant professional groups involved inside the school when there are allegations of incompetence: in Chapter 3 the head teachers, in Chapter 4 the teachers said to be incompetent, and in Chapter 5 their teacher colleagues.

It was the intention, in Study 1 of the Teaching Competence Project, to solicit the views and experiences of primary and secondary head teachers, first through interviews and then via questionnaires sent to a large national sample of heads. We began by interviewing a stratified random sample of 60 primary and secondary head teachers who had had experience of dealing with an incompetence case, from seven local education authorities. This provided preliminary information about the major research questions described earlier, as well as a base for the national survey, reported later in this chapter, to which nearly 2,000 head teachers throughout the country responded.

THE PRELIMINARY INTERVIEW STUDY

The 60 heads were interviewed using a semi-structured interview schedule. In addition to inviting heads to define incompetence, we asked them to address the major questions in our research, focusing on particular cases of incompetent teachers, and describe the events: how they became aware of the problem, what characterised it, what happened and what had been the outcome. The reason for concentrating on actual cases throughout this project is that it allows us to elicit conclusions from real life events, or at least from informants' perceptions of them, rather than engage in armchair theorising. As with all interview data in this research the interviews were analysed by the four members of the research team on a 'rate until agree' basis, that is, discussing cases until agreement was reached about the interpretation of them. In view of the sensitivity of the research topic, interviews were not recorded, but detailed shorthand notes were made and written up as soon afterwards as possible.

Several features which were to recur in later studies emerged in these preliminary interviews. One was the importance of the context in which teaching takes place. A case study described below tells of a teacher who did very badly in one school but later taught effectively in another. A secondary head in a middle-class suburban area expressed the influence of surroundings very vigorously: 'Three quarters of the teachers here would probably be "incompetent" if they were in some of the rougher schools in this area.'

Another particularly striking element that became painfully clear during certain interviews was the tremendous angst and strained relationships that could ensue. One head was threatened with violence by the husband of a teacher. Few heads had received anything that could be called 'training' for what they were to meet. One described how she arrived at her new school only to be presented with a petition signed by every parent of a particular class asking her to sack the class teacher. He would turn up to school in the morning and go home sick at ten past nine. She persuaded him to resign, but was torn between what she saw as her first and most important duty, to the children and parents, and her second responsibility as the senior manager of a professional colleague clearly suffering from severe stress.

All heads regarded their duty to the children in their school as a clear first priority, not one respondent expressing any other point of view. Most, however, were able to empathise, particularly with teachers who were suffering with personal or health problems, or broken marriages. When they finally got rid of the teacher, many were consumed by guilt and feelings of personal failure, however much colleagues or governors assured them they had done the right thing, as these two heads reveal:

> I feel I've taken the issue on. I've resolved it for the school . . . But you always have this feeling 'How can I put them out of their job?' This teacher has two children, is a single parent with a mortgage . . . But at the end of the day you have a professional duty to the students . . . It's much easier to deal with stroppy (incompetent) teachers . . . You can be hard then, not feel so much stress about it yourself.

Dealing with an ineffective teacher is the hardest thing a head ever does. You have to make yourself unpopular and you face the danger that the teacher will enlist support from other colleagues and you end up with a split within the school.

Inadequate or unsuitable classroom discipline, an issue which was mentioned by virtually every constituency of people interviewed later, recurred frequently. The emphasis on it became even more marked when heads were asked to talk about actual examples of incompetent teachers. Their accounts of events often indicated that poor control of pupils' behaviour formed part of their 'taken-for-granted' definition of incompetence, even if they did not refer to it explicitly in their definition. One head, for example, defined incompetence as 'Not achieving the objectives of a lesson', but went on to describe a teacher whose lessons were chaotic, with children throwing things and fighting. Another, whose definition was given as 'systematic low attainment despite guidance', told of a teacher who 'couldn't control a class'.

Poor personal relationships was another major factor. Some heads referred to bad relationships with parents, with teaching colleagues or, more importantly and more frequently, with pupils. As one said, 'Liking children is fundamental to the job'. Lack of commitment to the job, or to the policies, aims or ethos of the school, and personality deficiencies were also mentioned, as was inability to recognise and address any shortcomings. Most heads specified several factors which, alone or combined, would lead them to conclude a teacher was incompetent, with one head listing eight.

We referred in Chapter 1 to the many changes that had taken place in education in recent years, especially in the school curriculum. The catch-all phrase 'inability to deliver the curriculum', mentioned by over a quarter of heads, could refer to inadequate teaching methods, the teacher's own inadequate subject knowledge, or to pupils' failure to achieve. In most instances, the defining characteristic of incompetence was not the behaviour of the teacher, but the achievement of the pupils, an element that was subsequently to be scored very highly by heads in our national survey.

Not all of those thought to have inadequate class control were permissive teachers prepared to let anything go. Some had rather rigid personalities and unrealistic expectations of what children should be expected to do. They alienated their pupils by relying too heavily on 'chalk and talk'. They shouted and harangued children, expecting them to sit and listen, regardless of how boring or badly planned the lesson was, and when they failed to do so, the teachers blamed the pupils, rather than examining their own practice.

Several heads drew attention to the fact that some teachers have a good knowledge of their subject but may be unable to teach it in an interesting way:

They may know their subject well, but just can't get it across and make it interesting.

She was a very able scientist, but she had discipline problems.

He got on OK at his previous school, just concentrating on his subject, which he loved, but he didn't have the ability to inspire children who weren't well motivated to begin with.

Non-conformity was not seen as a major issue, but eight heads included in their definitions failure in areas we categorised as 'non-adherence to school policies, ethos and aims'. The overwhelming concern, however, reflected in heads' definitions of incompetence and in the examples they gave from their own experiences, was of teachers who were unable to organise a class in a way that enabled them to maintain order, enjoy good relationships with their pupils, and teach them effectively in an interesting way.

What was particularly striking in these preliminary interviews was the sheer complexity of most cases, leading to a long drawn out and sometimes frustrating procedure, which did not always produce a resolution, as this secondary head teacher's description shows:

I talked it through with the head of department, then I sat down with the member of staff, saying I was concerned with the damage and saying what is good practice . . . We set a time limit . . . We needed to be formal and present evidence. Some broad targets were set. The head of department did say things improved for six weeks, but then they slipped again. In the past it had been left at this stage, [but] when it slipped again, [they] talked about targets and then I was alerted.

I explored the evidence. We talked through some of the difficulties. We went through a long period of monitoring and support. That had not proved to be effective. We went to informal monitoring with targets – set ourselves half a term. We offered support from the science adviser, but the teacher wasn't interested in it, though he did take some support from the head of faculty.

But when we looked at the targets again, it was clear he wasn't meeting the targets, although some progress was made. [There were] clear targets and clarity of evidence . . . I indicated at a meeting that targets weren't met. I involved County, set targets, they weren't met, County personnel were present. I set another set, with County personnel, they weren't met.

He declined to have a friend or union rep present at the meetings. County recommended that we give him a third time-line. They said that if we went into a final warning there would be difficulties because he had a stress related doctor's note.

He received a final warning, and then he went off sick.

One important area of focus in the Teaching Competence Project was on positive outcomes, where teachers had been helped to reach an acceptable level of competence. In later stages of the project this was studied in more detail, especially in the national survey of head teachers described below. Head teachers were asked if there was any approach that had worked especially well in their specific case. The most commonly mentioned element was the advice and support provided by other school staff to the teacher concerned, particularly professional support, but in some cases emotional support too. Some heads also singled out the local authority staff, both personnel officers and advisory teachers, for praise.

Personal stress to the head and the emotional impact on the teacher involved were also seen as hugely constraining factors. Both primary and secondary heads saw teaching as a tougher job than it used to be, and felt their own role was far from easy. One head said that she went 'to hell and back', while another felt it blighted his family life for 18 months. They were very concerned about their own health and that of the teacher concerned. The extreme emotional tone of many of these cases was another theme that was to recur many times.

THE NATIONAL SURVEY OF HEAD TEACHERS

The interviews with 60 primary and secondary head teachers, undertaken right at the beginning of the Project, explored and clarified some of the major issues and procedures. Study 1 of the Teaching Competence Project also included a national survey of head teachers, designed to draw up an authoritative and detailed picture from a large stratified random sample. As there are many more primary schools than secondary schools, and based on our previous experience of national survey returns, we sent out questionnaires to a 1 in 8 random sample of all primary heads and a 1 in 5 random sample of all secondary heads in England. This produced a total sample size of 3,017. Responses were obtained from 1,966 heads, an extremely high return rate (65 per cent) for such a long and detailed questionnaire, especially given the severe pressures under which head teachers were working. As with the interviews described above we asked heads to report in great detail on a specific case of alleged incompetence, had they encountered one.

Many heads said they had not had to deal with a case of incompetence in the last ten years, but some 654 heads described in detail at least one case in which they themselves had been directly involved. Thirty of the heads described two cases, so we are able to report in this chapter an analysis of 684 case studies in total. Since heads were asked to report on a case they had encountered over the last ten years, many of the teachers they describe are no longer teaching. Furthermore, we do not know and cannot guess the experiences of the 1,051 heads (35 per cent of the sample) who did not reply, so it is simply not possible, from this study, to make an estimate of current numbers of allegedly incompetent teachers nationally. To do this would require a different kind of research.

One major interest in the research was to discover what happens when teachers thought not to be competent actually improve, so there were separate sections for heads to describe either someone who improved, or a teacher who did not. The questionnaire was designed to cover several elements, including personal information about the heads themselves, as well as details of the teacher alleged to be incompetent, the different phases of the process and the end result, if there was one.

The questionnaire was largely quantitative, as the categories had been drawn up from our previous studies, like the interviews we had conducted with 60 head teachers, but there were also questions where respondents could express themselves freely, in their own words. The following information was elicited:

- personal information about the length of time they had been in a headship
- type of school in which they worked with the allegedly incompetent teacher
- how the heads defined 'incompetence'
- what number of cases they had dealt with
- how competence was monitored in their school
- details of one particular teacher alleged to be incompetent – age, experience, etc.
- aspects of teaching regarded as unsatisfactory
- how the teacher's problem had come to their attention
- the response and behaviour of the teacher
- who else was involved in the case
- what the outcomes were
- a retrospective analysis of how the process could have been improved.

As Table 3.1 shows, there was roughly a 60/40 per cent split between primary and secondary respondents, with a mixture of different types of location, both urban

Table 3.1 Breakdown of case studies reported by 654 head teachers (of whom 30 described two cases, one teacher who improved and one who did not), a sample consisting of 684 teachers altogether

Total number of heads describing one or more cases		654
Number of local education authorities		122
Primary school heads	61%	
Secondary school heads	39%	
Rural schools	15%	
Urban schools	61%	
Mixed	24%	
Teachers who were thought to have improved		161 (24%)
Teachers who were thought not to have improved		523 (76%)
Total number of teachers described		684

and rural. Teachers who did not improve, in the view of the head, outnumbered those who did by about 3 to 1.

Some 1,312 heads said they had not had to deal with a case of incompetence. Of the 654 who had had experience of such a case, 70 per cent had dealt with either one or two instances in the last ten years. A further 15 per cent had encountered three cases and the remaining 15 per cent four cases or more. Altogether they had had experience of 1,519 cases, of which nearly 80 per cent were completed (1,204 completed, 315 current). The 684 detailed histories reported below were all taken from this set of 1,204 *completed cases*, none was still in process.

In terms of their experience of headship, the 654 respondents were split roughly into three thirds: 30 per cent had five years' experience or less as a head teacher, 32 per cent had been heads for between five and ten years, and 38 per cent had over ten years' experience. The sample was almost exactly a 50–50 split of female and male heads. Two thirds had been in their first headship at the time of the case they were reporting.

The quantitative data from the questionnaire are reproduced below mainly in the form of simple tables of frequency and distribution. It would have been possible to apply certain statistical tests to some of the grouped data, but after a number of trial tests we decided against this. For example, there was a strong belief, among certain groups of teachers, unions officers and others, whose views and experiences are reported in later chapters, that a change of head teacher could often lead to allegations of incompetence. We divided heads into three roughly equal groups, according to their experience of headship: those with four years or less, those with five to ten years of headship and those with longer service. We then ran a series of chi-square tests on certain key variables, like whether formal proceedings had been instituted, or whether the teacher had agreed with the head's assessment.

Sometimes a hugely significant chi-square was obtained, but it was not possible, from the quantitative data, to pick out whether the statistical significance had an educational significance, since we could not know whether a case had occurred immediately a new head took up post, or if there were cases that had commenced but were still incomplete where new heads were in post, and so on. Similarly, attempts to compare statistically the outcomes for male and female teachers might have been problematic, since there are far more women than men teachers in primary schools in particular and the sample had not been selected on the grounds of gender. Despite having a large sample, therefore, we decided to present the quantitative data in the form of tables and use qualitative analysis, rather than raw statistical tests, to explore some of the issues and subtleties.

Heads' definitions and identification of incompetence

Written definitions

There are two ways one can elicit definitions of incompetence from head teachers' replies. The first is their *written definition* in response to the direct question 'What, in your experience, are the major characteristics of an "incompetent" teacher?' The second method is to analyse the descriptions of real life cases they have encountered. This offers an *operational definition*, since these were the actual factors they identified to be characteristic of a specific case. We describe these responses later, in the section 'Cases encountered by heads'. There can sometimes be differences between written and operational definitions.

Table 3.2 shows the six most common written definitions from a random sample of 50 per cent of all replies. The careful sifting and sorting of several thousand freehand statements, some of which can be quite lengthy, is extremely time-consuming, so it was not possible to do a full content analysis of the qualitative responses of the total sample. All the qualitative analysis in this chapter, therefore, was undertaken on this same random 50 per cent sample of 327 questionnaires. Each of the tables states the sample size.

The notable differences between the written and operational definitions of incompetence are shown in Table 3.4 (p. 55). The written definitions are given in Table 3.2, though we attach greater weight to the operational definitions in Table 3.4, since these are based on actual cases, rather than on speculation or stereotypes.

Table 3.2 Most frequently mentioned indicators of incompetence, from a random sample of half the responses (327 questionnaires, of which 288 offered definitions)

Factor		Percentage mentioning
1	Classroom discipline	65
2	Planning and preparation	40
3 =	Relationships with pupils	24
3 =	Quality of pupil learning	24
5 =	Subject knowledge	18
5 =	Professional commitment	18

Most heads saw incompetence as consisting of a cluster of factors, not just one single one, as the quotes below reveal, and this was reinforced by the analysis of actual cases, as will be discussed later:

> Inability to relate to children and stimulate interest/excitement in learning. Inability to understand process of children's learning. Inability to differentiate work. Unable to promote high expectations in behaviour and work. Lack of subject knowledge.

Poor classroom organisation. Poor class control. Low expectations. Inability to deliver the curriculum through lack of planning, poor subject knowledge and failure to capture the children's interest. Inability to communicate effectively with parents about children's performance.

Inability to organise resources or to structure learning tasks and assessments. Poor class control and relationships with parents and pupils. Poor management skills and understanding/use of good educational practice. Inability to work within school policies.

Identifying incompetence

The first intimation that there might be a problem with a particular teacher came mainly from complaints and from the head's own informal monitoring, as Table 3.3 shows clearly. Three of the four most common sources of complaint were fellow teachers, parents and pupils themselves. Both formal and informal monitoring by the head or senior managers, such as deputy heads, were also informative, as were unsatisfactory test scores and examination results. Inspections by the Office for Standards in Education (OFSTED) come low in the rank order, as do pre-inspections, prior to a formal visit from inspectors (in tenth and twelfth positions respectively).

Table 3.3 How the head teacher first became aware of the problem (684 cases)

First source of information	Percentage of cases
1 Complaints/comments from other staff	67
2 Informal monitoring by the head	61
3 Complaints from parents, made in person	60
4 Complaints/comments from pupils	49
5 Problem inherited when head took up post	45
6 Formal monitoring by head	42
7 Informal monitoring by senior management	40
8 Formal monitoring by senior management	29
9 Unsatisfactory test/examination results	18
10 OFSTED inspection	15
11 Complaints directed through governing body	14
12 Pre-OFSTED inspection	13

A little below half the heads (45 per cent) said that they inherited a problem when they arrived at a school, a feature which occurs a number of times in this research. New heads seem particularly conscious, on arrival in the school, of those who seem less than competent. Equally, as Chapter 4 will show, some teachers alleged to be incompetent may complain that they had been fine under the previous head, but experienced a clash of values, beliefs, practices or personality, when the new head arrived.

Types of case encountered by heads

The types of case described were very varied. Some dragged on interminably, others were resolved more speedily; some involved certain kinds of perceived weakness, others involved different ones. The genesis of the cases did show some common or predominant distinguishing features, however, and we try to highlight these below.

Who spoke to the teacher first?

Head teachers said that they themselves took the responsibility of raising the issue with the teacher concerned. Two thirds of heads (66 per cent) said that they were the first person to tell the teacher officially that there was thought to be a problem. The next most likely person to raise the matter first with the teacher was a head of department or curriculum co-ordinator (15 per cent), while in third place was the deputy head (9 per cent). Others who later became involved were most unlikely to be the bearer of the first message (LEA officer = 4 per cent; school governor = 1 per cent).

Formal or informal?

Individuals have their own definition of 'formality', but in most cases (59 per cent) heads stated that the matter was first discussed informally. In over a quarter of cases (28 per cent) it was first raised in a formal context. In only 2 per cent of cases was it first discussed during a formal appraisal.

The nature of the problem – operational definitions

Table 3.4 is a very important one, because it shows the many factors thought to lie at the heart of the allegation of unsatisfactory performance. This is the nearest we can get to operational definitions of the concept 'incompetence', because Table 3.4 is based on head teachers ticking a list of areas in which they thought a particular teacher's performance was unsatisfactory. In most cases several categories were ticked, confirming that incompetence was rarely seen as unidimensional.

There is a particularly strong focus on pupils' learning, and it is noticeable that the two highest categories are low expectations and poor progress. Classroom discipline, which is often cited as the most common indicator of incompetence by different constituencies in written definitions, actually comes in fourth place in this list of operational definitions.

What was the background of the teacher?

The sample contained teachers who taught all year groups, from Reception up to A level classes. It is not possible to elicit any pattern across subjects, because

Table 3.4 Areas in which teacher's performance regarded as unsatisfactory (684 cases)

Factor	Percentage of cases
1 Expectation of pupils	65
2 Pupils' progress	64
3 Planning and preparation	58
4 Classroom discipline	57
5 Inability to respond to change	51
6 Differentiating work according to pupils' abilities	50
7 Monitoring and assessment of pupils	49
8 Relationships with pupils	48
9 Managing classroom resources	43
10 Adhering to school policies	34
11 Relationships with teacher colleagues	32
12 Commitment to job	29

primary teachers usually had to teach the whole curriculum and it would not be wise to make inferences about the smallish numbers in certain secondary subject groups, as this would involve too much speculation. For example, although there are few teachers in the sample who taught music or religious education, these are subjects with fewer staff in a secondary school than is the case in mathematics, science or English. Since many teachers teach more than one subject, any attempt to calculate relative percentages would not be well founded. Teachers might, in any case, teach more effectively in their major subject than their minor one, though there were examples of people whose subject knowledge was good, but who still had difficulties.

Nor should anything be assumed from the gender breakdown of the sample (54 per cent female and 46 per cent male). There were more primary than secondary teachers in the sample of 684 cases, and infant schools, for example, are almost exclusively staffed by female teachers, so the small majority of female teachers is not of any significance. Table 3.5 shows the distribution of teachers across age groups and length of teaching experience at the time they were judged to be incompetent. There are separate figures for those teachers the heads believed had later improved their performance, about 24 per cent of the sample, referred to in future as the 'improvers', and the 76 per cent thought not to have taught better, labelled the 'non-improvers'.

Table 3.5 needs to be interpreted *with considerable caution*. As a result of the high level of recruitment to the teaching profession in the 1960s and 1970s, about two thirds of teachers nationally were over the age of 40 in the late twentieth century, so the concentration of teachers in the 40–49 and 50–59 age groups is to be expected, as is the bias towards the '20+ years' experience category. The patterns are not, therefore, quite as striking as they may seem. Although teachers labelled 'incompetent' are more likely to be in the 'middle-aged' bracket, so was the whole teaching profession at the time of enquiry. What

Table 3.5 Age and teaching experience of non-improvers (76 per cent of total sample of 684 teachers) and improvers (24 per cent of total sample)

	Non-improvers %	Improvers %
Age group		
20–29	11	12
30–39	17	21
40–49	33	43
50–59	24	16
60+	2	2
Missing data	13	6
Teaching experience		
Under 1 year	7	5
1–3 years	9	11
3–5 years	5	6
5–10 years	11	14
10–15 years	12	14
15–20 years	12	15
20+ years	26	26
Missing data	18	9

can be said, even allowing for there being more missing data (where respondents failed to supply the information) among the non-improvers than the improvers, is that teachers who improved were slightly more likely to be in their forties, while those who did not improve were a little more likely to be in their fifties.

How did the teacher react to the allegation of incompetence?

Being told that one is regarded as incompetent is not something that people find easy to accommodate, and head teachers reported a variety of reactions. In 44 per cent of cases the head believed that the teacher concerned agreed with the assessment of the situation. But this overall figure conceals a crucial difference between two groups of teachers, those who later improved, and those who failed to improve what they did. Whereas teachers who subsequently, in the judgement of the head, improved their performance, and those who did not, showed similar features on many other measures, here was an example of a critical difference between the two groups. A total of 63 per cent of the 'improvers' were stated by heads to have agreed there was a problem, compared with 38 per cent of the 'non-improvers'. In the eyes of head teachers, recognising that all is not well can be an important part of successfully addressing a problem, while denial is seen as an obstacle. Intensive analysis of a random sample of half the questionnaires showed a number of noteworthy differences between the improvers and non-improvers, as Table 3.6 shows.

Table 3.6 Percentage of 327 heads mentioning various reactions of non-improvers (76 per cent of total sample) and improvers (24 per cent of total sample)

Responses to allegation of incompetence	Non-improvers %	Improvers %
Addressed issues raised/took on board the advice/went on courses	33	56
Did nothing/not a lot	25	0
Went on sick leave for a period, then worked to improve	16	6
Refused to accept there was a problem	16	3
Contacted union	14	13
'Emotional' response	4	7
Did not at first accept there was a problem, later worked to improve	2	21

The eventual improvers not only addressed the issues raised, but were much more likely to listen to advice or agree to go on courses, even if they did not initially accept that there might be a problem. It was much more common for the non-improvers to appear to do nothing or very little, to refuse to accept the head's judgement, or to go on sick leave. Table 3.7 shows a number of very marked differences between those who eventually improved and those who did not. Most notable is the category 'Always receptive to support and advice', which embraced 44 per cent of improvers, but only 19 per cent of those who did not improve. The latter group was more likely to have been unreceptive to support and advice from the beginning, or to have become so part way through the process. By contrast the improvers, even if they had resisted help initially, became much more willing to accept it as time went on.

Table 3.7 Reactions to advice (684 teachers)

Reactions to advice	Non-improvers %	Improvers %
Always receptive to support and advice	19	44
Initially receptive but later became less receptive	32	13
Initially unreceptive but later became receptive	7	32
Always unreceptive to support and advice	26	6
Missing data	16	5

Heads described a series of emotional reactions from a small number of teachers to being confronted with an allegation of incompetence, including tears, sulking and the withdrawal of co-operation. In the case of improvers, however, this negative reaction was more likely to be short-lived, especially when the gravity of the situation became clearer, or when support increased confidence, or firm action forced the issue, as these comments from heads below reveal:

Tried to improve but lapsed again after first meeting. Support given but ignored advice. Second monitoring and meeting – more support and advice given. General improvement – not perfect but acceptable.

She knew there were problems, but lacked confidence and strategies to deal with them. She made no rapid changes, and initially was hostile to any suggestions to change her practice.

Strop! Became quite rude and indifferent – worked 'to rule'. Went early, came in late, etc. It reached a stage when I had to have a formal meeting and minute everything said in front of my deputy head and county adviser. This 'shocked' the person and we turned a corner.

Reactions of eventual non-improvers are given in the following comments from heads:

(a) Sent an increasing stream of children to the head.
(b) Ignored the problems. Stated that nothing was wrong; no discipline problems even though pupils running around and over furniture.

Became very angry with pupils and staff. Turned down offers of support from head of department and head. Problems continued and parental/pupil complaints increased.

She was a very intractable person and there was a strong personality clash with her first head of department . . . (who left) during the informal stages. The acting head of department was a close, long-serving colleague and progress was slow for 18 months when a new head of department was appointed. After a settling in period, formal proceedings began. By then the teacher accepted her shortcomings and genuinely tried to overcome them – not to much avail!

What help or support was made available?

Heads were asked specifically what strategies had been used to help the teachers improve their performance. Table 3.8 shows the main strategies employed. While senior managers were more likely to be involved with those who subsequently did not improve, those who did improve were more likely to be offered regular meetings, the chance to see fellow practitioners thought to be good at their job, to be sent on in-service courses, or to be observed during their own lessons.

Many heads described at length what they and their colleagues had tried to do to support the teacher, and careful thought appeared to have been given. In several cases the more senior members of staff, as well as outsiders, had been involved. For some heads signalling to the teacher that the senior people were

Table 3.8 Main strategies used to support teachers (327 heads)

Strategy	Non-improvers %	Improvers %
In-house support and advice	31	35
Target setting	28	31
Observation of teacher's lessons	21	27
Sent on in-service training course	19	27
Given opportunity to observe good practice	21	26
Offered regular meetings	10	22
Involvement of senior staff with support/advice	28	22
Support from Local Education Authority advisers	23	21

actively seeking to help was regarded as an important psychological element of the response. In several cases these strategies were associated with a degree of success:

> Discussion with head and deputy head. [Teacher] knowing that the head and deputy head *wanted* the teacher to succeed. Observation by deputy head. Deputy head and head working with the teacher. Regular feedback meetings. Following *small* targets of success.
>
> (teacher improved)

In about a quarter of cases the teacher was given time out of the classroom to go on courses, witness good practice in the school or elsewhere, visit the doctor, or was offered some alleviation of duties, given a smaller or easier class. Sometimes these strategies paid off, but this as not always the case, as the contrasting outcomes of the two cases below reveal:

> Identification of key problem as perceived by head. List of concerns. Action list of strategies to help remedy the situation. Programme of informal/formal observations. Monitoring by Head of Department . . . Visit by LEA adviser to comment on performance and offer advice. Visits to see good practice in school and other schools. INSET and course attendance.
>
> (teacher improved)

> Support from team leader and deputy head who helped with daily/weekly planning. Class observations with follow-up meetings and written feedback by head. Smaller class than rest of the team. No challenging pupils included in the class. The best teaching area. Regular time off school to visit medics. Relief from taking any curriculum responsibility for two years.
>
> (teacher did not improve)

Lesson observation was also tried, often by a specially selected 'mentor'. There was usually a specific focus on particular strategies, some of which seemed elementary. However, since three quarters of the teachers in the sample were thought not to have improved, many of these attempts were said to have failed. Most heads appear to have made considerable efforts to offer support, though a small number simply became exasperated or rejected the very idea of assistance, as these two contrasting cases show:

> Head monitored progress of some pupils. Suggested various strategies for improved performance. Suggested less Draconian approach, smile at parents – be more welcoming. Monitored teaching, classroom control. Regular meetings for personal support – suggestions of meetings with a mentor, an adviser, a doctor . . . Several mentors were used (each one gave up after approximately six months). This teacher was a drain on everyone's personal reserves.
>
> (teacher did not improve)

> [I used] no strategies. The incompetence related to failure to adhere to school policies/procedures over marking of GCSE homework, deadlines. I inherited the situation but I had on record other administrative and professional failings.
>
> (teacher did not improve)

Who else became involved?

Within the school the major responsibility for what happened was taken on by heads themselves. They were assisted in two thirds of cases, however, by their senior colleagues, such as the deputy head, and in about one third of cases by other members of the teaching staff. As Table 3.9 shows, the most common external involvement was from LEA advisers or advisory teachers (58 per cent), union officials (48 per cent) and officers from the LEA personnel department (48 per cent).

The chair of governors was reported to be involved in 40 per cent of cases, which seems a low figure, given the responsibilities of the post. We cannot

Table 3.9 Who else was involved, other than the head (684 cases)

	Others involved	Percentage of cases
1	Deputy head/senior management	67
2	LEA advisers/advisory teachers	58
3 =	Teacher union	48
3 =	LEA personnel department	48
5	Chair of governing body	40
6	Other members of staff	37

explain, from this study, why the chair was not included more frequently. That would need a different enquiry, as heads were only asked to describe in the questionnaire who was involved, not why a particular group or person was or was not involved.

How long did the process last?

There has been a great deal of concern about the length of time taken when a teacher is alleged to be incompetent. A balance must be struck between the common law notion of 'natural justice', which decrees that anyone accused of something must be given due notice and a fair hearing, and the rights of those who, if the allegation turns out to be true, may be suffering the consequences of poor practice.

In 1997 the Labour government, when it began to initiate discussion about and legislation on incompetent teachers, proposed a two-term process, plus a 'fast track' option, which could lead to dismissal in as little as four weeks. In the national survey head teachers' views were solicited, and they were also asked about the length of time they had spent on the cases they described in detail.

It is notoriously difficult to put an exact time on a process which may have had a diffuse beginning, rather than a single spectacular event, and which may be protracted at the end. However, with these reservations in mind, Table 3.10 is a summary of what head teachers themselves estimated to be the duration. It shows that fewer than 20 per cent of cases were thought to have been concluded within a year. The two largest categories occupied between one and three years (46 per cent), with '1–2 years' being the largest single group (27 per cent). About a fifth of cases (21 per cent) lasted three to seven years or longer.

Table 3.10 (A) Time elapsing from identification of problem to conclusion of case; (B) Heads' views about the length of the process (684 cases)

	Percentage
(A) Total length of process	
0–1 term	4
1–2 terms	9
2–3 terms	6
1–2 years	27
2–3 years	19
3–7 years	16
7+ years	5
Missing data	14
(B) Heads' views on length	
Process was too long	55
Process was too short	1
Process was about right length	27
Missing data	17

As Table 3.10 also reveals, most head teachers (55 per cent) felt that the process was too long, with only 1 per cent of respondents believing it was too short a period. About a quarter (27 per cent) said that the length of time was about right. Heads were invited to give a freehand account of their views on government proposals for quicker procedures and we did a content analysis of a random sample of 50 per cent (327) of the 654 questionnaires returned.

Approximately 55 per cent of this sample had offered their views, and positive statements about faster dismissals outnumbered negative reactions by about three to one. Some heads felt it was too early to judge, or admitted that they were not familiar with government proposals. The following statements are illustrative of the points that many heads made in *favour* of a shorter process, though some expressed concern about whether this would work, especially if teachers went absent through ill health, and several made a plea for continued support and a fair, not just fast, system of judgement:

> There must be a faster method of removing teachers whose actions actually damage pupils' attitudes and therefore progress. Many teachers, when faced with situations recognise this and are grateful for support. What is not acknowledged is that the present system becomes too prolonged, adversarial, demotivating for staff body as a whole.

> Very much in favour of the 'faster track' but I suspect that once cases are started the staff member will go off 'sick' – how do we then proceed? I am not aware that government proposals will deal with such a situation.

> A helpful proposal, but we must be able to guarantee support first before we fast track teachers out of the profession.

Fewer heads were opposed to shortening the period of time, but many expressed the same reservations about 'fast track' dismissals uttered by union officials and LEA officers and reported in Chapters 6 and 7. They were especially concerned about where they would stand with a four-week dismissal case before an industrial tribunal. About six months, or two terms, was commonly mentioned as being more feasible. These comments below were typical of those that were negative about proposals for quick dismissals, teacher illness often being mentioned as a complicating factor:

> Would be very unsure of acting so quickly in most cases. Teachers are rarely totally incompetent and support has to be offered and chance given for them to improve. Unions, etc. expect different levels of support to be offered. Given the stress these cases cause, two terms is preferable but I'm not sure if it's manageable. Teachers may improve only to 'slip away' again. Also in many cases, I think, staff go off ill and it's difficult then to give required time for improvement without causing stress.

Don't like the phrase 'fast track' – such methods should only be used in extreme cases of incompetency, i.e. where there is a real threat to 'life and limb'. A structured scheme of guidance support and counselling – involving LEA inspectors/advisers – working with agreed target dates over perhaps a six month period is the fairest way of dealing with incompetency.

Were predetermined procedures followed?

The vast majority of head teachers (80 per cent) followed a set of procedures that had been agreed by their LEA or by the governors within their school. One matter of concern, given the sensitivity of the situation, was that about one head teacher in six (17 per cent) followed no predetermined procedures, but rather improvised actions as the case progressed, or said that existing procedures were regarded as inappropriate. Table 3.11 shows the breakdown of 'Yes' and 'No' answers to the question about following predetermined procedures.

Table 3.11 Responses to the question: 'Were you following a predetermined procedure when dealing with this problem?' (684 cases)

Was predetermined procedure followed?	Percentage
YES – LEA procedure	60
YES – School's own procedure	20
YES – Other procedure (unspecified)	3
NO – Procedure improvised as case progressed	15
NO – Procedure available considered inappropriate	2

Some of the 'No' responses referred to more rudimentary cases that never really developed, where there was more informality and early improvement. None the less, it still seems a potentially hazardous approach, especially if events had gone awry.

Why did some teachers not improve, while others did?

About three quarters of the teachers described by heads were said not to have improved, while a quarter did reach an acceptable level of competence. Training and retraining are important but expensive matters, so a cluster of items in the questionnaire invited a freehand response to direct questions about why some teachers appeared to fail, what strategies worked particularly well, and whether certain constraints may have been in operation. Table 3.12 shows the content analysis of the freehand responses of a random sample of half the head teachers (327 cases) describing their beliefs about why some teachers did not appear to be able to improve what they did.

Table 3.12 Most common reasons for teachers not being able to improve (327 heads)

Reason why some teachers did not improve	Percentage
1 Denial – would not accept there was a problem/did not act on advice	19
2 Personality factors – should never have been a teacher	16
3 Unable to change/adapt to national curriculum etc.	13
4 Health problems/stress	10
5 Not committed/lazy	9
6 Personal problems, demoralisation, lack of confidence, burnout	8
7 Context – in the wrong age range/position/school	4

Detailed comments illustrate these points more clearly. Table 3.4, laying out the areas in which the sample of teachers' performance was regarded as unsatisfactory, showed the *symptoms* of perceived incompetence, while the illustrative quotations below indicate a few of the perceived *causes*, as seen by the same head teachers.

Denial

Would not accept that there was a problem. Competency had never been questioned formally before, even though she had been taken out of classes and given support duties. Was given a good reference, which was untrue. Teacher always blamed the children.

Square peg in a round hole who refused to believe he wasn't 'round' even when complaints came from students, parents and other members of staff. Oxbridge graduate who had/has communication problems.

Personality

She was in the wrong job to begin with. She could not relate to children and had no understanding of how they learned.

Should never have entered teaching as he did not like pupils and found it difficult to communicate with anyone. It would appear that he had been failing for *many* years before I joined the school and inherited the problem.

Unable to change

I believe she found all the changes of the national curriculum too demanding and not necessary.

In primary education things have moved on at an unacceptable pace and he was just unable to cope with the demands and pressures.

Health and personal problems, stress

Psychological problems meant he never sustained the effort needed to improve. He ran away from pressure – taking time off, lying about being ill.

She lost control of the class and was never able to regain it. She had a good track record before this, but I believe the stress of the job and the change of schools proved too much.

Not committed/lazy

He had lost interest in the job. He wanted to do things his way which was inappropriate, and he failed to meet the needs of all his students.

Lack of commitment to the job. Deeply unhappy as a teacher. Lack of organisational skills.

Context – wrong age range/position/school

Promoted beyond her abilities in a 'difficult' school. Came from FE and found 11–16 beyond her.

Unused to demands of teaching a large mixed class – had been used to small private school groups.

What approaches appeared to work well?

It would be easy to take a substantially negative view of these findings, especially given that only a quarter of the teachers described were judged to have improved their teaching and reached an acceptable standard. However, we were particularly concerned to identify any particular approaches thought to have been successful. As might be expected an analysis of our random sample of half the freehand written responses (327 heads) showed more offering examples of successful strategies from the improver than the non-improver group. Yet although 82 per cent of heads describing an improver gave examples of approaches they thought had worked particularly well, so did 59 per cent of heads describing teachers not thought to have improved. All was not thought to be hopeless, but there were certainly huge difficulties.

The major categories involved support of one kind or another, but the rank order was different for the improver and non-improver groups. Table 3.13 shows

Table 3.13 Most successful approaches for improvers and non-improvers (327 heads)

Strategy (improvers) %		Strategy (non-improvers) %	
I In-house support	43	LEA support	29
2 Positive, sensitive approach	20	In-house support	15
3 Openness/honesty	9	Union/head relationship	12
4 Monitoring process	9	LEA/school procedures	12
5 Observing good practice	7	Keeping detailed records	10

what were regarded as the five most successful factors for each of the two groups. The prominent position of 'In-house support', as a strategy that was thought to work well with those who improved, confirms what union officers said, reported in Chapter 6, about the importance of positive or negative expectations from other people, particularly if the head wanted someone to succeed, rather than fail.

Since the actual wording of the question, however, was 'Is there anything that you felt worked particularly well?' it has to be pointed out that, in the case of the non-improvers, 'worked well' was not always interpreted by heads as meaning 'helping the teacher'. Some 10 per cent of heads said that 'getting rid of the teacher' had worked well.

Analysis of the freehand statements also shows that strategies that work in one context may not be effective in another. For example, offering a high level of support, observing someone's lessons, encouraging them to watch others, giving detailed and honest feedback, all these may lead to success with a teacher who actively seeks to improve, but fail if the teacher is acutely stressed, resistant, or simply appears not to have the inner resources to change existing practices. In these cases grinding attrition can result. Table 3.12 above listed reasons why teachers did not succeed, and the statements below, describing both improvers and non-improvers, confirm the importance of the need for a positive context for success, where several favourable conditions overlap.

In-house support

> A close working relationship between a senior manager and the teacher concerned. The short term but high level of support was particularly effective.
>
> (teacher improved)

> Care and support given by deputy head responsible for induction.
>
> (teacher did not improve)

LEA support

We had a wonderful adviser who helped wear Mr X down!

(teacher improved)

The support from the LEA adviser to myself as the head and to the teacher was excellent. My chairman of governors also worked very closely with me.

(teacher did not improve)

Positive, sensitive approach

Support from co-ordinators and senior staff. Teacher was not made to feel a failure.

(teacher improved)

Trying to remember that whatever the problems made for the school (and there are MANY), the incompetent teacher is a person with feelings.

(teacher did not improve)

Openness/honesty

Being consistent, open and honest. Keeping clear records of incidents and meetings and action points.

(teacher improved)

Honesty tempered with kindness. It did help having an individual who was honest about his problems.

(teacher did not improve)

Union/head teacher relationship

The sympathetic and understanding shared approach of the LEA and the National Union of Teachers. I was well supported by LEA/governors and could deal in an honest and reasonable fashion with the NUT.

(teacher did not improve)

LEA/school procedures

Using the procedure in a constructive way to improve the teacher's performance.

(teacher improved)

The LEA's framework was a useful shield to depersonalise the situation.

(teacher did not improve)

Monitoring process

> Observations and feedback – reflecting the positive as well as weaknesses – useful discussion. Keeping a duplicate book as an observation log – copy kept and copy (main) given directly to the teacher – no suspicion of 'covertly' kept records.
>
> (teacher improved)

> Teaching myself in the department – gave me a much better insight of the problems and enabled me to talk from first hand knowledge.
>
> (teacher did not improve)

The outcomes of the cases

There was no single end result to allegations of incompetence. When head teachers were asked to describe what had eventually happened to the cases that were not current they reported a dozen different outcomes. In addition to the 684 detailed cases described, heads recorded what had happened in a further 520 cases in which they had been involved, giving a total sample of 1,204 teachers for this particular analysis.

Table 3.14 shows the outcomes in rank order of frequency under different categories. In some 80 per cent of completed cases the teacher had left the school for one reason or another. The largest single outcome was early retirement, a popular option which became less readily available when the conditions for it were changed after March 1997. In any case, it is not usually an option for younger teachers, largely being available for those aged over 50. Ill health retirement was the second most common end result. Heads had frequently referred to physical or psychological stresses, and in many of these cases the teacher's doctor

Table 3.14 Summary of outcomes of 1,204 cases (not just the 684 detailed case studies, but rather all completed cases mentioned in the replies) reported by 654 head teachers

Outcome		Percentage
1	Took early retirement	20
2	Retired on the grounds of ill health	17
3	Reached acceptable level of competence	16
4	Resigned, moved to another post	14
5	Resigned and left teaching profession	13
6	Resigned and looked for another post	6
7 =	Made redundant	3
7 =	Dismissed	3
9 =	Still in post, case never resolved	2
9 =	Given different duties in same school	2
11	Redeployed by LEA	1
12	Other outcome	3

had been involved. These two major reasons accounted for about 37 per cent of the outcomes between them.

The second largest group, accounting for about a third of all cases, was teachers who resigned, most frequently to take a job in another school (14 per cent), or leave the profession altogether (13 per cent), but some teachers (6 per cent) resigned to seek a different post even before finding alternative employment. Table 3.14 shows that these two major results, retirement or resignation for one reason or another, were the outcome in 70 per cent of cases. The remaining 10 per cent of those who left their post consisted of very small groups like redundancy and dismissal (3 per cent each), or redeployment by the LEA (1 per cent), a diminished option since schools assumed more responsibility for their own staffing following the 1988 Education Act.

While 80 per cent actually left their post, about 20 per cent of teachers remained in it, the vast majority (16 per cent of total sample) because they were regarded as having improved their performance to an acceptable level. In some 2 per cent of cases heads practised a mixture of support and damage limitation by assigning them to different duties, while a similar percentage of teachers (2 per cent) were still in post and the head appeared to have reached some accommodation of their perceived shortcomings, or even given up.

A separate analysis of those teachers who were thought eventually to have improved their performance reveals a mixed evaluation by heads. The greatest success was obtained by a small group (4 per cent) subsequently classified as being 'very good', and a bigger group (9 per cent) said to have become 'good'. The two largest clusters, however, were those described as 'acceptable' (39 per cent), or 'acceptable but with some problems remaining' (42 per cent).

How can the process be improved?

The 654 head teachers who took part in this study had had direct experience of being centrally involved in a case of alleged incompetence. They were able, therefore, to capitalise on the many benefits of hindsight. All respondents were invited to reflect on the whole process, to reflect on how they and others might have acted differently to be more effective, what constraints existed, what help they might have needed and whether training would have been beneficial. One common factor in all these responses was that they felt they needed more support, something we reported above from the interviews with head teachers, many of whom recounted graphically the harrowing nature of the experience, both for them and the teacher concerned. A feeling of isolation came through strongly in those interviews, and it features again in this national sample.

What might heads have done differently?

The overwhelming response to this question was that action should have been taken earlier. Once ignored, the problems simply escalated. There was no

Table 3.15 Rank order of action heads would have taken, with the benefit of hindsight (percentages are of those who said they would have acted differently, not of whole sample) (327 heads)

What would be different		Percentage
1	Taken action earlier	47
2	Been more forceful/more direct	12
3 =	Taken more formal approach	9
3 =	Not appointed the teacher in the first place	9
5	Involved the LEA sooner	8

difference in this sentiment between heads describing teachers who had improved and those recording cases where the teacher had left the profession. Table 3.15 shows the rank order of most common responses, from our analysis of the freehand comments of a random sample of half the questionnaires, in response to the question 'With hindsight, is there anything that you would have done differently?' Just under half said they would have changed what they did.

With the benefit of hindsight many heads concluded that they had prolonged the informal stage for too long. They had often hoped the situation would improve, only to find that a more focused and structured approach was necessary, in which detailed written records became crucial, and this also applied both in the case of those who improved and those who did not. The initial tension in the process comes when head teachers instinctively want to act as a caring manager, but then find that this has not worked. Since the switch from informality to formality can be a painful one, it is often psychologically blocked and delayed. The beliefs of heads after the event were extremely consistent, as the selection below shows.

Taken action earlier

I should have gone in a lot sooner. I gave the teacher the benefit of the doubt and as a result children were damaged.

Been more forceful, more direct

I would not have listened to the advice of my own union at the outset. Appeasement did not help at all.

Taken more formal approach

I would have minuted every complaint made by colleagues and inspectors and I would have formalised the initial monitoring and made sure that I confronted every situation – keeping a diary of events, discussions, etc.

Not appointed the teacher in the first place

> Not appointed him in the first place, but this was a vacancy which was advertised and interviewed for three times before this decision was made. Pressure, therefore, of insufficient applicants for the post.

What might others have done differently?

In about 40 per cent of the freehand comments of a random sample of half the questionnaires, beliefs were expressed about what others might have done differently. Mostly these comments reflected a wish for greater support from different constituencies, as Table 3.16 shows.

The key people from whom support is most sought are mostly LEA advisers and fellow head teachers, as well as senior colleagues in the school. As was reported in Chapter 2, many heads, in interview, had spoken of the sense of isolation they had felt, so support from others who could understand, or who had relevant experience, was thought to be vital. It must be remembered, however, that 60 per cent of heads did not make any suggestions about the actions of others, so the views below are those of a minority of respondents, albeit a significant one.

LEA – should have provided better support to head

> I would have welcomed a LEA officer/adviser who would have given advice on how to help the teacher and how to conduct the incompetence procedures. Unfortunately the advisory service knew nothing (or very little) about the procedures and Personnel Department knew nothing about the teaching side. I was, therefore, always needing two types of advice from different departments.

Previous heads – should have tackled situation

> An early acknowledgement of the problems – *much* earlier. It was clear from final reports that this teacher had been teaching in the same area for almost 30 years and had frequently been through similar procedures.

Table 3.16 Rank order of action heads believed others should have taken (percentages are of those who responded to this item, about 40 per cent, not of whole sample) (327 heads)

	What others should have done differently	Percentage
1	Better support from LEA	31
2	Previous head should have tackled situation	12
3	Teacher should have been more receptive	10
4 =	Line manager could have been more effective	8
4 =	Honest references should have been given	8

Teacher – should have been more receptive to support and advice

> [Teacher should have] been more open about problems affecting performance and receptive to help. Not put up barriers to genuine and sympathetic handling.

Honest references should be given

> The teacher who resigned has since taken up a teaching post in another LEA. No references were requested. The reference contains a comment about the action taken by the school. I feel there should be a legal requirement to take up references prior to employment. I am sure there are now other groups of children who are being damaged by this teacher.

What were the constraints?

The most common constraint mentioned by the 62 per cent of heads who made freehand comments in this section was legal issues and fear of running foul of the law, followed by the time-consuming nature and complexity of events, as Table 3.17 reveals. A further point was to do with *relationships*, between the head and parents, governors, the teacher alleged to be incompetent and other members of staff.

Sometimes relationships were very positive and heads found it difficult when they liked the teacher concerned as a person, but had to take action on professional grounds. This intricate nexus of complicated and conflicting relationships could tear at the heart of well-being. Heads were especially wary of the teacher's union and the need to follow procedures. They also resented the massive amount of time and energy required. The teacher's real or invented illness was seen as a complicating factor, especially when prolonged absences interfered with the sequence of the disciplinary procedures they were supposed to follow. Equally stressful was the need, for confidentiality purposes, to conceal from other teachers what was being done, especially when there was a belief among them that the head was taking no action at all. The comments below amplify and highlight different aspects of these points and the other factors listed in Table 3.17.

Table 3.17 Rank order of constraints faced by heads (percentages are of those who responded to this item, 62 per cent, not of whole sample) (327 heads)

Constraints		Percentage
1	Legalities and employment law	21
2	Amount of time consumed	12
3 =	Length of procedures and long timescale	10
3 =	Teacher unions	10
5	Absences of teacher	9

Legalities of procedures/employment law

Danger of mishandling situation leading to, e.g. accusation of constructive dismissal, leaves head very uncomfortable and vulnerable to litigation through a point of law rather than the issue of incompetence.

Amount of time consumed

Time factor: the proceedings were almost inevitably drawn out and I wrote over 30 memos, letters to LEA, unions et al. It was incredibly time consuming. All in all the man was observed/inspected six times!

Length of procedures and long time scale

The number of stages to be worked through while the children still suffered.

Teacher unions

Knowing that if I got one of the stages wrong, the teaching union involved would have stepped in.

Absences of teacher

It is very difficult to proceed when the teacher has the backing of the medical profession and receives sick notes for two weeks at a time over a prolonged period of time. The medical profession only hears one side of the story therefore working conditions/practices are grossly misrepresented. It is impossible to proceed with capability procedures when the teacher has medical and union backing to request a gradual re-integration to teaching through part time work.

Relationships with different groups

(A) The teacher alleged to be incompetent

The fact that I liked the teacher – he was essentially honest and very willing to help at extra-curricular and PTA events.

(B) Other teachers

The school was at a low ebb when I arrived, as the previous head had resigned following an OFSTED inspection. Relations with staff were difficult, as there was so much to sort out. I did not have the full support of the management team to undertake this task – the first time a teacher's practice had been questioned at the school.

(C) Governors

The wife of one governor tried to organise a petition against me for dealing with the incompetent teacher. One governor, a friend of the teacher, tried to organise a governors' meeting without me. It was horrendous. I felt totally friendless and wished I'd copied my predecessor and let the bad teacher drift on!

(D) Parents

Parents/others complained of 'curriculum issues' that I had to be seen to be dealing with while not saying that this member of staff was on support for just such issues, and indeed had targets for some. The inability to let other staff know that the situation was being dealt with – and that the senior member of staff involved was not 'getting away with doing nothing and being paid a lot'.

What would have helped?

Many heads were extremely concerned about their own vulnerability and so wanted a better understanding of the procedures involved, reflecting their anxiety about falling foul of the law. This might take the form of personal assistance from an outsider, or even something as simple as a flow diagram, or a guide to the stages of the process. It was symptomatic of the essential loneliness of their experience that heads often sought external assistance. Some wanted an independent external assessment of the teacher's performance, from the LEA or OFSTED, on a daily basis at critical times, while others would have welcomed a support group, or even a personal mentor, preferably someone who had experienced an incompetence procedure at first hand:

> A 'friend' to discuss things with from the LEA. The LEA were super with advice – and support – so were the Diocese – but someone professional 'on call' who understood and whose job it was to support! Colleague heads were wonderful too – but we've all in our way got our problems and don't like to burden each other too much!

The need for training

One of the questions in the questionnaire asked head teachers 'Have you received training in dealing with cases of incompetence?', while the following question asked 'If no, would you have liked training?'. Of the 82 per cent of the sample of 654 head teachers who responded to the first question, one third (33 per cent) said that they had had some training. The two thirds who had not had any training were strongly in favour of it being available, 89 per cent of them saying that they would have liked training, and this applied to experienced as well as to new heads. Indeed, some felt it was important for deputies to receive training as well:

> As a recently appointed head the issue of teacher competence is a new area for me. Training would seem to be central – yet because it is the responsibility of a head, it is the one issue that at present a deputy has no involvement in. As such it would seem to me: (1) Deputy heads need to be trained – especially given the number who will be acting heads in the present climate; (2) It should be part of the training for a head's qualification; (3) Existing heads need 'remedial' training. Fairness, clear steps and a reasonable timetable would seem to be essential in dealing with competence.

General observations

Head teachers were asked if there were any general or further points they wished to make. Some commented on the increased demands that the profession now faced, so that notions of 'competence' had moved to a higher level of demand. Even if the quality of teaching had improved, many believed, it might not have improved sufficiently to match the increase in demands on the teaching profession:

> There is no doubt that teaching quality in schools and colleges is much higher now than it was 10–15 years ago. All my head teacher and principal colleagues endorse this and agree that tolerance of incapability is low. With more students taking exams and assessments at all levels, there are also fewer places to hide in schools and colleges. The 'consumers/customers' are also more demanding and rightly so as recognition widens that educational success is a key factor in future career success, etc.

Most wanted to put the issue of incompetence in perspective, arguing that it was a very small minority of teachers, and that they felt that, in general, their colleagues were industrious and competent, though some feared for the future, especially if the quest for higher competence merely produced safe orthodoxy and conformity:

> I fear the cloning of the profession. Most of my best teachers (when I was a pupil) were distinctly eccentric and some were charismatic. They could now be seen as incompetent.

A number were concerned about the negative image of teachers sometimes portrayed in the mass media and the escalating pressures that this produced. They feared that these pressures could turn competent practitioners into incompetent ones:

> There are few teachers now who do not *feel* incompetent. We all struggle to fulfil ever unreasonable job descriptions and cope with continually being labelled 'failing' by OFSTED, overwork, and the press. Many quality members of the profession have taken early retirement to escape this spiralling pressure/stress . . . More labelling of teachers as incompetent will only serve to demoralise further a profession more demoralised than I can ever remember and contribute to the self-fulfilling prophecy of the 'blame-fail' ideology/culture we live in.

Some heads were critical of initial training and induction, feeling that certain teachers should not have been allowed into the profession, or should have been identified as being at risk in their first post. Others were concerned that teacher shortages, especially in certain subjects, could lead to the employment of those who just manage to pass their course and would normally have difficulty obtaining a post:

> My own experience of three cases as a head (and several other, often unresolved cases, from earlier in my career) is that it is at the *point of entry* to the profession that problems are not picked up. I'd welcome more stringent entry requirements – not just in terms of academic strengths, though this should not be ignored – but also as regards *inter-personal skills, sense of innovation, acceptance of change, autonomy*, above all 'being interesting in the classroom' so pupils don't fall asleep or become disruptive.

Many heads described in detail the traumatic impact of events on themselves and their family, just as heads had done in the interviews reported above. Usually, however, they said they would go through it all again in the interests of their pupils and the school. It was especially difficult when the teacher concerned was in a senior position. Several heads found themselves going through incompetence procedures with their deputy or with a head of department or senior teacher, and this caused particular stress:

> It took an enormous amount of time, was very stressful for me (it only hit me the following term when a minor illness became unexpectedly worse and I became clinically depressed). Because the member of staff was the deputy head, there was no management support for me within the school and it was very divisive for the staff who agreed she was useless but felt sorry for her. She talked publicly about what I was doing and I could say nothing. The LEA and Diocese were very helpful and encouraging. The governors were all

rather scared, they very much wanted her dismissed but didn't really want to be associated with the process. It was awful but worth it and I would do it again.

One issue that concerned heads was not so much the teacher who was clearly failing, but rather the person who was just on the borderline, doing enough to avoid formal proceedings. In the case of older teachers, some heads would have welcomed a humane process of withdrawal, or possibly even transfer into a different role:

Part of the problem is that people who were once quite good at their job become 'tired'. There should be somewhere or some way that they can be transferred to a different role within the profession if they wish, before formal proceedings have to take place. Early retirement at 50 with enhancement should be an option for those who request it. Twenty-five plus years in the job is punishment enough without further hassle, etc. In-service sabbaticals for length of service should also be a possibility to infuse some new life into the 'old dog'.

Finally one head described with approval the situation in another country which appeared to take some of the pressure away from the head and the school:

I like the sound of the system used in Australia. The head has a competency and skills appraisal check for every teacher. This is applied every year. When a teacher 'fails' this check, the issue is taken away from the head. An independent panel then takes over. They assess the teacher, set targets and achievement times. If not achieved, further targets and shorter time limit set. If not achieved, teacher's contract terminated. I like the independent nature of the assessment body as this removes personality clashes and prejudice claims between head and teacher.

SUMMARY

This chapter reports a study of head teachers in primary and secondary schools in England. A number of the major findings from the national survey are listed below:

*   A sample of 654 head teachers reported in detail a case, during the last ten years, of a teacher alleged to be incompetent; 30 reported on two cases (total sample of cases = 684).
*   One quarter of these teachers were believed to have improved later, three quarters not.
*   First indications of a problem came from complaints from other teachers, parents, pupils themselves, and from the head teacher's informal monitoring.

- Low expectation of children, poor pupil progress, inadequate planning and preparation, classroom indiscipline, inability to respond to change, were the most common problems.
- Teachers who later improved were more willing to acknowledge a problem, were more receptive to advice; non-improvers often denied there was a problem.
- Most common strategies were in-house support and advice, target setting, observing teacher's lessons, sending on courses, giving opportunity to observe good practice.
- Many cases (46 per cent) took from one to three years; one in five cases took longer; a majority of heads believed this to be too long and would have preferred six months to two terms.
- Most schools followed a predetermined procedure, but one in six did not.
- The two most common outcomes of cases were retirement and resignation (70 per cent), though the early retirement option (20 per cent of cases) is no longer so readily available.
- Of the teachers who subsequently reached an acceptable level of proficiency, 13 per cent became 'good' or 'very good'; 42 per cent became 'acceptable but with some problems remaining'.
- With hindsight many heads believed that earlier action would have helped.
- Heads welcomed government legislation, but felt fast track dismissals might be too quick.
- Heads were worried about employment law and would have welcomed more external help.
- Only one third of heads had received training in the field, though 89 per cent of the rest would welcome it.
- Heads were concerned about the huge stresses on themselves, the teacher, other staff, pupils, parents and governors, often fearing for their own health and that of others.

Chapter 4

Teachers alleged to be incompetent

It was no easy assignment to elicit information from teachers alleged to be incompetent. Most had been emotionally bruised by the events in which they found themselves enmeshed and some said it was traumatic even to recall them. Many of those who replied said they were deeply stressed. Just as the head teachers, described in Chapter 3, reported considerable strains on themselves and their family, so too the 70 teachers in this study said that they had found the experience devastating.

Some of those who initially had been willing to participate in the research said that revisiting the events caused them too much distress to complete the questionnaire. One teacher telephoned to apologise for not returning the questionnaire, explaining that it had triggered a panic attack from which she had been suffering periodically since the allegation of her incompetence. Others who had completed the questionnaire also wrote of the stress caused to them merely in recalling the events.

Study 2 of the Teaching Competence Project was designed to analyse their views and experiences, and it was with some trepidation that we embarked on it. We decided early on that observation of the teachers in their classrooms was not feasible, as it would be too intrusive. Instead more sensitive methods were needed. The main tool of data collection, therefore, was a detailed questionnaire, but we also carried out a small number of in-depth interviews. In some instances teachers also provided us with copies of the relevant documentation, which was often copious in volume.

SAMPLE

The sensitive and confidential nature of allegations about someone's professional competence means that it was not possible to ask LEAs, teacher unions or head teachers to put us in touch with teachers who had been the subject of or were currently undergoing incompetence procedures (also referred to as 'capability procedures', both in official documents and in informal settings). In order to contact such teachers, therefore, a request for volunteers was made in the Times Educational Supplement, to which we received 80 responses. These must have been people still in touch with education to have seen the appeal, either directly, or through contacts. We then wrote to these volunteers giving them further information about the Teaching Competence Project and enclosed a questionnaire, together with a freepost envelope for its return.

Two independent bodies involved in supporting teachers alleged to be incompetent indicated their willingness to inform teachers with whom they were in contact of our research. We made available to these organisations some questionnaires and freepost envelopes for distribution to those who wished to participate in the study. In total, 70 completed questionnaires were returned. This is an opportunity sample, therefore, of 70 teachers who were available and willing to provide information, not a truly random sample of all teachers alleged to be incompetent.

Separate questionnaires were designed for current and past cases. Both questionnaires contained sections requiring respondents to give details relating to their age, sex, years of teaching experience, the type of school they had taught in, positions of responsibility held. Respondents were also asked a series of questions intended to allow them to describe the events surrounding the allegation of their incompetence and to indicate whether they agreed with it. Details were sought concerning the head teacher, other parties who became involved in the events and the type of procedures followed. Data were also collected on the outcome or the anticipated outcome of these cases.

In addition, the teachers were asked to reflect on the way in which events had been handled by themselves and the others involved, and to consider whether any improvements could have been made. Several of the questions involved responding to a set of predetermined categories, but others invited a freehand response. Many respondents wanted to tell their story in their own words, so there was plenty of space for freehand responses. Tables 4.1 and 4.2 show the breakdown of the sample in terms of whether their case was current or completed and the gender split.

Sample details

No inferences can be drawn from the ratio of female to male respondents, as there are far more female than male teachers in primary schools, especially in the early years, and the overall gender profile for the total teaching staff in public sector nursery, primary, secondary and special schools is about two female to one male teacher (DfEE 1996 p.31).

Eighty per cent of teachers in the sample were over the age of 40, and a similar percentage had taught for ten years or more. About half of the teachers concerned had been teaching at the same school for over five years when the allegation was first made. In 10 per cent of cases, they had been at the school for over 15 years. National figures show that about two thirds of the profession were in the 40+ bracket during the period under review. One would expect, therefore, most respondents to be predominantly middle-aged, like the profession itself.

Table 4.1 Types of cases

Type of cases	Number of questionnaires returned
Current	26
Past	44
Total	70

Table 4.2 Sex of respondents

Sex of respondents	Percentage
Female	63
Male	37

As will be reported in Chapters 6 and 7, however, both teacher union and LEA officers believed that, along with newly qualified teachers (NQTs), older teachers are more likely to be the subject of incompetence allegations. They argued that this is because a number of older teachers 'burn out', are less committed, become unable to adapt to changes in education, a view in part supported by what head teachers said. Some teachers in this study, however, suggest that it is because they have become too expensive for their school to employ, but we have no related evidence to support or refute this belief.

Completed questionnaires were received from teachers in infant, junior and primary schools, and from the secondary and tertiary sectors, together with six cases of teachers in special schools. In the primary sector, teachers from all year groups were represented. In the secondary/tertiary sector, most subjects were represented. Table 4.3 gives details of the type of school in which respondents taught.

Since the teachers who took part in this research were all volunteers, they may not be representative of all teachers who have been alleged to be incompetent. In only 4 of the 44 completed cases in this survey had the teacher reached a level of competence acceptable to the school management (that is, less than 10 per cent). Of the remainder, two were given different duties in the same institution,

Table 4.3 Type of school taught in at time of allegation (70 cases)

School	Number of cases	Percentage
Primary sector	26	37
Secondary sector	32	46
Tertiary sector	2	3
Special schools	6	9
Independent schools	2	3
Peripatetic teacher	2	3

but the rest (38 teachers) had left their school. By comparison, the survey of head teachers, reported in Chapter 3, which was based on a national stratified random sample, showed that about a quarter (161 out of 684 individual cases, 24 per cent) had reached a level of performance acceptable to the head.

Most of the teachers stated that the allegation of incompetence and the subsequent events had had a profound effect on their personal and professional lives which they wanted to share. The sample may, therefore, be skewed towards those who disagreed very strongly with the allegation of incompetence, or felt the procedures adopted were ineffective and/or unfair. None the less this study does provide an insight into the experiences and perceptions of a group of teachers whose views are rarely heard. It also raises issues about the way in which these cases are initiated and handled by school management and others, such as LEA staff and teacher associations.

Although the 70 teachers had been, or were at the time, alleged to be performing unsatisfactorily in some or all aspects of their teaching post, what soon became clear, as the responses were analysed, was the uniqueness of each case. No two cases were exactly the same: there were differences in the ways in which the allegation had been made, in the teacher's reaction to events, in the support offered and the teacher's response, in the way that procedures were or were not followed, the different parties that became involved, the nature of their involvement, and in the outcomes. We have grouped some data into tables, but much of the story is qualitative and individual.

TEACHERS' ACCOUNTS OF EVENTS

Definitions and identification of incompetence

In this research there have been areas of agreement and of disagreement between different groups and constituencies. The perceptions of those who are accused of incompetence may, in some cases, be diametrically opposed to the perceptions of those who make the allegations. A head teacher, for example, may see a particular teacher as lazy and incompetent, while the teacher may feel an unsupported victim. It must be said, however, that our interviews with head teachers and the national survey of their views and experiences, reported in Chapter 3, showed that many heads could empathise with teachers, in some cases regarding them as friends, even though they had to take action against them.

One of the key findings of this research has been that the lack of a universally accepted definition of 'incompetence' may result in different interpretations of the term at different times and in different schools. In about a quarter of the cases described in this study, teachers indicated that they did not have a job description at the time of the allegation of unsatisfactory performance. They also expressed concern about the basis on which some of the allegations were made, about one in six stating that no in-house monitoring took place. Teachers'

Table 4.4 In-house methods of monitoring teaching performance (70 cases)

Method of monitoring	Number of cases	Percentage
Informal monitoring by head/ senior management (SM)	14	20
Informal monitoring by head/SM + appraisal	13	19
None	11	16
Formal monitoring by head/SM only	10	14
Appraisal process only	9	13
Formal and informal monitoring by head/SM + appraisal	6	9
Formal monitoring by head/SM + appraisal	4	6
Formal and informal monitoring by head/SM	2	3
Missing data	1	1

description of the methods used by their schools to monitor performance generally are set out in Table 4.4. In this and other tables percentages may not add up to exactly 100 because of rounding individual categories up or down.

As Table 4.4 indicates, aggregating the 'Informal monitoring' and 'None' categories shows that over a third of teachers (36 per cent) stated that no regular *formal* system of monitoring was in place in their school. 'Not really done. Only head could do it but he plays no role in classroom practice or curriculum' (primary teacher). In only six schools was there reported to be comprehensive monitoring of performance.

Although this is a relatively small and skewed sample, and therefore the findings should be treated with caution, there is an indication that formal monitoring of performance may be taking place less in primary schools than in secondary schools. Fewer than half the respondents referred to the appraisal process, yet there is a statutory requirement on schools, under the *Education (School Teacher Appraisal) Regulations 1991* (DES 1991), to carry out appraisals for all teaching staff on a two year cycle, and the observation of a teacher's classroom practice is a mandatory element of this. The relatively low level of compliance was confirmed by head teachers. Just over half (57 per cent) of head teachers, responding to the same question in the national survey, said that appraisal was carried out in their school.

Notification of problem with performance

Teachers were asked by whom and how they were informed of the alleged problems with their performance. In two thirds of cases the head teacher had raised the issue with the teacher, in 20 per cent of cases – nearly all in the secondary sector – it had been either the deputy head or head of department and, in 10 per cent of cases, a LEA officer. OFSTED and HMI inspections were reported as other channels through which the allegation of unsatisfactory performance had been made, but these accounted for only a very small number.

There was a fairly even split between the respondents, nearly half, indicating that the matter had been raised with them informally and a similar number saying they had first been told at a formal meeting that their performance was currently unsatisfactory. Five teachers reported their shock at receiving the allegation in a letter, without any previous warning, while three stated that the issue had been addressed as part of the appraisal process.

The use of the informal conversation is one aspect of the process that needs to be addressed. Individuals have their own definition of 'formality', but in our national survey of head teachers 59 per cent of heads stated that the matter was first discussed informally. Head teachers may avoid formality in an attempt to minimise confrontation or distress, but some teachers reported that they had not initially realised how potentially serious their position was. By the time they were aware of this, events had overtaken them. Teacher union officers stressed how important it was that head teachers and line managers should be explicit in their initial conversations with teachers about areas of weakness and possible outcomes if improvements were not achieved. These perfectly reasonable expectations put head teachers in a difficult position. If they act precipitately they are seen as insensitive and authoritarian, if they proceed gently their message may not be understood.

In 1997 local authorities were asked by the Secretary of State for Education to review and revise their capability procedures in the light of the *Report of ACAS Working Group to consider an outline capability procedure for teachers* (1997). This framework document discussed the 'informal' and 'formal' stages of the process and stated clearly that 'informal' does not mean 'ad hoc':

> It is important that professional performance problems are clearly identified and given appropriate consideration and support at the earliest possible stage. The nature of the problem, its level of seriousness and cause(s), must be investigated and identified by structured information gathering and systematic recording.

If this approach had been followed, no teacher should have been in any doubt about the allegation, the support to be offered, and the next step, if improvement was not achieved. It became clear during interviews with LEA personnel officers, reported in Chapter 7, that even where LEAs had comprehensive capability procedures in place, there had been a need to take some head teachers back to the beginning of the process, to make sure that the required procedural steps had all been followed.

Areas of performance regarded as unsatisfactory

The teachers were asked to indicate which areas of their performance had been alleged to be unsatisfactory, distinguishing between those that they perceived to be 'major' factors and those that were 'minor' factors. Table 4.5 sets out the findings, the ranking denoting the frequency with which the different elements were cited as 'major' factors.

Table 4.5 Areas of teachers' performance regarded as unsatisfactory (70 cases)

Area of performance	Major Factor %	Minor Factor %	Not a Factor %
1 Classroom discipline	53	6	41
2 Planning and preparation	32	22	46
3 Pupils' progress	29	15	56
4 Relationship with colleagues/ team members	27	7	66
5 Management role	25	6	69
6 Adherence to school policies	24	13	63
7 Expectations of pupils	24	12	64
8 Monitoring and assessment	22	12	66
9 Relationship with pupils	21	10	69
10 Management of classroom resources	18	21	61
11 Differentiation	18	15	67
12 Relationship with parents	15	9	76
13 Curriculum role	15	4	81
14 Commitment to job	15	4	81
15 Classroom display	13	12	75
16 Ability to respond to change	9	10	81
17 Subject knowledge	7	9	84
18 Homework	6	4	90

As Table 4.5 shows, classroom discipline problems were cited in first place, followed by 'inadequate planning and preparation' of lessons, with 'unsatisfactory pupil progress' in third place overall. The first four factors are similar to the first four rankings of head teachers, though the order is different and 'relationship with colleagues/team members' is present instead of 'expectation of pupils'. Table 3.4 in Chapter 3 showed the first four factors, according to the national sample of head teachers, to be as follows: (1) Expectation of pupils, (2) Pupils' progress, (3) Planning and preparation, (4) Classroom discipline. Teacher union officers, LEA staff, parents and pupils also identified classroom discipline as a major factor, as later chapters will show.

Teachers' own assessments

Respondents were asked whether they had agreed with the head's assessment of their performance. Given that the teachers were all volunteers, and many felt

Table 4.6 Teachers' reactions to allegation of incompetence (70 cases)

Teachers' reactions	Number of cases	Percentage
Did not accept there was a problem with their performance	54	77
Felt the management's diagnosis of problem to be wrong	4	6
Accepted the management's assessment of the situation	12	17

strongly that they had been unjustly accused of unsatisfactory performance, it was not surprising to discover that, as Table 4.6 shows, about three quarters of them (54 out of 70) had not previously considered that they had a problem with their performance, and a further four believed the management's specific diagnosis of the problem to be incorrect.

Of the 16 who did accept that there had been a problem, however, all except one indicated that their own diagnosis was a lack of effective social control over pupils' behaviour, poor classroom discipline. Only two of these teachers (current cases) reported that action was being taken to help them improve their class management skills, though others said that they had informed the school management of their difficulties, but received little or no support:

> I am not a very assertive teacher and needed help with discipline on occasions. Most times I was unsupported and told that the problem was that I did not teach properly, which was why the children behaved badly, so I was given little support for indiscipline.

Several of the 54 teachers who did not agree with the school management's allegation of unsatisfactory performance cited as evidence what they saw as concrete indicators of their effective teaching, including references to the head teacher having praised their performance:

> The head had remarked on two occasions at formal meetings that she considered I was 'an excellent teacher'!

> In November the head referred to me as 'highly competent' and had full praise for all my work.

> I had the best A level results in the college for five consecutive years.

Teachers who disagreed with the assessment of their competence were asked about the allegation that their performance was unsatisfactory. A wide range of explanations were offered which included: a belief that there was a conspiracy; bullying and victimisation; scapegoating; racial discrimination; incompetence or vengeance by the head; unjustified complaints from parents; clashes of philosophy; pupils being unwilling, or unable, to learn or behave well; inadequate resources; the need to make staffing cuts as a result of financial pressures.

It is not possible to give here a full account of all the comments made by teachers. Those cited below have been selected to represent several different types of explanation given, as well as the strength of emotion displayed by many of the teachers who responded:

> My second in department and the male deputy were great friends and wanted me to leave so that my second could have my job. (conspiracy)

> I have written evidence from one of the six people on the interview panel when I was appointed (a parent governor), that the head wanted a young internal male candidate to be given the head of department post. The other five members of the panel felt I was the best candidate. I faced persecution, intimidation, unreasonable demands from very early on. Another teacher commented that 'the head has a hit list and you are obviously at the top of it'. General discipline in the school was dreadful. (bullying)

> I felt I was being victimised. Since the head came to the school, discipline had deteriorated. Some staff were not given any support and were openly criticised. No confidence and low morale was inevitable and [there was] much tension in the school. (victimisation)

> I taught a child whose father was a governor of the school and whose mother was an advisory teacher. They assumed he was 'exceptional' but testing proved he was average. I was blamed . . . I was then given a very difficult class behaviourally. They had always been difficult, but I was blamed again. Procedures were started against me. I have received four visits from the inspectorate and received positive feedback. The adviser stated that I was 'miles away from incompetency'. (scapegoating)

> Chance – a largely absent and difficult sixth form student, an awkward and emotionally upset parent and a new head. The parent blamed me for the fact that her son had left home and accused me of being rude to her on the phone. I was head of sixth form. (unjustified complaint)

> I believe that, following my role as [union] school representative, in more than one incident between the head and other [union] members, relations between myself and the head deteriorated. I became the subject of repeated scrutiny and any bad lesson I taught was immediately seized upon, whilst my good teaching was largely ignored. (vengeance)

> I was told I was 'too independent' in my thinking and working. (non-conformity)

Very large class – 35 children, 12 of whom on special needs register. No additional help (new head had terminated contracts of ancillary staff). Very small classroom. Several children had caused discipline problems throughout their school career. (pupils' fault)

I think the school needed to lose a member of staff in their reorganisation and I was probably having the most discipline problems, so they wanted to get rid of me. At least they thought I was an easy target. (financial pressures)

In discussion with head teachers, LEAs and teacher union officers, it became apparent that the arrival of a new head at a school could become a significant factor in the initiation of capability procedures against a teacher. Explanations for this were that a new head, without the 'baggage' of long-term personal relationships with the staff, was more able to confront a teacher about perceived weaknesses. Examples of cases were also cited where a new head, with a philosophy of teaching and learning which differed from those of existing staff, demanded changes in these areas. Teachers who said they had been valued by the previous head suddenly found themselves a focus for criticism. Table 4.7 sets out the amount of time in post of the head teacher concerned.

Table 4.7 Length of time head had been in post when allegation was first made (70 cases)

Number of years in post	Percentage
Less than 1	21
Between 1–3	19
Between 3–5	13
Between 5–10	23
Between 10–15	7
Between 15–20	6
Not applicable (teacher peripatetic)	3
Missing data	8

Table 4.7 shows that 40 per cent of cases were initiated by heads who had been in post for less than three years. This figure looks high, but many new head teachers were appointed during the period under review, so it is not possible to corroborate the 'new broom' belief with any certainty. Many of the teachers themselves did not appear to perceive this as a key factor, though a few did refer to the short time in post of the head.

Teacher's receptiveness to support and advice

Despite the majority of the respondents' vehement rebuttal of the allegation of incompetence, none reported themselves as being 'always unreceptive' to

Table 4.8 Receptiveness to support and advice (70 cases)

Level of receptiveness	Percentage
Initially receptive, but later became less receptive	31
Support and advice were not available	31
Always receptive to support and advice	29
Initially unreceptive but later more receptive	7
Missing data	1
Always unreceptive	0

the support and advice on offer, as Table 4.8 shows, though head teachers saw defensiveness and denial as a major obstacle. About a third of the teachers believed that support and advice was not available. Another third (31 per cent) reported themselves as 'initially receptive' to the support being offered, but less prepared to accept advice as events progressed.

Although it might have been expected that the four teachers who eventually reached an acceptable level of competence would have been among those who were 'always receptive' to support and advice, in fact, none of the four believed themselves to be in this category. A number of the comments made by respondents revealed lack of trust and challenged the very concept of 'support and advice', which they sometimes perceived to be harassment:

> What appeared to be support and advice seemed to be used more to make a case against me, rather than in good faith.

> I was always receptive when I trusted the person giving the support and advice and was sure of their good will. The later 'support and advice' was more like harassment and was very difficult to be receptive about.

It may be that some teachers were resistant to acknowledging that support and advice were being provided, or alternatively that what heads consider to be support and advice was simply not perceived as such by the teachers. Teacher union officers referred in interview to a blurring of 'support' and 'monitoring', and the need to make a clear distinction between the two. Some heads may wish to believe that support and advice have been provided to show they were following procedures properly, since most LEA capability procedures require some element of support for the teacher. Prising out the reality from contrasting and sometimes conflicting accounts is not at all easy. The difference between 'support' and 'harassment' may become emotionally clouded depending on the role of the informant.

Procedural issues

There was evidence from interviews with local authority and teacher union officers that, even where capability procedures existed, head teachers were not

Table 4.9 Was/is the head teacher following a predetermined procedure when dealing with this case? (70 cases)

		Percentage
Yes	LEA procedure	36
	School's own procedure	9
	Other	6
No	Procedure improvised as case progressed	36
	Procedure available considered inappropriate by head	I
Don't know		13

always aware of, or did not follow them. Table 4.9 shows that many of the aggrieved teachers in this sample expressed similar beliefs, with over a third (37 per cent) stating that no predetermined procedure had been followed by the head following the allegation of incompetence. It might be the case, of course, that heads were indeed following a set of agreed procedures, but the teachers involved were simply not aware of them, as some of them admitted (13 per cent).

A number of teachers believed that, even where procedures were available, heads did not always use them properly and some felt strongly about any deviations from them:

> The procedures are not worth the paper they are written on. There is no protection in schools which have a weak governing body. The procedures are far too open for abuse by senior management who do not seem to have to account for their behaviour. After 15 years' successful teaching my confidence has been seriously undermined and I am now having to rebuild my career.

In the national survey of head teachers, one in six heads said that they had not followed any predetermined procedure, but rather improvised at each stage. There may be disagreement among the different parties about the exact number, but there is agreement on all sides that some head teachers do not follow the procedures that have been laid down. Effective communication between the head and the teacher about procedures being followed is vital if teachers are to understand the seriousness of the allegation and to understand their own rights and position.

Capability procedures comprise two parts, the 'informal' stage and the 'formal' stage. Respondents were asked whether formal proceedings had been instituted in their own case. Table 4.10 sets out the findings.

It can be seen that, even in the 44 completed cases, where the outcome had been that 38 teachers had left their post, formal proceedings were said never to have been instituted in about 40 per cent (18) of the cases. Of these 18 teachers,

Table 4.10 Were/have formal proceedings (been) instituted?

	Current cases	Completed cases	Percentage of total sample
	n = 26	n = 44	n = 70
Yes	10	25	50
No	16	18	49
Don't know	0	1	1

five had retired on ill health grounds, three had resigned and moved to another teaching post, two had reached an acceptable level of competence, two had taken early retirement, one had resigned and was looking for another teaching post, one was moved to a different post in the same school, and one, at an independent school, had been dismissed. In other words, many of these teachers left during the informal stage of the process, before the formal stage had actually been reached. Even where the formal stage had been initiated, it was extremely rare for a case to result in an actual dismissal. In the 26 cases still taking place at the time of enquiry, formal proceedings had already been instituted against ten teachers.

Time scales

The 44 completed cases had taken varying periods of time from the initial allegation to its conclusion. Table 4.11 shows that the most common length of time was one to two years, although eight cases had taken over three years.

Many head teachers had said the process had taken too long and this sentiment was echoed by these teachers. Eleven of them felt that the process had been too long, though five believed it was too short. There were clearly different perceptions as to what was a 'reasonable' length of time for the process. Only three of the 44 teachers reported that the time scale had been 'about right'. Twenty-nine teachers stated that the events should never have taken place at all, since they did not consider there was a genuine problem with their performance.

Table 4.11 Length of cases from initial allegation to conclusion (44 cases)

Time scale of case	Number of cases
Less than 1 term	1
Between 1–2 terms	9
Between 2–3 terms	6
Between 1–2 years	12
Between 2–3 years	6
Between 3–7 years	8
Missing data	2

Teachers who had actually reached the stage of formal proceedings were asked to state the length of time from the beginning of the formal stage to the end of the case. In over half the 19 cases for which we have information, matters still took over a year to bring to a conclusion. In the outline capability procedure proposed in 1997 by the ACAS working party, cited above, there is the recommendation that once the capability procedure has been formally activated, the maximum period for dealing with cases should normally be no more than two terms (paragraph 2.3). Only six of the 19 cases which involved formal proceedings would have met this requirement.

Accounts of other parties' involvement in the events

In the course of the studies undertaken previously in this research, it had become apparent that a number of other parties become involved in cases where a teacher is deemed to be performing unsatisfactorily. LEA officers, both personnel and advisory, are often called in by a head teacher. Teachers, in turn, frequently seek advice from their union representative, and it is quite common for deputy heads, particularly in primary schools, to become involved in a support and monitoring role. Table 4.12 details the people who became involved in the cases described by the teachers.

The prominent first position of the union in this hierarchy is not surprising, but chairs of governing bodies are thought to be less centrally involved, though they may have been without the teacher knowing. In their responses, some teachers simply described the type of role played by the different parties, while others referred to the quality of the involvement and the perceived benefits or

Table 4.12 People involved in the capability cases (70 cases)

People involved in case	Percentage
Teacher union	87
LEA advisory staff	66
Deputy head/senior manager	64
LEA personnel officers	57
Chair of governors	33
Other members of school staff	30
Other governors	16
Chair of school's Personnel Committee	10
Occupational health	6
Solicitor	4
LEA inspector	4
Independent teacher support organisation	4
Chief Education Officer	4
Counsellor	3
LEA Racial Equalities Officer	1

otherwise. Many comments reported the part played by local education authority staff and teacher association officers, and these provide a useful point of comparison with the interview data collected by the research team from those same groups. What emerged from analysis was that, while no one body was consistently praised or condemned, in the case of both union representatives and LEA officers, there was more criticism than appreciation.

LEAs

The teachers who expressed positive feelings about the role of the LEA talked in terms of the 'fairness' shown and the support offered. One teacher, who had resigned from his post and had then been helped to find another teaching position by his LEA, described the role of the authority's staff: 'Personnel officer – absolutely fair in his dealings. Tried to do his best. Advisory teachers – gave support and good ideas.'

A primary teacher, who reported that her head teacher had not been prepared to accept that her inability to cope with class discipline problems was, to a large extent, caused by a recent divorce and difficult teenage children at home, wrote warmly of the support she had received:

> Both the union and the LEA adviser were *excellent* in their constructive support. They both witnessed my tears, despair and swearing at the impossibility of the situation – my humanity, in fact. I wouldn't have kept my head above water without them.

More often, though, LEA officers were criticised for the way in which they handled teachers. The following comment, typical of others, was made by a teacher undergoing capability procedures at the time. It reinforces the point made by teacher association officers that the process should be handled sensitively, with praise being given, where possible, if improvement is the true goal of the procedure:

> LEA adviser [is] more concerned to pick up on negative aspects rather than areas where improvements have been made. She will shift goalposts from visit to visit and positive points from discussion afterwards don't often appear in written feedback – very disheartening.

LEA staff were also often perceived as 'taking the head's side' or not ensuring that the head had followed procedures correctly:

> A group of parents came to my door one evening. They had heard about it [the competency procedure] from a parent who was on a governing committee and they wanted to offer me support. Practically every parent in the class wrote to the head, to the chair of governors, etc. A little later 3–4

advisers came to school, I believe to give support to the head. One had to write a letter on the visit, part of which said 'Everyone but one teacher is performing well' – I believe this was for the parents' benefit, and to support the head.

In response to a question asking if there was anything which would have been helpful that was not available to them at the time, some teachers felt that it would have been useful to have the services of a counsellor, with whom they could discuss in confidence both their professional and personal feelings – a sort of 'educational Samaritan', as one respondent put it. A number felt this was a service the LEA could and should provide.

Teacher unions

Press accounts of teaching sometimes portray unions as pressure groups whose duty it is to defend an incompetent teacher, whatever the merits of the case. Yet this is not what union officers themselves believe, as Chapter 6 will reveal. Nor were these teachers' perceptions of the effectiveness of their union representatives universally favourable. There was a complete polarisation of views and experiences. Some teachers had found their union representative to be an invaluable support and source of advice. Often, however, the praise was for finding the teacher an exit with dignity, in the first of the two cases below with a good reference attached:

> Union rep invaluable. Negotiated for a good reference in exchange for not carrying out incompetency procedure formally.

> The union rep was on the ball and informed. However, all he could do was advise early retirement.

By contrast, several respondents were unhappy with the representation they had received. Some described their union representatives as 'useless', or accused them of collusion, believing that union officers were more concerned with maintaining good relations with the head and LEA. Their expectation was that they would be defended vigorously, but the union was depicted as unquestioningly accepting the diagnosis of the school management of the teacher's incompetence and seeing its role in terms of advising teachers of the best options for leaving their post:

> Union rep was pretty useless. He seemed to be on the head's side and didn't turn up for a second meeting.

> Support and advice re procedure/alternatives given by union but, in the end, I felt they colluded with the LEA in procuring a redundancy package for me.

[Union was] sympathetic but ineffectual – having recently lost a case against the same school, they were unwilling to take any action.

Some teachers indicated that the procedures adopted by their school prohibited them from being represented by anyone other than county council recognised trade unions. In a number of cases, the teachers had turned to other bodies, like teacher support groups which represent teachers who feel that their union has let them down. A representative of one of these teacher support groups stated, in interview, what she saw as the unions' limitations:

A union won't wholeheartedly challenge a head or an LEA, or they'll only challenge up to a certain point. After that, they are much more interested in compromise agreements, a teacher retiring. They say to the teacher, 'Well, you can't stay in that school, can you? Let me broker some sort of deal for you.'

In the interviews carried out with officers from the six teacher associations, to be reported in Chapter 6, it was clear that many union officials felt it was actually part of their role to make a judgement about the competence of the teacher, and to tailor their subsequent suggestions for action accordingly. They justified this approach by citing concern for the pupils' education, which, like head teachers, they saw as their first priority. This stance was then seen by aggrieved teachers as divided loyalty, or as treacherous collusion with the very bodies with whom the teacher was in dispute. Confusion about roles and functions is yet another example, in this minefield of fraught personal relationships during incompetence allegations, of further differences in perception and conflicts of interest.

Colleagues in school

Comments relating to the involvement of other teacher colleagues in the school focused mainly on allegiances, on whether the teacher saw them as 'on my side'. Few teachers reported receiving the support of their colleagues. More indicated that their peers had been actively unsupportive, or had kept their distance. In some cases, it was fellow teachers who had apparently been the originators of complaints about the teacher's performance. Indeed, the national survey of head teachers had shown that heads were most likely to be alerted to incompetence allegations by a teacher colleague, and the views and experiences of teachers who have not themselves been accused of incompetence will be reported in Chapter 5. Several accused teachers, however, believed their colleagues had not openly supported them for fear of retaliation from the school management:

Most of the staff have expressed serious concern about the situation but feel intimidated and are scared to show support.

The deputy head was supportive at a personal level but he said to me, 'I have to be careful what I say or my job could be on the line'.

I believed, at the time, that that deputy head was trying to ameliorate the situation, but when the disciplinary allegations were made, they seemed to be for a number of things which he had been involved with, e.g. giving me permission to miss a meeting.

Governing bodies

While governors were involved in over a third of the cases described, respondents rarely described or commented on the nature of this involvement. The comments which were made were almost entirely negative, criticising governors' lack of knowledge of procedures, or their inability to distance themselves from the LEA and the head teacher, despite holding formal responsibility for the appointment and dismissal of teachers:

The whole basis of these types of cases depend on having free thinking knowledgeable governors. It appears that there is a good chance that teachers facing disciplinary action will be faced with a kangaroo court and have no chance of receiving justice until they go to a tribunal, at which point it is too late. The current 'anti-teacher' ethos does not support justice in this type of case.

Outcomes

Teachers whose cases had reached a conclusion were asked what the outcome had been and for information relating to their current employment status. Those who were still the subject of capability procedures at the time of the enquiry were asked what they thought the most likely outcome would be. Tables 4.13,

Table 4.13 Outcome of completed cases (44 cases)

Outcome	Number of cases
Retired on ill health grounds	12
Resigned – moved to another teaching post	8
Took early retirement	5
Reached acceptable level of competence	4
Dismissed	4
Was made redundant	3
Resigned – left teaching	2
Resigned – looking for another teaching post	2
Given different duties in same school	2
Other	2

Table 4.14 Subsequent employment status of teachers whose cases were completed (44 cases)

Employment status	Number of cases
In teaching employment	26
Not in employment	13
In non-teaching employment	3
Missing data	2

Table 4.15 Current cases in process – what teachers thought to be the likely outcome (26 cases)

Perceived likely outcome	Number of cases
Dismissal	5
Don't know	4
Retire on ill health grounds	3
Take early retirement	3
Reach acceptable level of competence	3
Resign – look for another teaching post	3
Be given different duties in same school	3
Resign – leave teaching	1
Redundancy	1

4.14, and 4.15 detail these findings, but percentages have not been used because of the smaller numbers involved.

Most (29) of the 44 teachers whose cases were complete had resigned or retired, while a further seven had been dismissed or made redundant. This finding closely matches the head teacher survey figure of 70 per cent in the two categories of 'resignation' or 'retirement', with relatively few actual dismissals. Table 4.14 shows that 29 of the teachers had found another post, 26 of these in teaching, though it was not always a full-time position, nor was it always to the liking of the teacher concerned.

There were 26 teachers whose cases were still in process and they were largely pessimistic about the likely outcome, most fearing they would be dismissed, retire, or resign. Only three expected to reach a level of competence acceptable to the head, as Table 4.15 reveals.

Only two teachers referred explicitly to a lack of support as the reason for their failure to reach an acceptable level of competence, but there was a very strong belief in the *causality* of being a victim: that the teacher had actually been made to appear incompetent by the allegation. This assertion of externally induced and reified incompetence, as opposed to personal responsibility, was the strongest of all the clashes between different groups' perceptions of reality.

It was decided that I was incompetent when I was competent. I was managed into failing. I was banned from teaching what I was qualified to teach and given a wide range of work outside my ability, training or experience. I was set up to fail. I knew this and told management that I knew this. It was part of the psychological warfare. Knowing what my persecutors were doing was an added strain.

What others, like head teachers, saw as a denial of their personal responsibilities, teachers themselves regarded as a rational explanation of events beyond their control. It was an exercise in the apportionment of blame: critics attached blame to the teachers, while they themselves assigned blame to others.

TEACHERS' REFLECTIONS ON EVENTS

What might teachers have done differently?

In common with the other groups interviewed in this research, teachers were asked whether there was anything that, with hindsight, they would have done differently. Many felt that they should have been more assertive in the early stages of the allegation. They reported feeling traumatised and even paralysed, ignorant about their rights, as these comments reveal:

I would have involved my colleagues more, told more of them and asked for their support. I kept quiet because, although I knew, in my conscious mind, that the whole affair was a nonsense, I felt strangely vulnerable.

[You need] knowledge of the legal framework. When you are in a class full-time, you don't have the peace of mind and the information necessary to rebuff the charges.

Several teachers claimed that the head had accepted complaints against them without attempting to substantiate that the allegations were valid, relying on the view of their head of department, or on the veracity of complaints from pupils or parents. This view was more commonly held by teachers in secondary schools, as head teachers are more likely to delegate certain responsibilities to other staff. Another complaint was about judgements on specialist teachers being made by someone not qualified in the field, which contrasts with the situation in medicine described in Chapter 2:

[There was] no means of defending myself against untrue accusations. No IT [Information Technology] inspectors allowed to come in and assess my work/performance when I requested it. Unqualified people allowed to make judgements on my performance as an IT specialist.

When teachers were given specific targets to meet there was no general consensus as to how this should be handled. Whereas some teachers wanted to be able to meet one set of targets before moving on to the next, other teachers and union officials regarded this as 'moving the goalposts'. What these teachers overwhelmingly wanted was 'more support': from their colleagues, from their LEA, from their union, from anyone, in fact, who would take their side against what they saw as formidable odds.

> [I was] continually under 'inspection' – which was negative. When I said my planning document took five hours to complete on a Sunday, I was told that, if that's what it took, I would need to take that long.

> [It would be helpful to have] less monitoring and more feedback . . . [fewer] targets to meet, or targets a few at a time and then get feedback if there's improvement.

Successful practice

It was a particular focus of the Teaching Competence Project to identify successful practice, since both training and retraining can be expensive, so anything that sheds light on the acquisition of greater competence is welcome. In order to identify what appeared to be successful practice in incompetence cases, from the vantage point of the teachers involved, we asked them if there was anything in the events which had taken place which they would describe as having 'worked well'. This notion was not always interpreted as being directly related to their classroom practice, as in some cases comments referred to personal support they had received. Twenty-eight teachers (40 per cent of the sample) were able to identify some aspect of their case. Eight of these referred favourably to the role played by their union, four spoke with appreciation of the support of colleagues and three felt that the capability procedure followed by the school had been constructive.

The comments made by the four teachers who ultimately reached an acceptable level of confidence were scrutinised to find out whether there were common threads which could be identified, but, while the experience had been a more positive one for the teacher quoted below, others believed that nothing had worked well.

> I enjoyed sessions with a very thorough and caring 'critical friend' teacher/ colleague. I learned much from her and felt this was a very good way forward. She came into one or two of my lessons and established a tick target sheet with me. I observed one or two of hers.

Constraints on teachers' actions and response to the allegation

Teachers were also asked what constraints, if any, they had felt when dealing with the events following the allegation of unsatisfactory performance. Most referred to constraints which were unique to their own case, but there were three constraints which were commonly mentioned, listed below in the order of frequency:

1   The feeling of isolation due to the confidentiality aspect of the process
2   A lack of union support/the need to pressurise the union to act (discussed earlier)
3   Personal circumstances, e.g. financial/health

Confidentiality

Confidentiality was sometimes self-imposed, as teachers felt they might jeopardise their legal position by talking to others. Others reported that they had actually been instructed not to discuss their situation with colleagues in the school. For these teachers their enforced isolation exacerbated the stress caused by the initial allegation of incompetence:

> I was reminded about never participating in discussions with anyone about what was actually happening.

> The deputy head and classroom assistant were unaware of the procedure. As problems arose the cards seemed stacked against me, despite all my efforts, most of the time.

Two teachers reported that it was their union that had suggested it would be better not to discuss the matter with colleagues. There were also instances of head teachers insisting on confidentiality.

As part of Study 4 of the Teaching Competence Project, we examined the capability procedures of a sample of LEAs. There was nothing in these to prohibit teachers from discussing their situation with others, should they wish to do so. In one teacher's case however, he was required to remain silent under his school's own separate 'Code of Conduct'. The ambiguity surrounding the confidentiality issue is a further example of some teachers alleged to be incompetent not being given full information concerning capability procedures and their personal rights.

External personal factors

Some teachers felt that a more sympathetic view should have been taken of their own, or family members' personal and medical problems, which they believed had affected their performance and continued to influence their ability to react to the allegation of incompetence. Those who were not old enough to opt for the early retirement route talked of having wished to resign, in order to remove themselves from the stressful situation in which they found themselves, but were unable to do so because of financial constraints:

> I had just gone through a divorce and a hysterectomy.

> My mother was seriously ill with major heart disease. [She was living with the teacher]. My mother-in-law suffered a massive stroke the day I was told of my alleged incompetence. I was later off sick, diagnosed as having clinical depression related to stress.

> Couldn't resign, because husband just been made redundant and we had three young teenagers and a large mortgage to support.

General comments made by teachers

In both questionnaires and interviews respondents were offered the opportunity to make further comments, if they wished. Many reiterated points already made concerning procedural issues and the quality of the involvement of LEAs and teacher associations and these have been incorporated into earlier sections in this chapter. The remainder could be grouped together under the following three headings:

1   Personal distress and trauma
2   Bullying and victimisation
3   'Surviving the ordeal' and regaining self-confidence

Personal distress and trauma

What has emerged as a common theme is the degree of emotional trauma teachers say they suffered. The first crisis occurs at the initial allegation of incompetence, while the second becomes evident during the period when their performance is under scrutiny. Most of the teachers in this study had been in the profession for many years. For the majority, this was, they said, the first time their competence had been called into question. Their accounts of their experiences and reactions paint a vivid picture of personal humiliation and depression:

> After 20 years of teaching and having been valued by parents, pupils, colleagues, governors and previous heads, I now feel completely demoralised because of a head who had been in the school for eight weeks.

> The whole beastly time from the inspection to finally being made redundant so damaged me professionally and personally. It is a totally isolating

experience being done for incompetency – I haven't even been able to tell my parents. I still have nightmares.

I was devastated. I have never been in trouble before – treated terribly by head, and with crassness by a LEA officer who should have realised I wasn't coping and called a halt. The whole thing was like being run down by a juggernaut – inexorable, heartless.

Bullying and victimisation

Allegations of bullying and victimisation appeared in a number of the responses and workplace bullying is an issue which has also received attention in the press. Teachers said they found it difficult to know how best to deal with someone who, in their view, was acting in an unreasonable manner towards them. Many saw themselves in a power relationship in which they occupied the subordinate position:

My head exploited my weakness to undermine my confidence and force me out of teaching after 25 years in the profession. Her actions were that of a bully, with all her actions camouflaged so that no suspicion could be pointed at her.

In my opinion this is a classic case of a young new head over-flexing his muscles and trying out his power. He wanted to shake my tree and certainly succeeded. When I look back now, I'm surprised at how frightening the whole experience was. I kept telling myself I could cope with it, but I couldn't.

'Surviving the ordeal' and regaining self-confidence

Twenty-six teachers whose cases were complete had indicated that they were currently employed in the teaching profession. Some reported that they were undertaking supply teaching or private tutoring, while others had found new full-time posts. A number described how they were slowly rebuilding their self-confidence in an environment where once more their knowledge and expertise were valued, and where they felt they were being successful:

The head at my new school has told me in writing that he values my contribution as a teacher and tutor.

I took early retirement . . . then . . . I spent a whole month applying for lots of office jobs, poorly paid and without success. I decided finally to give teaching another try and I'm happily supply teaching for two different LEAs. I notice how polite the pupils are generally in other schools.

I am now a member of the senior management team in another school. I have rebuilt my self-confidence, regained professional credibility, enjoy good relationships with my children, parents and colleagues. I have committed myself to making sure that nobody that I work with ever suffers the isolation and marginalisation that I endured.

This raises once again the question 'What is "incompetence"?' The teachers quoted above had all been alleged to be incompetent by their previous head teacher, yet say that they have now moved to other posts in different schools and are valued members of staff. This highlights two issues. First, there can be a high degree of emotional filtering when there is disagreement between head and teacher over whether there is a problem with the teacher's performance, or about the nature of the alleged problem, so it might be helpful to have access to an independent assessor who is trusted by both parties, but is not personally involved in the events. Second, before the introduction of Local Management of Schools, LEAs had the facility to redeploy staff, especially where the context was not appropriate for the teacher concerned and a more suitable environment could be found.

Teachers whose performance is unacceptable to a school's management are most likely to leave the profession, even if fresh circumstances might have improved matters, or they have to struggle to find a school willing to give them another chance. Redeployment is a sensitive issue which depends very much on the likelihood of someone doing better in another setting. For those unlikely to improve, it seems unfair to impose them on another school. In the case of teachers who might well improve, the opportunity to find a more suitable assignment seems to have diminished, though several teachers in this sample did manage to create a fresh opening for themselves.

FOUR CASE STUDIES

Although we have tried to elicit some common features among these 70 teachers, each was unique. The following four brief case studies, while illustrating certain recurring issues, show the individual elements of a group of teachers who are often grouped together, as if they are a single entity, but who, in real life, are distinct individuals.

Mrs Baker

Mrs Baker was a primary teacher with 30 years' experience when she was first alleged to have a problem with her performance. At a previous school she had held the post of acting head for a time when the head had been on sick leave. During her career she had taught all year groups and some mixed year group classes. At the time of the initial allegation, some 18 months prior to the interview with the researcher, Mrs Baker had been at the school for five years and was the teacher of a Year 5 class. She was also the special needs co-ordinator and third in the management hierarchy of the school. When asked how performance was monitored at the school, she said, 'That's difficult. We have had appraisal, but basically it's just the head coming in and seeing.'

In common with most cases investigated in this research, it had been the head teacher who had first informed Mrs Baker of the perceived problem with her performance. Accordingly to Mrs Baker, this had taken place during a routine meeting about special needs issues and the head had informed her that she was going to ask a phase adviser to come in and observe her lessons. Although Mrs Baker said she had not previously considered that she had a problem, she implied that there were discipline difficulties: 'I think it was the fact that no supply teacher wished to take the class, and it was said that that was my fault.'

Mrs Baker strongly denied that the blame for pupils' poor behaviour lay with her. She did, however, describe the class as 'horrendous'. In the following year, she was identified as not meeting the needs of the low ability Year 6 maths set that she taught. She again rejected this accusation, saying that she could only use the materials she had within the classroom and that she was being asked to teach maths in 'a different way to what I normally teach'. At the time of the interview, she had been moved to a Year 3 class and was told that her performance would continue to be monitored by the head and the phase adviser.

She believed that her absence on sick leave during the school's OFSTED inspection had caused resentment among other staff and felt that the head's actions against her partly stemmed from this. She described the events over the past 18 months:

> I have had visitations from phase advisers, and the head checking very frequently, but always the same subject, Maths, probably because I don't teach maths the same way as anybody else does in the school. [The head] will come in, sit down at the side of the classroom, and write notes all the way through the lesson . . . I don't like it. I feel I'm on teaching practice.

She described the feedback given by the head as destructive and demoralising, saying: 'What would be helpful, if they are saying "You're not doing this right", is to turn round and say "I would suggest you do it this way".'

Mrs Baker explained that there had been a change of phase advisers during the 18 months since the original allegation and that she seemed to receive different verdicts on her performance from different advisers. Having been told by one adviser that her performance was 'fine', the latest one had informed her that problems remained with her performance. In common with other teachers studied, there had been a pattern of sick leave. Mrs Baker said:

> Every time I seem to be ill, I then have somebody coming in to check on me. It's rather funny, OK, I've been teaching 30 years, and until these last three years I have had very little time off.

She believed that she was being hounded out of the school by a head who felt threatened:

> I'm a highly paid teacher. I've also been a head teacher, albeit acting. I was in an academic council working with the head who's the head of the school now, so we were on a par, and it's not an easy situation . . . I have more qualifications than the head and anybody else in the school, and that also doesn't go down well.

Mrs Baker pointed out that the national test results for her Year 6 class were higher than those of the parallel Year 6 class. The researcher was also shown documentation relating to the actions taken by the school. Mrs Baker claimed that written accounts of meetings were not faithful representations of the discussions which had taken place. A recent account of a meeting recorded that she had been verbally warned that, unless improvement was achieved, capability procedures would be started. Mrs Baker categorically denied that this verbal warning had been given and was awaiting a response from her union to a request for their advice on this issue.

As with other cases studied, the stress caused by being the subject of constant supervision, accompanied by worries about the eventual outcome, was militating against Mrs Baker's ability to improve to the level demanded by the school:

> I shall probably become ill because the stress is telling on me, and that is no good. I am becoming stressed out. I know that, I already have beta-blockers. I'm getting things that I never had before and, having been a healthy person, it doesn't go down well.

When asked whether the head teacher was following any predetermined procedure Mrs Baker said that she presumed so, but was not sure. Certainly, at the time of the interview, formal proceedings had not been instituted, even though 18 months had elapsed since the initial allegation. Mrs Baker did not know whether the chair of governors was aware of the situation. She felt that she should have contacted her union sooner, saying that she had not done so because she did not realise the seriousness of the situation.

She emphasised the feeling of isolation experienced by someone alleged to be incompetent, and called for a support network to turn to in these situations:

> I think there ought to be a club for teachers who've had the word 'incompetent' put on them. There should be a support network somewhere . . . a helpline, because one feels extremely isolated, and if you start saying too much, or you think if you start saying too much to certain teachers, they start thinking, oh, there must be some truth in it. You know, no smoke without fire . . . It is quite a big constraint, and it does alter your attitude to people and you think before you speak. I think I used to be the person in the

staff meeting who spoke the most, now I seem to be the person who probably speaks the least. It alters your personality.

When asked what she hoped the outcome would be, Mrs Baker emphasised her desire to continue teaching 'because I enjoy teaching, I enjoy the children'. She also needed to continue teaching from a financial point of view:

> I can't accept a loss on pay. The mortgage has got to be paid. You've met my mother, she's no youngster, and that is another constraint. She lives with me and had another stroke three weeks ago. There are other constraints.

Mrs Baker's case is representative of some older teachers who later in their career, to their bewilderment, find their teaching performance questioned. While her own comments suggested that there were problems with aspects of her teaching, such as classroom management difficulties with some groups and a resistance to change, as shown by her comments about the maths teaching in the school, there was also evidence that the process was being handled badly by the school and the LEA. The head had not explained to Mrs Baker what, if any, procedure was being followed, and the LEA had sent in different phase advisers who gave different feedback and advice and therefore caused confusion. There also seemed to be little understanding of the stresses caused to Mrs Baker by being involved in such events or awareness of her difficulties at home with an elderly relative. Early retirement not being a simple option, it may be that Mrs Baker will have to stay in this school until her health breaks down completely, which she sees as a poor reward for a teacher who has, in her view, been a valuable asset to the teaching profession for most of her career.

Miss Stanhope

Having been a teacher for 11 years, Miss Stanhope, in her thirties, moved to a new region of the country and took up a position at Blazedown Primary School. She had been teaching at that school for a little over three years when she received an official letter in which the head teacher listed areas of Miss Stanhope's performance which she considered to be unsatisfactory. The issues were, according to Miss Stanhope, 'mainly to do with presentation of work – how things looked, more than anything. She said the children's work was shoddy and their handwriting untidy'. She described her reaction to receiving such a letter:

> It was quite a shock! And I was angry, probably because no one had really said anything to me before. I just got this letter. Looking back, there may have been signs, but I hadn't picked up on them . . . And I'd been friends with the head and had supported her [when the head was the deputy] when she'd returned to the school after an operation. I had helped her settle back in – we worked in the same unit then.

Miss Stanhope suspected that the allegations of unsatisfactory performance were not to do with her teaching at all, but 'more because I was the union representative'. She explained that two years previously, she, with others, had caused the school to be closed down for a period due to health and safety issues. Although Miss Stanhope felt the items in the letter to be 'superficial and trivial', she claimed that she did her best to address the points raised. As far as she was concerned she thought everything was going well again, 'The head was treating me normally when we met on day to day things'.

Although she had requested a change to teaching older children, in the following academic year she found herself again working in the Year 1 unit, this time with the deputy head, and it was clear from her comments that the relationship was not always an easy one. During that year, LEA advisers were brought into Miss Stanhope's classroom. She described how one adviser gave her lots of suggestions which she then showed him were already an integral part of her planning. She claimed that a senior adviser who also observed her practice 'although he pointed out one or two things . . . seemed quite satisfied with my teaching in general'. Miss Stanhope had been angry that advisers had been brought in at all, as the head had given no indication that she felt things had not improved sufficiently. Ironically, since she herself was a union representative, when she contacted her union she found them 'unsupportive'. Their advice had been to do what the head teacher demanded.

The following year she was given a class of older children and she took on responsibility for two curriculum areas. She said, 'I felt much happier. I felt I was being successful'. She was devastated when appraisal of her teaching performance produced a highly critical report. She felt that the head teacher had been unfair in her feedback on the lesson observed and she admitted that relationships with the head 'broke down after that'. The head teacher then informed her that a parent had complained about lack of work being undertaken in the class. The stress of the situation became too much for her and she was signed off work by her doctor. She tried to find another post, but the head refused to write her a reference. Eventually, the LEA suggested retirement on ill health grounds. She did not understand how this was possible, 'I said to them I wasn't ill enough for that, but that's what happened.'

Like many teachers in this situation, she felt ashamed and had been unable to talk about what was happening to her: 'I kept it to all to myself until the end, apart from just a couple of friends in teaching. It was just such an awful thing to admit to my family.'

Once she had told people she said she received 'lots of support from friends and family' and eventually decided to find a new career, but the events had taken a tremendous toll:

> I was devastated. After all, it was a huge chunk of my life and I liked being with the children. It badly affected my health. I had severe bouts of depression both towards the end of my time at the school and afterwards.

Unlike in Mrs Baker's case, Miss Stanhope had been kept fully aware of the procedure being followed by the school, but she suspected that was probably because she was a union representative and the head would have expected her to check that procedures were being properly adhered to. She felt the procedure itself was fair, but raised an important issue: 'The procedure was a good way of going about it all. But no one ever questioned whether the head was right in her assessment of the situation.'

She argued strongly for independent assessors in these situations, perhaps from another school, to judge the veracity of the initial allegation.

The events surrounding Miss Stanhope's exit from the teaching profession had occurred some seven years prior to the interview with her. Since then she had been employed in a number of different types of employment but had recently made the decision to take a higher degree and embark upon a new career. Although some considerable time had elapsed since the events, recounting them to the researcher caused Miss Stanhope a great deal of emotional distress.

Mr Davis

A primary school teacher in his forties, Mr Davis had been teaching for over 15 years. He was, at the time of the allegation of incompetence, teaching a Year 6 class. He claimed that he was the victim of bullying and intimidation by the head, reporting that there was 'continual harassment and all aspects of my work were criticised'. The head was new to the school and in her first headship. According to Mr Davis, since her arrival, the ethos of the school had suffered:

> Discipline had deteriorated. *Some* staff were not given any support and were openly criticised. This led to a lack of confidence and low morale was inevitable. There was much tension in the school.

He explained that the school contained a large number of difficult children but under the previous head, support had been made available in the classroom to all staff. This support was withdrawn by the new head to some of the staff. He reported that these members of staff felt they were being 'pushed out of their jobs'.

Following a period of verbal criticism of his practice by the head, Mr Davis received a formal written warning from her alleging incompetence, of which he claims senior staff and governors were not informed. The criticisms continued, and he felt his authority as a teacher was being undermined by comments made by the head in front of pupils. The deputy head was asked to observe some lessons and according to Mr Davis was 'satisfied with my work'. He was initially receptive to the support and advice offered, but became less so as events unfolded and the head continued to allege unsatisfactory performance, until the relationship between the two eventually broke down completely: 'I couldn't discuss anything with the head. I went to a relative's funeral (with permission) and I was stopped a day's pay. I just felt victimised.'

Believing that there was no means by which the situation at this school could be retrieved, Mr Davis applied for a post at another school, but did not get the job, because, he claimed, of a telephone call made by his head. He subsequently became 'very anxious and depressed', accompanied by high blood pressure. He said: 'A job which I loved became a dread.'

His union's advice to him was to take early retirement on ill health grounds and two years after the initial allegation had been made he left the school. He said he should have applied for another teaching post as soon as he saw the 'warning signs'. He explained why he had not:

> I battled on hoping that the Head would be pleased with my work. When I realised that whatever I did, however hard I tried, she would not be satisfied, it was too late.

Mr Davis claimed that other staff had 'suffered' in the same way as he had. Four staff retired on ill health grounds in just over one year, others had retired early 'or been fortunate in finding another post'. He felt, in these circumstances, there should have been more concern shown by the school governors and the LEA about the way in which the school was being managed. Of course, it may be that this particular head had been appointed by the governors and LEA with the expressed remit of acting to raise standards. Unfortunately, due to the confidentiality of these cases, it was impossible to contact the head to investigate her account of the events.

Mr Peters

Mr Peters taught mathematics in a large secondary school and held responsibility for KS4 mathematics. He had taught at two schools before moving to Platt Secondary and had been in post there for nine months when he was first alleged to have a problem with his performance. His head of department asked him to 'pop in for a chat' and told him that there were concerns about his class management strategies and his relationship with pupils and parents. He reported what the head of department said: 'The words used were "There appears to be a complete breakdown of relationship with your lower school classes (Year 7 and 8)".' Mr Peters rejected the head of department's assessment: 'Clearly pupils challenge teachers from time to time and there are many different strategies a teacher might employ – and I was employing them.'

A follow-up meeting was suggested and arranged but, for some reason not provided by Mr Peters, this did not take place. Mr Peters reported that he spoke privately with two other members of the maths department, sharing the comments made to him by the head of department. He said 'they sought to encourage me about the things I was doing and suggested that the head of department was not correct'. In Mr Peters' case, no support or advice was made available to him either regarding classroom discipline or his relationship with pupils. He presumed he had reached a level of competence acceptable to the management because no one ever told him that he had not. He had felt vulnerable in the period following the accusation and he would have liked knowledge of the competence procedure in place at his school. He did not know whether the head of department was following any procedure when the first meeting was held.

Mr Peters is unusual among the teachers in this study. He was one of only four teachers in the whole sample who believed he had improved sufficiently in the view of the school's senior management. However, he stated that he had not been told officially and consequently was still unsure whether his performance was being monitored in some informal way of which he was unaware.

SUMMARY

This chapter reports the analysis of data collected in a questionnaire and interview study of a sample of teachers who had been alleged to be incompetent. Salient points are listed below.

- The sample consists of 70 primary and secondary teachers who had been alleged to be incompetent, of whom all were volunteers – 44 were completed cases, 26 were taking place at the time the questionnaire was completed.
- Over a third of respondents indicated that no formal system of monitoring of performance existed in their school. Over a quarter said they did not have job descriptions at the time the allegation of incompetence was made.
- The head teacher was most frequently the person who had informed teachers of the perceived problems with their performance, although in secondary schools this role was sometimes taken by the teacher's line manager.
- In nearly half the cases the teacher reported that the matter was raised with them during 'informal' dialogue; some said that this meant they had not realised the seriousness of their position until it was too late.
- In over a third of the cases described, teachers believed that no pre-determined procedure had been followed by the head after the initial allegation of incompetence. Formal proceedings had been instituted in 25 of the 44 completed cases.
- Many teachers had left their post during the informal stage after an allegation had been made. Retirement and resignation were the two most common outcomes.
- The four most common areas in which teachers said they had been alleged to be incompetent were: 'classroom discipline', 'planning and preparation', 'pupil progress' and 'expectations of pupils'.
- Over three quarters of the teachers rejected the allegation of incompetence. Their own explanations of the reasons for the allegation included: conspiracy;

bullying and victimisation; scapegoating; racial discrimination; incompetence or vengeance by the head; unjustified complaints from parents; clashes of philosophy; pupils being unwilling, or unable, to learn or behave well; inadequate resources; the need to make staffing cuts as a result of financial pressures.

- All teachers reported themselves to be receptive to support and advice offered, although some stated they became less so as events proceeded.
- Other constituents most frequently mentioned as involved in these cases were LEA staff and teacher unions. Criticisms were made by some teachers of the roles played by these, and a number felt that there was collusion between their union representative and the head teacher.
- A number of teachers called for an independent assessor to provide an objective judgement of their performance.
- Little reference was made to governing bodies, but such references were predominantly negative, teachers feeling that governors did not understand either the details of their case or the procedures involved.
- Of the 44 completed cases, only four teachers had reached an acceptable level of competence.
- Reasons given by teachers for their apparent lack of improvement reiterated the claims that the initial allegation had been incorrect, that school management were conspiring to remove them, that it would have been impossible to satisfy the head, that they were the victims of bullying and intimidation.
- Of the 44 teachers whose cases had concluded, 29 had found employment elsewhere, 26 of these in teaching, though it was sometimes part-time or occasional work. Several teachers said that their work was now highly esteemed in their new post.
- With hindsight, many teachers wished they had challenged more forcefully the initial allegation.
- Most teachers believed they should have demanded and received better support: from the LEA, from their union, from their colleagues. There was a call for better legal advice.
- Some teachers reported that the confidentiality aspect of the procedures left them feeling isolated and vulnerable, unable to share their misery with others, or gain support and advice.
- Overwhelmingly, the teachers in this survey felt misjudged and mistreated. Many described medical conditions of themselves, their partner, or close members of their family which they felt had affected their work, but not been taken into consideration.

Chapter 5

The role of professional colleagues

In the national survey of head teachers, reported in Chapter 3, it was found that the first intimation that a teacher was not performing adequately was most likely to come from a fellow teacher. We had not intended, in the original research design, to study the views and experiences of those teachers who had worked alongside a colleague regarded as incompetent, but it became clear, as the research progressed, that they often played an important part in the events, and not just at the initial stage. Some became confidants, while others displayed overt hostility, or were seen by accused teachers as colluding with senior management in the school. Whether fellow teachers are hostile or supportive of those colleagues regarded as incompetent is another unexplored area in this whole field.

It was decided to ask the same questions on the same topics as with other groups, so letters and questionnaires were sent to a random selection of head teachers of 300 schools, 210 primary and 90 secondary, located in 15 LEAs in different regions of England. The letter asked the heads to pass the questionnaire to a member of their staff who, they believed, might have had experience of working alongside an under-performing colleague. It is possible that this procedure may have produced a sample with particularly strong feelings about what happened, but many of the findings are similar to what other groups report. As ever it was stressed both in the letter and on the questionnaire that all responses would be treated as strictly confidential. A freepost envelope was provided for the return of the questionnaire.

In total, 137 questionnaires were returned, but in 42 cases the head teachers had themselves filled out the questionnaire, even though the instructions clearly stated that it should be done by a teacher, so these were not included in the analysis. There were 57 completely documented cases, 31 returned by female and 26 returned by male teachers. The teachers they described were also fairly evenly split by gender (27 female and 30 male). The respondents were, on the whole, very experienced teachers. Just over half of them (52 per cent) had been teaching for over 20 years and three quarters were over the age of 40. Thirty-four of the cases reported took place in primary schools, the remaining 23 in secondary schools. This chapter is based on the written accounts from this sample of 57 fellow teachers.

Since this chapter describes teachers writing about other teachers, wherever possible, to minimise confusion, the term 'respondent' or 'fellow teacher' will be used to describe the teachers whose views and experiences were being sought (that is those not, themselves, regarded as incompetent, but who have worked alongside someone said to be incompetent), and the term 'teacher' will normally be used to describe the practitioner alleged to be incompetent.

WORKING ALONGSIDE AN INCOMPETENT COLLEAGUE

Perceived areas of weakness

In line with the other studies undertaken during this research, we asked the respondents to indicate which aspects of the teacher's work had been perceived to be unsatisfactory, thus providing *operational definitions* of incompetence. The most frequently mentioned areas of weakness were very close to those cited by head teachers in the national survey, the first five rankings being almost exactly the same, as shown in Table 5.1.

Table 5.1 Most frequent areas of weakness – data from fellow teacher and head teacher questionnaire surveys

Fellow teachers	Head teachers
1 Expectations of pupils	Expectation of pupils
2 Classroom discipline	Pupils' progress
3 Pupils' progress	Planning and preparation
4 Relationship with pupils	Classroom discipline
5 Inability to respond to change	Inability to respond to change

Fellow teachers, like head teachers, felt that the problems occurred in clusters, rather than singly. Poor planning was accompanied by inadequate or sometimes overly authoritarian control over behaviour, or negative relationships with pupils, as these responses show:

> The teacher was having discipline difficulties as well as general classroom management. Quality of work was poor and expectations were low. Quality of teaching and planning was also less than acceptable and the teacher was struggling to come to terms with the idea of the national curriculum, differentiation and quality teaching.
>
> (primary)

> No preparation of lessons. Not meeting national curriculum targets. Not attending meetings. Dictation in lessons – unstimulating for students.

Teaching the class as if all students are the same. Never offering praise or support. Over-disciplinary. Not completing documentation or administration. Not working with colleagues. Refusal to use IT at all. Not meeting exam board requirements. Not marking/setting exam work. Not setting/marking homework. Non attendance at parents' evenings. Not keeping self up to date with new issues/developments in the subject and in teaching in general, etc., etc. I could go on!

(secondary)

How respondents became aware of a colleague's problems

Just as the causes of ineffective teaching were often clustered, so too were the pieces of evidence for it. When asked 'How did you become aware of the teacher's problem?', respondents often referred to several cues, ranging from noisy classrooms to complaints from pupils and parents:

Moderation of work across year group. Parental discontent. Colleagues' discontent – 'carrying' the problem into subsequent year groups. Planning not handed in or incomplete. Tasks not achieved in curriculum responsibility area – always 'bluffing' way out of 'situations'.

(primary)

Classroom noise. Review of exercise books. Complaints from pupils and parents and staff. Performance at meetings. I was aware of problems before he was appointed to the school and fought in vain against the appointment.

(secondary)

These findings closely mirror those of the national questionnaire survey of head teachers. Head teachers, too, reported complaints from staff, parents and pupils in their four most common means of identifying an unsatisfactory teacher. The data were further scrutinised to investigate whether there were any differences between primary and secondary fellow teachers' accounts of identifying a colleague having a problem. Across most of the categories there was very little difference, but only primary respondents, since they could usually ascribe poor pupil behaviour to one former teacher, rather than several, reported having become aware of an under-performing teacher by 'inheriting the class'.

Confronting the problem

Fellow teachers are in a difficult position. Sometimes they are of the same, or even of lower rank than the teacher accused of incompetence. Yet the process is often handled by the most senior people in the school hierarchy. In 50 of the 57 cases in this study the respondent indicated that poorly performing teachers had been informed, by someone, of the concerns about their performance. Of the remaining seven cases, two respondents reported that the teacher's poor performance had never been addressed by the school management and five did not know whether the matter had been raised with the teacher.

In the majority of these 50 cases where action was taken, it was the head who discussed the issue with the accused teacher, either alone or with other members of the senior management present. Occasionally, a LEA adviser was present. In six cases the identification of the teacher's problems arose during an OFSTED inspection and was dealt with by the head and the inspection team. There were often strong feelings of hostility expressed by respondents about the whole matter of teaching with someone not performing competently, and one of the respondents felt especially angry that his own earlier warnings had gone unheeded:

> The matter was addressed not by the first head, whom I informed – I was told to 'mind my own business' and not be unprofessional. OFSTED highlighted her incompetence to the new head.
>
> (primary)

There were 14 cases where it had been the line manager's responsibility to raise concerns initially with teachers about their performance. As might be expected, all but three of these had occurred in secondary schools.

Action reportedly taken by schools

When asked whether any steps had been taken by the school to address the problem with the teacher's performance, most (86 per cent) respondents indicated that the matter had been addressed in some way. The action most frequently described was 'support and advice', 'close/regular monitoring' and 'relief of pressure on teacher'. The category of 'support and advice' most commonly referred to help with planning and preparation, or the teacher had been given the opportunity to observe what was regarded as 'good' practice, either within the school or at another school. Less detail was given of what the 'monitoring' had comprised, but observation of lessons and regular meetings were mentioned.

In the majority of the cases, respondents thought that their school management had invested a great deal of time, energy and resources trying to help the alleged incompetent reach an acceptable level of competence. Three had been given non-contact time for planning and one respondent reported that 'problematic' children had been removed from the teacher's class. In a further three cases teachers had been given different duties, classes or age groups. One criticised 'easier' options, saying that this evaded the issue: 'The teacher was made into a supernumerary! Not dealt with directly by head or deputy although problems were well known.'

Sometimes the respondent had been personally involved in the support, and the last of those quoted below had observed 42 lessons:

I, as Head of Department, had weekly meetings to help him plan lessons and to advise him of good practice. He was regularly observed and given feedback – both positive and negative. He was given the opportunity to observe other lessons in both his subject and others. The whole department made themselves available for answering any questions and giving ideas.

(secondary)

Teaching was closely monitored by head teacher and ultimately the advisory and inspection service.

(primary)

I [the deputy head] observed 42 lessons and attended 18 meetings with the teacher from September to February.

(secondary)

Outcomes of the cases described

Table 5.2 sets out the outcomes of the 57 cases described in this survey. Once again, the pattern reported in other chapters is repeated, with the most typical exit route for under-performing teachers being retirement, either early, or on ill health grounds, with dismissal only occurring in two cases.

Table 5.2 Outcomes of cases encountered by fellow teachers (57 cases)

Outcome	Number of cases
Early retirement	8
Retirement on ill health grounds	8
Resigned, left teaching	8
Current case – no outcome yet	7
Resigned, moved to another teaching post	6
Still in post, never resolved	4
Reached acceptable level of competence	3
Dismissal	2
Resigned, looking for another teaching post	2
Resigned, next job not known	2
Temporary contract not renewed	2
Other	5

Far from wanting to draw a protective cover over teachers thought to be incompetent, fellow teachers, like head teachers, believed unequivocally that their own first duty was to their pupils. In the 41 cases where the teacher had eventually left the school, 31 respondents expressed satisfaction at this outcome, mostly because it removed a source of dismay and aggravation, but sometimes because it was thought to be a good solution for the teacher involved:

I have always erred on the side of harmony and have felt that dismissal was very harsh, particularly on a personal level for someone with a wife and family to support. However, looking at the mess in which the science department found itself when many other departments were moving forward, and looking at the way in which pupils were being 'short changed' (particularly in terms of results and their perceptions of science) the decision was clearly the right one.

(secondary – teacher was dismissed)

The atmosphere in the school has improved markedly so I am pleased that we are now able to move on without issues of competency hanging over us. The teacher herself has found a school that is easier to teach in, so she may well feel more motivated and able to cope with change.

(primary – teacher resigned, moved to new teaching post)

Strong feelings were also expressed when incompetent teachers had been allowed to leave their school via the early retirement, redundancy or the resignation routes, with their reputations intact and, furthermore, in some cases to continue to work in the profession. This was a noteworthy feature when the teacher concerned had blamed others. Those given some kind of early retirement deal aroused particular antipathy:

He took the easy way out and was rewarded with a pension!

(primary – teacher opted for early retirement)

It was probably the easiest solution for the school, but the person did go to another school on supply (long-term) and caused similar problems there.

(primary – teacher's temporary contract not renewed)

I have mixed feelings. On a *personal* level I feel great sympathy. I liked him and there's the 'But for the Grace of God . . .', BUT . . . I feel there are many people, including this person, who are not capable of teaching. Lots of expensive, time-consuming support won't change this. In schools with ridiculous shortages of basic resources and huge class sizes, this time and money could be better spent. In other professions people who 'can't do' leave. It does not seem fair that if you 'can do' in teaching, you work until you're 60 and leave with only what you have paid for, but if you 'can't do', schools will find ways of pensioning you off. (I'm planning a nervous breakdown at 50!)

(secondary – teacher retired on grounds of ill health)

Some respondents expressed concern about the length of time it had taken for the issue to be resolved and were critical of the procedures undertaken. In only two cases was the school accused of neglecting to provide appropriate support to the teacher. The overwhelming response to the outcomes of these cases was that it had been beneficial for the school that the teacher had left. The four cases reported as never having been resolved led to frustration and desperation among the other staff. Even those respondents who had worked alongside a teacher eventually judged to be reaching an acceptable level of competence were hardly fulsome in their response to this outcome:

> I'm not entirely satisfied – member of staff concerned is now performing better – but there's still room for improvement.
>
> (secondary)

Effects of under-performing teachers on other staff

The effect of an under-performing teacher on other staff in the school was thought to be profound. Forty nine (86 per cent) of the 57 respondents said they had personally been affected in some way, of whom 30 had themselves been involved formally in the action taken by the school, mainly because they were the teacher's line manager and so were involved in monitoring, advice, or the actual capability procedures. The overwhelming majority, 46 (81 per cent) of the 57 respondents, believed that the events had had an effect on other staff in their school, almost all believing this to have been negative.

One secondary head of department gave a graphic account of the problems that occurred when one of her teacher colleagues failed to carry out the teacher assessment for a GCSE examination. Pupils complained that they did not want to be in his class any longer and she had to assess the ungraded coursework herself. The teacher then went off sick and she could not get a supply teacher to cover his work. What irked her most was that the head felt sorry for the absent teacher.

Respondents' own part in the action taken by the school had often been a time-consuming responsibility, involving classroom observation and checking that targets were being met. Of those involved with the formal capability procedures, several said they had personally 'prosecuted' the incompetence case, or been asked to present evidence at hearings. Many respondents had offered emotional as well as professional support, which could drain their own reserves. They felt particularly bitter when the teacher reacted negatively:

> Advice on curriculum issues given by me to staff in general was received negatively which made progress difficult. Her self-defensive attitude made communication and progress an uphill struggle.
>
> (primary)

> Acting as mentor in the closing stages of the disciplinary proceedings was depressing. I was in a 'mentor' role, which meant I should give support, but the teacher concerned was so demoralised and had such a poor

understanding of the situation that it was frustrating and seemed to be a rather fatuous exercise. It also worried me that I was gathering evidence which would contribute to dismissal.

(secondary)

Only one respondent expressed criticism of the process undertaken by the school. This was a head of department in a secondary school, who supported the teacher:

The procedure was very badly handled throughout. Hence, I had as little to do with it as possible. And, as a member of the same union, I preferred, as it were, to 'help' the person involved and to ensure fair treatment.

The general view of most respondents, however, was that one incompetent teacher can have a hugely detrimental impact on a whole school. Comments reported the practical implications for their colleagues in the form of increased workloads and considerable emotional impact. Absences among teachers alleged to be incompetent created additional work and duties. Many respondents reported that the children had become more difficult to teach and a disruptive class could affect other teachers. Even when the under-performing teacher had departed from the school, some teachers were still left coping with the consequences:

Those who took over the class had rather a chaotic mess to sort out, both curriculum-wise and from the point of view of controlling the children, retraining them, etc.

(primary)

It took up a lot of staff's time advising/helping. Also a lot of time giving help to his students outside lessons! The year after he left *all* his groups were almost impossible to handle and took a lot of teacher effort to restore to proper behaviour.

(secondary)

There was concern and frustration not only about the impact of the teacher concerned on children's learning, particularly in primary schools, where the impact of an under-performing teacher could blight a child's education for a whole year, but also on the reputation of the whole school, the department, or the fellow teacher responding. At a time when school inspections were often given prominence in the local press, or when the school or subject department were trying to recruit pupils, reputation was regarded as very important, and fellow teachers were anxious not to see their own being sullied by someone else.

One described how the English department went from being a 'flagship' department to a failing department in the space of 18 months. Others in secondary schools lamented the effect not only on examination results, but on pupil choices of subject. Many in both primary and secondary felt that the good name of their section or department had suffered badly. They reported that other members of staff were resentful that a teacher was under-performing and apparently 'getting away with it'. Such comments came mainly from primary schools, where staff take on many responsibilities. It was especially galling when the teacher concerned was being paid more, supposedly for additional responsibilities.

The resentment at someone prospering who did not appear to deserve it was heightened in one primary school where no action was taken to address the teacher's perceived problems. He was thought to have been given a good reference, enabling him to become the deputy head at another school. The staff at his original school reportedly found it 'demoralising and frustrating that someone so incompetent could be allowed to remain in post and ultimately achieve promotion'.

It was only a minority of respondents that spoke in support of the accused teacher. Some were able to empathise with a fellow practitioner in distress, while others were not happy at the way someone was being treated in the school. One repercussion of an under-performing teacher and the actions taken to address the problem was a deterioration in the relationships among other staff. A number of predominantly primary fellow teachers, reported that staff relationships had deteriorated with the emergence of 'different camps':

> There are many other members of staff who will now not go into the staff room.
>
> (primary)

> Some staff members felt that the teacher involved was treated unfairly. Others felt it should have been dealt with many years before and she should not have been allowed to carry on as long as she had. Relationships have suffered.
>
> (primary)

What should have been done differently?

Over three-quarters of the 57 respondents felt there were things others involved in the events should have done differently. There was an overwhelming consensus that under-performing teachers need to be identified early, that steps to support and monitor their practice should be put in place swiftly and that the process, once instituted, should be carried out speedily.

Only one respondent believed that the teacher concerned should have been given more time to improve, although five felt that the level of support given had been unsatisfactory, while two called for a more rigorous procedure to guard against inappropriate appointments and the use of temporary contracts was suggested to facilitate the removal of unsatisfactory teachers. In general the level of tolerance by fellow teachers was relatively low:

Despite concerns about this teacher's performance, nothing was done until an OFSTED inspection took place. I feel too much time was given to this teacher to improve and too little action taken when this teacher avoided meeting targets and routine observations by taking days off sick.

(primary)

I believe that if the interview process had included a class teaching session he would not have been appointed to junior school teaching. He had no training or experience. His engineering background led more naturally to college or secondary school.

(primary)

Since respondents were often in a central position to see what was going wrong, they were asked what they thought *should* happen when a teacher is under-performing. Many provided comprehensive answers to this question indicating that teachers often have clear opinions about this issue. Below is a summary of the factors most frequently mentioned:

- Regular monitoring of teaching should be in place to allow early identification of problems.
- The teacher should be given a clear account of the areas of concern.
- Achievable targets should be set within agreed time limits.
- A programme of support and advice should be put in place, including the opportunity to see good practice in other classes/schools, team teaching, in-service training, LEA advisory support.
- Regular monitoring and feedback should take place.
- If improvement does not follow within a 'reasonable' time (40 out of 57 suggesting one, two or three terms), formal procedures should be put in place.

In addition, one respondent insisted that 'schools should have clear policies, so that staff know against what boundaries they are being judged', and two called for the early involvement of unions, a secondary head of department reporting that he had found union representatives' advice 'invaluable'. Several mentioned that it would be useful for the teacher to have access to some sort of counselling service, a facility also called for by a number of teachers who had themselves been alleged to be incompetent, reported in Chapter 4. Although only five respondents explicitly used the word 'dismissal', it was clear that the overwhelming majority believed strongly that persistent under-performance should not be tolerated.

Time scales

Of the 684 cases described by head teachers in Chapter 3, some 46 per cent had reportedly taken from one to three years to resolve, and a majority of heads felt this was too long. Like many of the heads, teacher respondents stated a preference for a six months to two terms time scale. Scrutiny of both the quantitative and qualitative data revealed some interesting patterns. All but two of the 22 secondary teachers opted for either one to two terms or two to three terms. No secondary teacher considered less than one term to be appropriate. In a secondary school, however, only one subject area may be affected. The largest single group of respondents supported the two to three term time scale. It was their view that this period allowed appropriate support and advice to be given and provided the teacher with adequate time to improve:

> One school year should be sufficient to see whether a colleague is able to improve performance. All problems may not be solved, but significant progress should be seen.
>
> (primary)

> Problem is identified and discussed with teacher. On some simple points, improvement needs to be monitored immediately or in the first month. At least a term and a half of support is essential to allow a fair chance but after this, if there is no recognisable improvement in performance, dismissal procedures can commence.
>
> (secondary)

When it came to longer and shorter time scales, there was a noticeable division among respondents from primary schools. Certainly the comments of primary teachers selecting a short time scale showed little patience with incompetent colleagues. Paradoxically, however, the majority of respondents advocating periods longer than a year were also primary teachers. There seemed to be a contrast between those primary fellow teachers who felt strongly that incompetence should not be tolerated beyond a term and those who wanted to give their peers every chance to reach an acceptable level of performance. The two teachers below illustrate this fundamental difference of view, the first believing that a term was plenty of time to get rid of the truly incompetent, the second favouring more than a year:

> The children's needs must come first. In my experience teachers who are incompetent do not have the ability to become competent. This is different from teachers who have one or two areas of weakness which can be addressed and supported – these are not 'incompetent' teachers.
>
> (primary)

> If the time scale is too short this could lead to putting even more stress into what is already a very stressful situation. Also, there are times when classes are large and difficult children can have an effect on your performance. More time may also lead to sorting out personal problems and therefore improve teaching performance.
>
> (primary)

Selection and monitoring

Many respondents felt that the teacher experiencing problems was either in the wrong kind of school, the wrong sort of post, or should not have qualified in the first place. There were strong calls for teacher training institutions to fail students who are clearly unsuited to the teaching profession. If selection by the school had failed and the person appointed experienced difficulties, several respondents stressed the need for a better system of monitoring performance in schools, both locally and nationally, to allow early identification of problems before they escalated:

> Effective monitoring, appraisal and evaluation of teaching and learning within a school ensures that the necessary support for any teacher facing problems is in place at a very early stage.
>
> (primary)

> We [the profession] badly need agreed procedures. I believe we need something similar to the GMC in medicine to monitor standards nationally and maintain standards. It is in the interests of everyone involved that these situations shouldn't depend on which school, how interested your line managers are and how strong or weak the senior management team is.
>
> (secondary)

Lack of tolerance?

Fellow teachers appear to be the least tolerant constituency when it comes to incompetence. It was very noticeable, from our analysis above, that there seemed to be relatively little sympathy from respondents for teachers who were, in their view, under-performing. Few showed much empathy with teachers experiencing difficulties, and even when they did mention mitigation, the overwhelming mood portrayed was one of intolerance. The reasons for this seem clear: respondents felt that children's welfare must come first; many experienced frustration and embarrassment at the damage, as they saw it, to their school's, their department's, or their individual professional reputation; several resented the drain on their own and their colleagues' time and energy, especially if they became involved in actual capability procedures.

The first comment below expresses the generally 'tough' attitudes and feelings described by many respondents, while the second one represents one of only two fellow teachers who offered any consistently sympathetic view, citing the importance of context on performance:

> All teachers should be asked by management to pose themselves one question: 'If I had my own children in this class, would I be happy with the quality of the teaching that they are receiving?' If the answer is 'no' – then action should be taken.
>
> (primary)

A lot of pressure is put on to teachers at the present time to achieve set targets, some of which are unattainable, owing to the deprived areas in which a lot of teachers work. Then teachers are labelled as incompetent as they appear to have 'failed'. Other teachers seem to have a lot easier life teaching in 'leafy suburbia' without the discipline and social problems. They are seen to be successful and competent. If these teachers' roles were reversed, who would appear competent then?

(primary)

SUMMARY

This chapter reports a questionnaire survey of a sample of fellow teachers who had worked alongside a teacher alleged to be performing unsatisfactorily. A number of salient points are listed below:

- The total sample comprised 57 teachers who reported experience of working alongside a member of staff who had been perceived to be under-performing. All were volunteers. Sixty per cent taught in primary schools, about 40 per cent in secondary.
- In common with the definitions of incompetence provided by head teachers in our national questionnaire survey of primary and secondary schools, the indicators of incompetence most frequently mentioned by respondents were: expectations of their pupils; classroom discipline; relationships with pupils; pupil progress, inability to change.
- In most of the cases described, it was the accumulation of a number of different factors that resulted in concern about an individual's performance. The most frequently mentioned were: pupil behaviour, parental complaints, students' complaints/comments; colleagues' complaints/comments; own observations of teacher.
- In 50 of the 57 cases described in the survey, the allegedly incompetent teachers had been informed of the concerns surrounding their performance.
- In 32 of these 50 cases, it had been the head who initially raised the issue with the teacher, either alone or with other members of senior management present. In 14 of the 23 cases taking place in secondary schools, the line manager had taken on this responsibility.
- The provision of 'support and advice' was mentioned in 28 cases, and 'regular monitoring' in 22 cases. Eight respondents explicitly mentioned target setting. In 11 cases, respondents reported that steps had been taken to relieve pressures on the teacher such as provision of classroom support; movement to different duties/age group; non-contact time.
- The outcomes of the cases described repeat the pattern which emerged from the head teacher questionnaire survey. Early retirement and retirement on ill

health grounds had been the most common exit routes for under-performing teachers. Dismissal had occurred in only two of the 57 cases.

- In the 41 cases where the teacher had left the school, over three-quarters of respondents expressed satisfaction at this outcome, mostly for the sake of the children and the school, although some also felt it was best for the teacher concerned.
- Frustration was expressed by some teachers that an incompetent colleague had been allowed to leave the school via the early retirement, redundancy or resignation routes with their reputations intact, and, in some cases, to continue to work in the profession.
- In the three cases where teachers had reached an acceptable level of competence, the respondents clearly felt that their performance could at best be described as 'satisfactory'.
- Criticisms were expressed by many of the respondents about the length of time it had taken for the issue to be resolved. They were very concerned about the impact on children's education of an under-performing teacher.
- Most respondents believed a period of between one and three terms was an appropriate time scale, though some primary fellow teachers supported longer and shorter time scales.
- It was clear that one incompetent teacher can have a huge impact on a whole school and 30 respondents said they had been formally involved with the action taken by the school: providing support and advice, monitoring performance, involvement in the actual capability proceedings. These responsibilities had been time-consuming and, in some cases, had taken an emotional toll on the respondent.
- Well over three quarters of the respondents believed that the events had had an effect on other staff in their school: additional workload caused by the incompetent teacher's absences from school; coping with deteriorating pupil behaviour; worries about pupils' learning; repercussions for the repu-tation of a department or whole school; deterioration in staff relationships with 'camps' emerging; distress at seeing a colleague in such a situation.
- Respondents were asked what they thought *should* happen when a teacher is identified as under-performing, and the most commonly mentioned factors were:

    - regular monitoring of teaching should be undertaken to allow early identifications of problems
    - the teacher should be given a clear account of the areas of concern
    - achievable targets should be set within agreed time limits
    - programme of support and advice should be given, including the opportunity to see good practice in other classes/schools, team teaching, in-service training, LEA advisory support
    - regular monitoring and feedback should take place
    - if improvement does not follow within a 'reasonable' time, formal procedures should be put in place

- – although only five teachers explicitly used the word 'dismissal', it was clear that the overwhelming majority of respondents to this survey believed that persistent under-performance should not be tolerated.

- Most respondents expressed intolerance of their incompetent colleague, with only two of the sample offering significant sympathy.

Chapter 6

Union officers

Most teachers alleged to be incompetent turn to their union. They have joined a teacher association partly to be protected and supported by it, should they ever encounter problems. There are few problems more pressing than a threat to their livelihood, so aggrieved teachers expect their union to back them strongly. Unions may be viewed differently by the various constituencies involved in incompetence cases, however. Many head teachers said, in the national survey, that they were apprehensive about them, worried they would be exposed if they took a wrong step during the procedures.

In the public mind unions defend their members uncritically, even if they are in the wrong. Yet some teachers alleged to be incompetent accused them, in Chapter 4, of colluding with the head and the local authority. In this middle section of the book, Chapters 6 and 7, we report the views and experiences of two groups of professional officers, from teacher unions and local authorities, who often play an important part in incompetence cases, but who work outside the school.

Despite their central role, union officers are frequently neglected in educational research. It is relatively rare for them to be interviewed, or for teachers to be asked about the role of their union. In matters of incompetence, however, it would be foolish not to solicit their views and experiences. This chapter reports part of Study 4 of the Teaching Competence Project, in which we interviewed a sample of 21 teacher association officers representing the six major teacher and head teacher associations:

- Association of Teachers and Lecturers (ATL)
- National Association of Head Teachers (NAHT)
- National Association of Schoolmasters/Union of Women Teachers (NASUWT)
- National Union of Teachers (NUT)
- Professional Association of Teachers (PAT)
- Secondary Heads' Association (SHA)

A letter was sent to the General Secretaries of each of these six teacher associations explaining the focus of the Teaching Competence Project and requesting their permission to talk to some of their field workers who had dealt with incompetence allegations. Officers located in different geographical areas were interviewed, in case there were regional variations in the way in which competence cases were handled, though, in the event, differences in practice were more related to individual styles and preferences than to regional location.

The people interviewed ranged in experience in their union post from one year to over 20 years. The majority had come into this employment after being part-time officials and teachers themselves, though a small number were legal executives. Field officers described their role as 'broadly based', giving advice and support to members facing a variety of difficulties in their employment, as one put it: 'professional casework of almost any kind, whether health, discipline, competence, professional relationships, grievances'.

A semi-structured interview schedule was devised which addressed the key areas we were investigating. Teacher association officers were asked to define incompetence, talk about the number and type of cases they had encountered and their outcomes, discuss the events relating to specific cases, describe their own role. Since the two head teacher union officers deal with heads and deputies, their main focus was on helping these. Teacher unions do have heads and deputies who keep their membership, but their officers' main focus was on the individual teacher.

DEFINITIONS AND EXPERIENCES OF INCOMPETENCE

Definitions

Some officers felt it was not part of their role to define 'incompetence', while others gave very general definitions. A number were more detailed in their description, and several talked not of the symptoms of incompetence, but of the causes. Those officers who stressed that their role was not to give an opinion on what is or is not incompetence, explained their position as being reactive, merely responding to someone else's *de facto* definition:

> I don't have a personal view. In law, 'incompetence' is whatever the employer decides it to be.

> 'Incompetence' is the definition of the management at the time . . . It's not within my role to tell a head teacher, 'That's not an incompetent teacher'. If it's come to me, the head teacher has already defined it.

Among officers who were prepared to give a personal view of incompetence, many talked in general terms of teachers 'unable to reach a minimum standard of competence' and 'failing to deliver an adequate service in the classroom'. Where officers gave a more detailed account, their descriptions were similar to those mentioned by the head teachers interviewed in the first phase of this research and related to: planning and preparation, classroom discipline and organisation, teaching of the curriculum, teaching methods and pupil progress.

Others took a pragmatic view related to their job defending members, so it was not the *symptoms* but the *causes* and *contexts* of incompetence which under-pinned their own definitions. In some cases the management of a school was blamed for inappropriate appointments in the first place, resulting in what one officer called 'square pegs in round holes'. Reference was made to both in-house appointments and the recruitment of new staff to posts for which they were inappropriate:

> For example, someone would be employed as a special needs co-ordinator but without any qualification for special needs. Six months afterwards the school management will decide that he is failing but will fail to provide the necessary support.

Since the definition of 'incompetence' was not always clear, it became a context-bound concept, relating to the time and/or the place in which a teacher was located. Some teachers were alleged to be incompetent, a number of officers believed, because of a clash of values and beliefs, often with a new head teacher, a recurring theme in this research:

> Examples have occurred where teachers who were considered successful in pupil management under one head teacher, when the head teacher changes and the philosophy changes, are suddenly deemed to be inappropriate in their management of pupils.

The changes taking place in education over the last ten years and the 'unreasonable nature of the workload that's being placed upon teachers' were felt to make demands which some teachers simply could not meet:

> The workload is just unrealistic . . . Teachers are expected to work at an intense level, but to maintain it for 40 years, and that clearly isn't possible. There is a burn-out syndrome among teachers and expectations of them which are quite unrealistic and unknown in other countries. Having taught in [another European country] I know that the standards there are extremely high, but the expectations of what teachers have to do are far less. If you add to this the fact that teachers are expected to work with scant resources and little prestige, it is not surprising they feel a sense of failure. The most lowly worker in a model office would expect a telephone and a computer terminal at their desk. Teachers are often restricted on how much photocopying they can do for themselves.

Other common causes of 'incompetence' were identified as factors external to the institution, such as the impact of a divorce, or the health of teachers or their family members. Some union officers said they had found that illness or problems in the home could induce a spiral of decline, with stress leading to relative failure in the classroom, producing in turn allegations of incompetence, leading eventually to further stress, ill health and an increasing pattern of absence. They felt that the capability procedures themselves, with all the paper-work needed, could then add to the stress, appearing to reify the belief that the teacher was completely useless, as these two officers relate:

> Delayed response to bereavement is quite a problem. A lot [of cases] are divorces, family problems. When problems are impinging from their private life on to their professional life, there's not a lot you can do anyway, even with all the support in the world.

> They can't cope with the assessment regime [during capability procedures], with having to demonstrate that all their lessons have been prepared and all fit into a programme for the term at least, or for the year, and demonstrate how they fit into the syllabus and schemes of work. Probably in two-thirds of cases there is an absence pattern, particularly when the monitoring pro-cedures start to take effect, especially if there is a requirement to demonstrate forward planning in detail. Because they will stay up late at night, night after night, doing that as well as having to keep up with the marking and all the other things. They have to be absolutely perfect! At any time someone can walk in and say 'Can I see your scheme of work, your lesson plans, your mark book, examples of work pupils have done?' and there aren't enough hours in the day to do all of that.

Many of the union officers interviewed felt very strongly that most teachers, if scrutinised closely, would be found to be under-performing in at least one area of their job at some point in their career. One officer who had been a teacher himself said:

> I've always thought that but for the grace of God almost any teacher can be judged to be incompetent in some respect by management . . . Once you start looking at individual teachers, then most will be found wanting in some respect.

It was a commonly held view that once teachers had been identified as being 'incompetent', the standards which they then had to attain were beyond what would be normally required of any other teacher in the school. Some officers also alleged that heads, when judging a teacher to be incompetent, took too narrow a focus of that teacher's performance, perhaps highlighting one aspect of their classroom practice, without acknowledging the teacher's overall contribution to the school:

Something that is missed in incompetence is the value of the person even while you claim them to be incompetent. I believe teaching is a 'whole', a school is a 'whole'. I'm not suggesting that you can leave an incompetent without taking any notice, but you have to look at what they're also putting in, and sometimes the less competent ones in the aspect that the head teacher is looking at are very good at putting an awful lot into the school, i.e. extra-curricular activities. And sometimes I say to heads 'What are you getting as a whole out of this?' Even if I could accept there were 15,000 incompetent teachers, I don't believe there are 15,000 who are putting nothing in.

In summary, whereas head teachers, when asked for a definition of 'incompetence', had usually ascribed responsibility to teachers, union officers talked more about causes. Heads often gave concrete examples of what they thought were deficiencies in areas such as planning and preparation, teaching and learning, and classroom discipline. Many of the union officers switched some of the blame away from teachers, insisting that the impact of external and internal factors on teachers' performance in school was often ignored by heads.

Types of case encountered by union officers

The types of case in which the interviewees had been involved covered the whole range of issues mentioned by head teachers in the first stage of this research: poor discipline, negative relationships with pupils, parents, and colleagues; insufficient planning and preparation; inadequate coverage of the national curriculum; inability to cope effectively with management responsibilities; poor exam results; failure to follow policy guidelines; paucity of classroom display. One officer estimated that 90 per cent of the cases he dealt with were about actual classroom practice, only 10 per cent being related to teachers failing in their managerial capacity.

Some interviewees identified trends in the evidence given to them about alleged incompetence, picking out particular aspects of classroom teaching that were currently important in the minds of heads:

Failure to differentiate work – very popular criticism in primary at the moment.

Discipline is the big issue at the moment in secondary and primary, as well as general management of learning.

It's now more about the delivery of the curriculum and also of recording outcomes adequately and this dreaded word 'differentiation' which is what you hear all the time from LEA inspectors and no doubt OFSTED reports – the idea that every child has an individual target.

It was the perception of some officers that more cases of alleged incompetence arose in primary schools than in secondary schools. One suggested that the explanation lay in the way in which the larger institutions were able to provide greater support for staff to address any weaknesses:

> I suspect that the larger staff of secondary schools and the larger structure do add to the in-house support to help individual members of staff. The smallish primary schools with high contact ratios are certainly not as well placed as secondary schools.

Others pointed out that the changes over the last ten years in education had had a greater impact on primary teachers than secondary teachers. For many older primary school teachers, the national curriculum has required them to teach subjects, like technology, which had not been elements in their own school and higher education, or initial teacher training. Indeed, many had themselves not studied science or technology beyond the age of 13. The burden of developing the knowledge and skills to teach all the national curriculum subjects to the required standard, together with the increased amount of paperwork required in assessment and recording, were seen as key factors in incompetence cases in primary schools.

Several of the union officers identified two different groups of teachers who were most likely to become the focus of incompetence cases, the newly qualified and the over 45 year olds, corroborating, to some extent, what came out of the national survey of head teachers. In the opinion of the interviewees, the newly qualified teachers facing capability procedures could be split into two groups: 'those who should never have been in the job in the first place' and those 'who have not been properly mentored or supported'.

Some felt that the motivation to adapt to change and improve performance diminished as teachers got older and had known, in the past, that there was a retirement route out of the profession. Others mentioned the specific problems of mature entrants to the profession, not always willing to conform to accepted practice. Mature entrants had comprised, for some officers, a disproportionate amount of their case load. The three quotes below are typical of these widely held views:

> There are two types of problems as I see it. One where the older teacher finds they cannot adapt easily to modern methods and the national curriculum. The other is the newly qualified teacher who comes in and finds they can't cope. It's controlling the children that's the problem. I haven't had too many [cases] who are in their 30s, except people who have come in as a second career.

> They [the incompetent teachers] are either at the very beginning of their career or towards the end . . . I reckon from about 45 being towards the end

of their career, because people are thinking of retiring around 50 to 55. The roughly 28 year olds to 43 year olds, you don't tend to get too many of those.

[The mature entrants] are more challenging. They won't just accept the system that's there. The mature student, with a wider experience of life, will be making comparisons with how they were treated by other employers and so if they don't like the management style, they'll say so! And that's where you get abuse of competence procedures and victimisation. Unfair incompetence procedures is a form of bullying by some heads.

What triggers an incompetence case?

Various triggers were mentioned by the interviewees for capability procedures being instituted against teachers, including complaints from parents, pupils and other staff. The two most commonly mentioned factors were school inspections and the arrival of a new head at a school. Many felt that OFSTED provided the trigger for some head teachers to take action either after the inspection, when a teacher had been identified as unsatisfactory, or before the inspection took place, in order to demonstrate to the inspectors that they were monitoring performance in their school and taking steps to ensure quality teaching and learning:

> Some head teachers haven't got a grip and panic pre-OFSTED. Suddenly there is an immediate descent into punitive measures after a teacher has been there for years. We ask why something hasn't been done before.

The impact of a new head was mentioned by a large majority of those interviewed as a key factor and this was viewed both positively and negatively. In some schools, teachers who had perhaps been performing below an acceptable standard for many years had been tolerated by the previous head because their personal relationship with the teacher made it difficult to confront the teacher about weakness. A new head, without tribal loyalties to the existing staff, was more able to come into the school and address problems where they existed.

It was also suggested, by a head teacher association officer, that the changing roles of head teachers meant that heads today were more likely to take action against incompetent staff:

> I think if a head sees himself or herself as the first among equals – the old view of the head teacher – then they're less willing perhaps to be involved in a sanction against a colleague. If a head sees him/herself as a chief executive and has been brought up, say, into a headship in the last five years . . . they're likely to have less sympathy with those people who can't hack it. And that's right and proper . . . And I think you will sometimes find a head new in post realises that they have problems that have never been faced and should have been dealt with years ago.

On the negative side, examples of cases were cited where a new head had arrived at the school with a philosophy of teaching and learning in conflict with that of the existing staff, calling for changes in matters such as behaviour management, or teacher/pupil relationships. Teachers who had been valued by previous heads suddenly found themselves criticised for teaching methods they had always used and which they had believed to be effective. A case described by one interviewee, summarised below, illustrates how a teacher can be viewed as incompetent in one school, yet competent, indeed valued, as a member of staff in another:

> A teacher with 20 years' history of teaching in various schools in one authority applied for and was appointed to an equivalent post in a school in a neighbouring authority. Within a very few weeks, or even days, the new head teacher was complaining that the appointment was not working out, that the teacher did not fit in to the ways of the school and did not follow rigidly the instructions of the head on such matters as producing lesson plans, etc. This climaxed when the head suggested that the individual teacher should look for a post elsewhere, at which point she complained to the governors. A local authority adviser was involved and it was agreed that the teacher should be monitored. The teacher then became very stressed and went off sick, complaining to the governors about bullying by the head teacher, but these complaints were not dealt with.
>
> While on sickness absence, the teacher applied for a post back in her original authority with the support of advisers from that authority, was appointed and has now successfully completed two terms in the new school ... This is, I think, a classic example of the difference in perception of what makes a good teacher between the head and the individual teacher. It also reflects, I believe, on a rigid management attitude towards dealing with professional approaches to the job of teaching and the fact that they may differ. It begs the fundamental question 'Are teachers professionals, or operatives?'

The union officers were asked how many cases of alleged incompetence they had become involved with over the last year and how many were currently taking place. It is not possible to draw any general conclusions from the figures they provided individually, but several did suggest that the number of incompetence cases overall was rising. It was felt by many respondents that this increase was partly due to perceived rather than real levels of incompetence in schools, and partly because of the way teachers' jobs have changed over the last decade. The view was put that the high profile given by the media to the concerns expressed by the previous and present government about educational standards had made heads and parents more likely to allege incompetence. There was, however, a consensus that recent changes in education, and what one officer described as the 'unreasonable workload placed on teachers today', had also led a rise in the number of 'real' cases.

Outcomes of incompetence cases

The variations in the size and organisation of the different teacher associations meant that there were differences as to when a particular association became involved in incompetence cases and this therefore affected interviewees' accounts of the outcomes of the cases they had been involved with. Some unions do not see the cases which are resolved successfully in the early stages of pro-cedures and only become involved in serious cases late in the formal procedure. One of the larger teacher associations explained that it tended to become involved earlier in cases than its fellow associations, so it saw more examples of the teacher reaching an acceptable level of competence and procedures being discontinued.

Comments from officers in different regions suggested a higher 'success' rate than the one in four improvers reported by head teachers in the national survey, several believing that, particularly with timely intervention, the figure could be nearer a half:

> The majority have been successful and have come off procedure. If you looked at the 16 cases [I have dealt with during the past year], six or eight of them would have probably come straight through without any further problem.

Concern was expressed, however, that as early retirement routes close down, so does the opportunity to make what many of the interviewees referred to, either implicitly or explicitly, as an 'exit with dignity'. There was a general consensus, illustrated by the comment of the two officers below, that a person who had given many years of service to education should be allowed a means of salvaging pride and self-esteem:

> I have, in the past, encouraged them to look at ill health retirement and say, 'Look, is there a reason for this [incompetence] and the stress that you're under? Go along and see whether the doctor will support an ill health retirement', and generally up to now that's worked well.

> My worry is that what was a humane way of dealing with someone who was not going to be able to cope [i.e. early retirement] will be shut off . . . If someone's done 30 years at the job and not done too badly at it . . . Nobody's actually said to them up to now, 'You're crap' . . . So what do you say, 'Sorry, you're going to get the sack'? It strikes me as an inhumane way of dealing with people.

Membership of the teacher associations is not confined to the state maintained sector and many teachers and heads in independent schools belong to a union. A number of officers pointed to differences in the ways in which independent schools dealt with cases of incompetence. One respondent, from a head teacher association, thinking more from the head's than the teacher's vantage point, expressed a sneaking envy of his members in the private sector, who appeared to have much greater autonomy and direct power than maintained school heads:

> Independent schools are more ruthless. The head teachers and boards of governors are more directly accountable to parents. Certainly, X locally, who runs his own school, hasn't thought twice about going to industrial tribunals. He said, 'If I lose £10,000 to get rid of someone who's costing me money, it's money well spent.' Few heads in the state sector would say that, and risk going to an industrial tribunal. At an independent school, if there are complaints from the customers, it could damage the viability of your school.

What factors are important in cases where teachers actually improve?

A number of different explanations were offered for why some teachers reach an acceptable level of competence while others do not. In some cases, union officers were unconvinced that there had really been a legitimate problem in the first place and it had been relatively easy to address the area of concern identified:

> Sometimes it is a management issue – an area where parents have very high expectations, particularly in primary. Too much was expected of staff. In one or two cases there is a difference of view, even down to standards of dress.

Others talked about teachers who had allowed themselves to become less conscientious in their job and for whom the very act of being placed on a capability procedure was sufficient to motivate them to make the required improvement and show a greater level of commitment:

> One head saw a head of department resting on rather faded laurels and not really keeping up with developments or encouraging the pupils to take an interest in the subject beyond what went on in the classroom, and also it was said that the results were getting worse, although it's always been a debate as to how far the teachers are responsible for results and how much the pupils are. And basically I think he needed a shake up . . . we've never heard of any problem since.

Many officers made distinctions based on the perceived causes of problems – the difference, for example, between teachers who had let their planning, preparation or marking slide, and those who were experiencing classroom discipline problems, which they often felt were the hardest matter to rectify:

> I think it's the teachers who have drifted down, got demoralised, haven't received any real support and recognised that, if they're going to make it,

they've got to put a lot of effort in, and they do . . . With control problems, if it's gone too far, you might as well pack up your bags!

Like head teachers, union officers saw *denial* as a major obstacle to improvement. Teachers who had improved, they felt, were generally those who were prepared to admit there was a weakness in their performance. Although the attitude of the teacher was considered to be significant, however, it could be affected by the way the school management handled the situation. Several union officers mentioned that in the cases where teachers had reached an acceptable level of performance, the head teachers had been genuinely committed to a positive outcome to the case, wanting the teacher to succeed and not merely going through the motions of the process with the explicit aim of removing the teacher from the school. The complementary factors, 'self-help' and 'support', are illustrated by these three quotes:

> You can only help them when they're willing to admit that they have a problem, that it's not somebody else's fault.

> It [likely success] is influenced by the way they are handled within the process. If the individual feels that there is genuine support, albeit for a deficiency which they would see as being a fair assessment of the problem that they have, then that 'slap on the wrist' acts as an incentive.

> Where you've got a good head, they won't just say, 'You're not doing the job properly'. They will put practical suggestions. A lot don't. A lot of the ones who improve have heads who want them to turn round.

Procedures

The role of the local education authority

There was some evidence that those authorities with what the teacher associations regarded as 'sound' procedures were more likely to have raised their head teachers' awareness of the procedures in place. In other authorities, teacher associations reported ignorance of their very existence by some heads:

> In some schools, people were asking me 'Are you telling me there are procedures?' So, in some cases, even where procedures existed, they didn't know about them.

Even where union officers felt that the procedures in place were well constructed and provided appropriate support, turning the policy into practice was occasionally problematic. Some reported that head teachers did not accept the importance of providing support even though both the LEA and union were stressing this requirement, and they were prepared to get quite rough with heads who did not offer support:

> I want to monitor whether the support has been effective. That has been resisted on a number of occasions as not necessary. Well, I'm afraid it is! If it's supposed to be a *supportive* procedure, then you've got to give support. I think it's more recognised than it was . . . And I think perhaps LEAs and head teacher associations are saying to their members, 'Look you've got to do what's necessary for support. You've got to spend some money.' Sometimes there's an inflexibility in terms of support. Schools that haven't got a lot of funds, especially primary schools, say they can't find the money. I say, 'Well, you'll have to find it!'

Differing views were expressed as to whether in-house or external support was more valuable in these cases. One union officer indicated that his union always encouraged the involvement of outside expertise 'just in case the head is getting at someone in particular – as a sort of honest broker', though he admitted that it was rare for an inspector or adviser to disagree with the head's diagnosis. He acknowledged this might well be because the head had been correct in the initial assessment. He also suggested that, as in some LEAs the advisory services have been converted into autonomous business units, needing to be 'bought in' by schools to meet their income targets, they might be less inclined to disagree with a head. Concern was also expressed by some officers that a school's limited financial resources could lead to inadequate in-house support, with no specialist advisers to help a teacher:

> I expect problems. How do I deal with that? I try to link them in to another union member who has expertise in that area locally and I do that through my local networking because I don't believe then that proper support has been provided to that member.

Separating assessment and advice

Union officers were keen to stress that head teachers and LEAs should ensure clear roles for key players. There should be no confusion between assessment and advice. Others felt that the monitoring process was sometimes unfair, pointing out the small amount of time that an external adviser, who was also monitoring, might spend in a teacher's classroom observing. Some interviewees pointed out that there were difficulties in the way in which head teachers approached the informal monitoring stage of procedures. The term 'informal' seemed to encourage head teachers to ignore the need to keep proper records of any support provided and the type and outcomes of monitoring.

A number of officers called for what sounded like a paradox: a 'formalisation' of the informal process, while still preserving its informal status. This usually meant keeping better records, and informing teachers of the implications of being in the informal stage: that it could lead on to formal proceedings, with dismissal the possible ultimate outcome if improvement was not achieved. Union officers explained that, when they were brought into the process, they would ask for evidence of any support and monitoring during the informal stage and, if it were not forthcoming, would insist the whole process should be started again. One officer stressed the advantages of approaching the informal stage in a proper way, saying: 'A lot will depend on what use is made of the informal stage. If the informal stage is genuinely supportive then a lot needn't go on to formal.'

Concern was raised about the diffuse nature of some posts, especially when there were no job descriptions for teachers. There were differences in viewpoint among officers about how these should be conceived: length, style, detail, purpose. Sometimes there were no descriptions at all from the school or the LEA, on other occasions what was written down was considered to be inappropriate:

> Not all schools or all staff have got job descriptions which therefore means that if they come into the 'capability' group, you say, 'Well, have you got a job description? Do you know what is expected of you?', and if they haven't, you say to the head, 'Well, we'll come back later when you've given them a job description, so they know what is expected of them'.

The role of the teacher associations in incompetence cases

The common popular image of the union officer, obdurately defending members and obstructing any process of removing them, was not entirely sustained in this research. Most officers interviewed said they saw their first duty as being to the children in the school and in Chapter 4 we reported that some teachers who had been accused of incompetence even claimed that there was collusion between their union and the head teacher or local authority. Interviews with union officers showed there was some truth in this belief, though the officers who did collaborate with heads or LEAs saw it as expedient and in their members' interest, putting them in a position to obtain the best deal with the least pain.

There were a number of ways in which the field officers interviewed became involved in cases of alleged incompetence. The most common means was through initiation by the member, either directly to the local officer, or through the union's referral system. Interviewees also reported that, in cases where stress or other types of ill health were a factor, the initial contact was often made by the member's spouse or partner.

Responsibilities to children and teachers

The majority of union officers wanted to emphasise that their role was *not* to keep an incompetent teacher in post. They stressed that they were always mindful of the rights of pupils to enjoy a quality education. Within this context they saw their role as supporting their member, ensuring appropriate support to overcome the alleged problems, and providing them with the best possible advice on the options available to them, as the comments made by officers from different unions illustrate:

> My primary motivation is that the kids in schools are going to get the best deal and my next very close second is naturally my support for our members. But my primary consideration is the welfare of kids in school. So, if I see a member failing, I would push them towards early retirement or to some alternative and if they say, 'I'm going to resign', I wouldn't say, 'Well, don't do it on any account!' I'd say, 'Think very carefully about your options, but that could be one of them'.

In general, the role of those representing teachers is seen as giving advice to their member about what the procedure comprises, advising them what they need to do, what the likely outcome is and what the options are. According to circumstances, they then represent their member at formal meetings. They saw an important part of their work as ensuring that procedures were adhered to and some mentioned the need to keep the atmosphere calm and professional, acting almost like a marriage guidance counsellor, especially in fraught circumstances:

> It is my role to ensure that the people involved in such a case do not fight, but that there is impartiality and objective judgement rather than passionate involvement.

> Sometimes people get very emotional and it's hard to stay cool, calm and collected, so I try to keep them to the point. Sometimes I get them to adjourn [the meeting] so that proper answers can be given.

There is another, largely unpublicised part to the union officers' work: the personal and pastoral support they provide to teachers, who are often distraught at being identified as incompetent. Many described this as their 'hand-holding role'. One explained: 'Part of our role is simply to listen to members who have problems and very often they have no one to talk to other than us'. Some officers explained that teachers with problems were often avoided by other staff in school, not because their colleagues were necessarily unsympathetic, but because there was a sense of 'contamination by association'. They did not see this particular pastoral role as a 'nine-till-five' assignment. The comment below is typical of that made by many of those interviewed:

> The majority of members want to speak to you in the evening. I had a call at 11.40 p.m. last night and I spoke to the same lady at 7.30 a.m. this morning. I don't have to do that. It's not part of the job. I have an answer-phone so it

could go on there, but I believe that if *I* was worried about something, I'd be chewing my nails down all night, so I like to feel they can ring me.

Different officers, different practices

Within the common framework of responsibilities, it became apparent that there were some differences in actual practice between union officers, even between those within the same union. Sometimes what they did was in direct contravention of what they were supposed to do, according to their union's instructions, but they saw themselves as front-line troops, having to back their own judgement in the field, often in very difficult circumstances. Many had been teachers themselves, so there was sometimes a natural desire to provide practical help and classroom advice to their members, even when they were not supposed to, as these two officers described:

> Due to my own personal experience and knowledge there are many times when I slip into my advisory role. I've always found people welcomed it.

> I did go in during the holidays and checked out his classroom, his displays etc. There were no problems there. He seemed to have the classroom well organised. I don't think he shared around tasks or gave responsibility to the children – that, I think, contributed. My message to him was that, until he did re-establish his position with the group and clarify that he was master, he would waste a great deal of effort. He tried to do this, but never fully succeeded.

By contrast with this last comment, another officer in the same union took the polar opposite view when asked if he ever gave practical advice on lessons:

> No. Categorically no! We would refer them to the person who's making the judgement so that they were following that advice, because that would be more successful than second-guessing what that person wants. But we don't see that as our role, anyway.

The 'hands off classroom practice' position held by this union officer, however, was in the minority among interviewees. Most felt that they had professional expertise and should be able to give advice to their members about their practice. Some even argued that it would be useful for them to observe their members teaching, even though they said their union would disapprove. A number were happy to breach policy, believing this was in the best interests of their members, though what they saw sometimes put them in a difficult position, producing a clash between roles such as that of judge, mentor, representative:

> The head asked me to [observe] and the member was also keen . . . I went in and watched what was going on in this particular class. It's a dangerous

position for the union to be in, incidentally. I have to tell you that, from what I observed, it was absolute chaos! The problem is then that you have a difficulty with your member, because you see exactly what the head teacher is talking about, but your role as the union rep is not to be the advisory teacher or to act as the head teacher. My role was to ensure that fair procedures were followed and to assist the member to reach a fair conclusion.

Collusion, or pragmatism?

Through the eyes of teachers who had been accused of incompetence, this last example could be seen as another example of collusion with the head or local authority. The union officer witnesses for himself what the head has complained about, but the member believes that his union representative should have been more vigorous in contesting, on his behalf, the original diagnosis made by the head. What the officer sees as a need to make a personal judgement and then act in a pragmatic manner, may be regarded by the member as treachery. Indeed, some of our accused teacher informants had abandoned their union and turned to an independent agency that was willing to represent teachers.

In a number of cases, teacher associations became aware of events even before their own member had contacted them, through informal networking. These backstage contacts were regarded as 'collusion' by some of their members, but as expedient or pragmatic, often for organisational reasons, by the officers themselves:

> I have a very good working relationship with the officers of the LEA and they would very often ring me up and say, 'Just thought I ought to let you know that you may be hearing from so and so', so the network was very effective. In some cases, I was then able to use my contacts with other people to say to them, 'If you can get to so and so, encourage them to get in touch with me because I think they need some help'.

> Sometimes we're notified by the school representative, sometimes we're tipped off by the LEA, sometimes you get documentation, as I did yesterday, from a head teacher about a meeting before you get it from the member! There are a lot of tip-offs. I probably know before the member thinks I know. Why? It's simple. They're looking for dates, and it's ourselves and the LEA officer who are going to have the difficulty with diaries. It's simply organisational.

One head teacher association officer's comment indicated that there could often be a close working relationship between the different unions involved in a case, whereby the union representative of the head teacher and that of the teacher could agree to broker a deal:

I find myself talking to representatives of other professional associations and that's where the dealing is done. You know, I give them a ring and say, 'Can we talk this through?' Teacher unions have to stick up for their members, advise them and negotiate the deal. It's not good for members to know that there's a cosy relationship, but we all talk to each other a lot. If members suspected the close relationship, they might doubt the independence of the advice.

There is a further ambiguity. While their official role is to represent their member's interests, it was either implicit or explicit, from comments made by interviewees, that the majority of union officers *did* make their own personal judgement about the member's competence. Their explanation for this judgement was that it enabled them to weigh up which was the best option for their member to take, and therefore to give the most appropriate professional advice.

Only a very small number of interviewees explicitly rejected deliberately making any personal judgement about a teacher's performance, acknowledging that their own values and beliefs could affect their perspective, as this officer indicated:

Our responsibility is to provide the framework that is fair for them to do that but we would not get into a judgement as to whether they were bad, good or indifferent. There would be danger in that approach because then you're bringing your own baggage and prejudices into that process. Much better to be objective and see yourself as a representative, listening to what the member's got to say and, if you think that the arguments are unwinnable, saying so and helping the member to structure their arguments, so they are reasonable and effective, but not actually saying, 'I think you should just pack your bags and go'. What I would say is, 'The forces are against you. If you look at the corroborative evidence, it seems likely that you are eventually going to be dismissed and, if you took your case to an industrial tribunal, it would get thrown out.' So we would put it all into a procedural context rather than stepping into their shoes.

Constraints

Union officers were asked about constraints on them when dealing with incompetence cases. A variety of issues were mentioned, many reiterating points raised earlier concerning poor procedures, hostile management, and inadequate support. In relation to support, concern was strongly expressed that there was a lack of appropriate knowledge and expertise available at LEA advisory level, and it was felt that this situation could become critical in the newer unitary authorities created in the late 1990s. Many of these were small and employed few advisory staff, so some officers feared for their members, saying, 'You wonder how they're going to survive – where's the support going to come from?'

Another union officer felt very strongly that school management should be prepared to accept its responsibility for providing support:

The constraint is that [school managements] don't want to spend the time that, in honesty, they ought to put in. Because we're saying this person will never work again. The very young, yes, maybe they will, they will get a new career, but if you're dismissed as a teacher in [this region] you won't get another job as a teacher. And at 46, 50, 52, what are they going to do in this part of the world? So I think they do deserve care.

Union officers' responses to shortening the time scale

In 1997 the incoming Labour government had decided to formalise procedures for dealing with teachers alleged to be incompetent through the Advisory, Conciliation and Arbitration Service (ACAS). The *Report of ACAS Working Group to consider an outline capability procedure for teachers* was published in 1997. Stephen Byers, the Minister of State for Education at the time, then wrote to all Local Education Authorities asking them to prepare capability procedures in line with the guidelines in the ACAS Working Group Report. The report made three proposals in particular, which were of considerable interest to people involved in incompetence procedures, and which will be mentioned again in this and future chapters. These were:

1 There should be a 'discrete capability procedure' which would be used for 'problems related to competence', not instances of unacceptable professional behaviour, as these should be treated under procedures dealing with 'gross misconduct'.
2 A *shorter time scale*: 'once the capability procedure has been formally activated, the maximum period for dealing with cases should normally be no more than two terms'.
3 A 'fast track' route 'in extreme cases where the education of pupils is jeopardised', recommending that the period given for improvement after a formal warning has been issued should be no more than four weeks.

Unlike the case of teacher appraisal, which was introduced into schools in England and Wales in September 1992, no national capability procedure was to be imposed. Instead the preferred approach was for capability procedures to be incorporated into other local procedures and policies, to allow scope for local decision taking. At the time of the interviews, the unions were in the process of interpreting the framework document in negotiations with their local LEAs.

There was a general welcome for separate capability procedures, but there were some differences of opinions expressed, even between officers in the same union, about the time scales recommended. While most of the officers interviewed seemed to be reasonably happy with a period of two terms, some felt strongly that improvement was not necessarily always attainable in that length of time. Other officers wanted to emphasise that two terms would only be acceptable to them if proper support and monitoring were available during that time and that a four week fast track time scale was totally unacceptable:

> I don't think it's realistic in terms of time. If it is intended to *improve* the performance of teachers, it doesn't give sufficient time. I think two terms is too short, because potentially you can be two terms from the beginning of the formal procedure and sacked at the end of the two terms. I think a year would be a more reasonable period of time.

> We all recognise that there are people who are in dire difficulties . . . kids swinging from the lampshades . . . I can't see how you can start with something that is that bad and get to good enough in four weeks, if you're giving everybody else two terms – and they're not as bad, it's illogical!

There was a general feeling that four weeks was in any case a 'newspaper headline' figure which gave a misleading impression and there was little possibility that anyone could or should be dismissed in this time. Some were comforted by this, others irritated by attempts to win over what they regarded as a tabloid press audience. From many of the officers' comments, it was clear that if a teacher alleged to be incompetent was dismissed after having been given only four weeks in which to improve, their member would be advised to take the case to an industrial tribunal.

There was also general agreement that if a teacher was identified as being so poor that a four week fast track process had had to be instituted, serious questions would be raised about the competence of the school management:

> One has to say that if a head came to us, say, as governors of a school, and said, 'I want to fast track this one' . . . I have to say we've got the wrong incompetent in front of us, because if a head has only just noticed that somebody is so incompetent that they have to go immediately, I would question the competence of the head.

SUMMARY

This chapter reports interviews with 21 teacher association officers, during which a number of issues emerged.

- Teacher association officers believe that more attention needs to be given to the causes of incompetence, which are, in their view, often neglected by head teachers:

- The many changes in education, with the introduction of a national curriculum and the increasing administrative responsibilities placed on teachers, were considered to have placed an unreasonable burden on the teaching profession.
- Better awareness by school management of external factors such as marital difficulties or health problems was called for.

- Two particular groups of teachers seem more likely to be the subject of incompetence allegations: newly qualified teachers and those aged 45 and over with many years' teaching experience.
- Union officers felt that the number of cases of alleged incompetence was increasing.
- Common to many of the cases they discussed was the impact of the arrival of a new head at a school, while school inspections were also seen as a major trigger.
- Concern was expressed that, with the closing down of the traditional early routes of exit for teachers, more dismissals would occur and severe personal hardship would result.
- Where teachers had reached an acceptable level of competence, five common factors were identified by union officers:

  1 the teacher acknowledged there was a problem and realised the outcome could be serious
  2 the teacher was receptive to advice and support
  3 the head genuinely wanted the teacher to improve
  4 quality support and advice was available, whether in-house or brought in
  5 the process was dealt with sensitively.

- Where teachers failed to improve, it was not only that the above elements were not in place. Other factors identified by the teacher association officers included:

  1 some teachers were simply 'not up to the job'
  2 external factors like divorce or health problems may be too big an obstacle to overcome
  3 some teachers were unable to understand what was required of them
  4 the capability procedure itself was too stressful for some, causing ill health.

- Some LEAs had not produced separate disciplinary and capability procedures and this was viewed as problematic by the teacher association officers. Even where procedures did exist, head teachers dealing with cases of alleged incompetence were not always aware of them, or had not followed them.
- Support for the teacher alleged to have a problem with performance was not always as comprehensive as it should be. Financial constraints on schools,

lack of will by the head teacher and, in some areas, a lack of advisory personnel at LEA level were cited as reasons for inadequate support and advice.

- Teacher association officers stressed that the right of pupils to a quality education was a high priority for them when dealing with cases of alleged incompetence, but it was their role to ensure that their member was treated fairly and that procedures were followed properly.

- There is evidence that, within the common framework of responsibilities of officers, a variety of practice exists. Many of those interviewed reported providing their members with practical advice on their teaching and some, apparently in direct contradiction to their union's policy, undertook classroom observation themselves, believing they had to use their judgement to make sensible decisions out in the field in what might be very difficult circumstances. Others explicitly indicated that they did not see these types of actions as falling within their role.

- The majority of officers indicated that they themselves made personal judgements about their member's competence and justified this by saying that it helped them to decide on the best advice to offer, while a small number rejected this position from both an ethical and practical point of view.

- Many officers confirmed that they were, for the sake of expediency, prepared to work in collaboration with other unions or with the head teacher and local authority. Though seen as cosy collusion by some of their members, officers justified it by saying that it could reduce time and aggravation. Teacher union officers were quite prepared to liaise with a head teacher, or with their local head teacher union representative in order to broker the best deal, as they saw it.

- The officers' responses to government initiatives indicated a welcome for the distinction made between 'capability' and 'disciplinary' procedures and a qualified approval of the two terms time scale recommended by the ACAS Working Group as the period for a teacher to improve, so long as 'proper support and monitoring' was carried out during that time.

- The majority of officers felt that a four week dismissal period was unreasonable and unworkable and indicated that they believed that an industrial tribunal would rule in favour of their member and against any head teacher initiating such a short fast track process.

Chapter 7

Local education authority officers

Local authority officers have been already been encountered, albeit indirectly, throughout this research account. Head teachers, teachers, union officers all referred to them. After the late 1980s, however, when funding was devolved from local education authorities to individual schools, their role in incompetence cases lessened, as more responsibility passed to heads and governing bodies. Although they still have a role to play, other groups see them as more in the background than the foreground.

The two sets of officers most likely to become involved in cases of alleged incompetence are (a) local authority advisers or inspectors, most of whom are former teachers who joined the LEA as subject or phase specialists, referred to generically below as 'advisers', and (b) local authority personnel officers, not necessarily people with teaching or classroom experience, but responsible for employees. Both groups were interviewed during the Teaching Competence Project as part of Study 4, which investigated the views and experiences of LEA and teacher union officers, and chairs of school governing bodies.

SAMPLE

LEA officers often have a wider experience of cases of poor performance than those who only experience events in one school. They are responsible for drawing up procedures to deal with teachers alleged to be incompetent, they advise head teachers and may be involved in monitoring and supporting teachers and setting targets for improvement. In order to study their perspective on events we contacted several contrasting types of LEA and arranged interviews with a total of 20 of their officers. These consisted of eleven personnel officers and nine advisers from eleven different LEAs. Both groups contained some senior officers, and the advisers included primary and secondary specialists. The LEAs consisted of new unitary authorities established in the late 1990s, as well as long-established rural and urban ones, and included two London boroughs.

Two semi-structured interview schedules were constructed, one for personnel and one for advisory officers. The two were very similar to each other, though with a slight difference of emphasis. The schedule for advisers allowed for more discussion of individual cases and work done within schools to help teachers improve, while the schedule for personnel officers dealt more fully with the LEA's actual procedures for dealing with poorly performing teachers.

LEA officers were asked to define incompetence, to talk about the number and types of cases they had encountered, as well as discuss the extent and causes of the problems, and the outcomes or resolutions. We were also particularly interested in their procedures and the training, support and guidance they gave to head teachers and governors.

DEFINITIONS AND EXPERIENCES OF INCOMPETENCE

Definitions

Requests for a definition of incompetence had caused members of other interview samples to pause for thought. Personnel officers were not always clear, but LEA advisers, by contrast, had their ideas on this subject formulated already, and most expressed very clear ideas of what incompetent teachers did and did not do. Advisers were well used to analysing lessons, often using a structured observation schedule. Several mentioned that failings had to be consistent. They did not want 'the occasional duff lesson on a Friday' to be taken as evidence of incompetence:

> I would define it in relation to a number of teaching competencies, both in terms of the quality of teaching and the outcomes in terms of learning. Because we do a lot of inspection and review work, we have used the OFSTED criteria which we have embellished and embroidered. That gives us the basis for any of our judgements, so it is very much OFSTED orientated. [We look at] four areas – teaching, response, attainment, progress (TRAP). Against each of those areas we have quite a fine analysis. When we go into lessons, we analyse these. It's all the standard stuff in relation to pace, expectation and so on. All these are broken down with the planning, the pitch and the match against each of those four areas.
>
> (adviser)

> It has different strands . . . Poor questioning, poor subject knowledge, and that often as a consequence leads to pupils' inattention and poor behaviour and then often those same teachers find it very hard to contain the poor behaviour which their own poor teaching has created.
>
> (adviser)

Some of the personnel officers, few of whom had any direct experience of teaching, did not feel qualified to give a definition of *teaching* incompetence. They deferred to others in more direct contact with events:

We are not expert on educational standards. We would rely on the schools adviser to provide that.

(personnel officer)

My job is to support on the procedural aspects. In terms of defining the incompetence, I have to rely upon the judgement of the head teachers or others involved.

(personnel officer)

When we compared LEA officers' definitions of incompetence with those of head teachers, teachers and union officials, many of the same criteria were mentioned: poor discipline, inadequate subject knowledge, failure of pupils to make progress, lack of differentiation, and poorly planned or delivered lessons. A small but interesting difference, however, was the omission of any mention of relationships with children or parents. Whereas head teachers and union officials would frequently include the need to get on well with children in their definitions, this was not the case with LEA interviewees.

Numbers of cases

In most LEAs, personnel officers' responsibilities covered the whole authority, whereas advisers were responsible for a particular subject area or age range and also for a certain number of schools for which they had pastoral responsibilities. Unless they worked for a large LEA, therefore, personnel officers were likely to be involved with all or most of the capability cases in their area. Their estimate of the number of cases they dealt with varied between two and fifteen cases per year. The range of current cases they were handling was from none to thirty. Advisers, on the other hand, were likely to be involved with fewer schools and therefore experienced fewer cases, reporting between one and four each year. Some higher-ranking officers in both personnel and advisory departments stated that they dealt with fewer cases because they only became involved with the most serious and intractable ones.

Like union officers they felt that there had been a slight, though not dramatic increase in the number of cases. Most did not regard teacher incompetence as a significant local problem:

There's been a slight increase, it would appear, but all this OFSTED business and teachers on '6' and '7' [the two lowest grades at the time] has not made a dramatic difference to us . . . I think that all heads will hopefully be challenging, in the right sense, the performance of teachers, but I suspect most teachers will rise to that challenge.

(personnel officer)

I think the whole problem has been overstated . . . The 15,000 figure quoted by [the chief inspector of schools] has done a lot of harm to the profession

. . . The way in which some key figures have presented this information and the way it has been taken on by the press have given a profile to the issue that is disproportionate to the problem.

(personnel officer)

The cause of the slight increase was not thought to be a deterioration in the quality of teaching, but rather the result of higher expectations, more rigorous inspections and the speed and extent of changes to the curriculum. In fact, the suggestion was made that standards were rising, and that now that schools were responsible for their own recruitment they were more careful in making appointments, as there was no chance of incompetent teachers being redeployed to other schools in the LEA, although they might, of course, move to another authority. School inspections were thought to have made head teachers more diligent in their supervision and management of staff:

I think OFSTED's made a difference and heads, partly as a result of OFSTED and partly as a result of the move generally towards a more monitoring role, are much more acting as co-ordinators, going into the classroom and doing formal observations and reporting back to teachers and setting targets. When you do that and see very poor performance, then you can't just pretend it's not happening. You have to be seen to do something about it, and I think because more people are doing it, it breeds a greater confidence again.

(adviser)

The effect of OFSTED was mixed. Its criteria were known and could be used, but one adviser remarked that it could make the job of tackling incompetence more difficult. Once teachers had been 'passed' by OFSTED, he felt, it was harder to substantiate a charge of incompetence against them. Although officers believed the number of cases being dealt with was not great, however, there was concern that only the worst cases actually came to light:

In our experience head teachers will not apply capability procedures to a teacher who is failing by 5 per cent or 10 per cent or even 20 per cent. The cases we deal with are teachers who are failing by 50 per cent or more. In some cases, you could argue, 100 per cent.

(personnel officer)

As officers usually became involved at the invitation of the head teacher, they were aware of individual school context differences: that some heads might ask for help in dealing with a teacher who would not be considered incompetent in another school. In other schools, poor practice might continue, with no intervention by the head and LEA officers unable to do anything about it. There was both direct and implied criticism of heads who were not willing to confront the problem:

> I think there's a tendency for head teachers to complain and not actually tackle the problem.
>
> (adviser)

> I think sometimes the head lacks 'bottle'. I think there needs to be the will there to do it, and I'm not sure there always is.
>
> (personnel officer)

As was the case with other groups, LEA officers had found that most incompetence cases involved teachers in their forties and fifties. Problems were also found with new teachers straight out of college, but fewer with those in their late twenties or thirties unless they were new to the profession, which coincided with what union officers had reported. Another similarity was that several officers mentioned finding more problems in primary than in secondary schools, though they did not conclude from this that primary teachers were more incompetent than their secondary colleagues. They put the difference down to the more restricted opportunities in primary schools for helping teachers having difficulties, or for mitigating the consequences of an individual's poor performance:

> In the primary sector you have less room for manoeuvre, to sideline, marginalise someone. So, if a class teacher is failing, then that is the life opportunities for a whole class for the year and invariably the heads will have to act. In a secondary school . . . I am sure it is a question of them moving someone to the side, reallocating duties, rather than having to go into the formal sphere.
>
> (personnel officer)

> In a secondary it's diluted . . . In a secondary people can be hidden in certain year groups, whereas in primary, and particularly in smaller primaries, everything is much more exposed.
>
> (adviser)

Few subject-specific points were made, but a modern languages adviser reported finding more cases of alleged incompetence than her colleagues because, she claimed:

> It's more difficult to teach modern languages than a lot of other subjects – it requires more skills and it's more teacher centred. You need to be an extra-vert and a good manager. You can't just sit there and hand out work books for children to do the lesson, like perhaps you might in maths . . . Teaching modern languages is a much more skilled teaching affair and, therefore, any teacher who has a weakness is more easily exposed.
>
> (adviser)

Identifying problems

Several LEA officers emphasised that, in their experience, incompetent teachers did not have one single problem, but rather several, confirming what was found in the national survey of head teachers. One adviser spoke of teachers 'hovering on the margins' of competence. Their preparation and planning might initially be identified as unsatisfactory, but when they were given help with planning, it became clear that their organisation and management of classes was also weak, so poor planning was merely a symptom of more profound problems, rather than the cause of them:

> Initially it may appear that the teacher has problems with classroom management. But when you look at the reasons, it may be related to a lack of appropriate objectives, or appropriate teaching methodology.
>
> (adviser)

> In a few cases there have been quite substantial discipline problems, but in most of them that hasn't been the major issue, it has almost been a by-product. It actually comes down to not being able to relate to the children and their learning.
>
> (adviser)

Some officers tried to identify the root cause of the teachers' problems. They spoke of stress, coming from the job itself, from external factors and from a combination of both. Stress related to teaching was linked in their minds with the initial introduction of the national curriculum and to the many subsequent changes to it. Disillusionment and diminishing commitment among older teachers were also associated by some officers with curriculum changes, media, public and political pressure, and an increase in administrative tasks:

> All that change didn't do much for morale in the service generally, and if you're not enthusiastic about your work then the commitment isn't there.
>
> (personnel officer)

> There is probably no other profession that has got so many people passing opinions and making judgements at the moment. It is putting a huge strain on schools and the people who work in education generally.
>
> (personnel officer)

With a wider experience of cases of alleged incompetence than most informants, other than union officers, LEA officials were in a position to recognise common features across cases. Like union officers and heads they identified *denial* as one of the most prominent, when teachers refused to accept that there was a problem. A personnel officer said:

It's more than low expectations. It doesn't matter how many times they are perhaps made aware of what the expectations should be, they don't seem to take it in and understand it. They don't understand that they are failing either. It's always someone else's fault. I've been involved in ten cases in the last fifteen months or so and every one is the same, the same basic things in different degrees.

An adviser spoke of the case of one teacher resolutely rejecting the suggestion that there was a problem, confident that he was:

. . . the best teacher in the school if not in the country. Therefore there was nothing that he could learn because there weren't any problems at all. There was no openness to suggestions, because that would be to admit there was something wrong.

(adviser)

Moving from a specific case to a general comment on teachers he thought were in a state of denial of their problems, he felt a sense of hopelessness if minds were closed:

They have a lack of awareness of what a good lesson might be. Even when they have fed back to them a detailed description of the lesson with its strengths and weaknesses they can't quite see why the weaknesses are weaknesses. So it's an inability to grasp it, and therefore an inability to think about what they might as individuals do to make it better. If they're sent off to look at other classes in the school, or other teachers in other schools where they are obviously being sent to see good practice, there's always a reason why they couldn't do that. So it's always the number of children with behavioural difficulties [that they blame], special needs children who can't speak English well. There's always something that happens on that particular day which is the reason why their lessons don't go well, whereas normally they would go well.

(adviser)

The role of the LEA

Since the introduction of Local Management of Schools (LMS), LEAs have been in a different and somewhat diffuse position with relation to the employment of teachers. Teachers themselves are often unclear about the standing of the LEA since financial devolution. They are appointed by school governing bodies and work under the direction of the head, who is also appointed by the governors, but the LEA pays their salaries from the school's budget. Some officers referred back, with a certain nostalgia, to the time, over a decade previously when LEAs were more fully and unambiguously in the 'employer' role:

We had something called the staff agency. That was where all the hopeless teachers were put. They were there on a supernumerary basis, farmed out to schools for short periods of time, and just moved around the LEA from school to school. It didn't cost the schools anything, they didn't expect too much from the teachers anyway, so everybody was happy.

(personnel officer)

Where LEAs were employers, we had more chance of moving staff, plus in the past we had peripatetic teachers you could move to support teachers.

(adviser)

Not all respondents saw the past in such favourable terms, however. Others believed it was right that heads had to deal with capability issues in their schools and not rely on the LEA to do the 'dirty work' for them. One said:

The problem has to be identified in a school and dealt with in a school. In the past, when it was just the LEA . . . these incompetent teachers would just move round from school to school because the LEA was the employer and had the power to direct.

(personnel officer)

For most LEAs redeployment is simply not an option, but though they are no longer in their former powerful and controlling position, they still have a significant part to play in dealing with poor performance. Part of this is the responsibility of producing official capability procedures, to inform head teachers and governors of the steps they should take.

Capability procedures

All the LEAs studied had procedures for dealing with incompetent teachers. Most had reviewed and rewritten them in the light of government requirements, and had based them on the 1997 framework produced, at the request of the government, by the Advisory, Conciliation and Arbitration Service (ACAS) described in Chapter 6. Some LEAs had agonised about procedures, and one was on its eighth draft. A number of LEAs only had to make minimal changes to their established practice, while others, which had previously combined procedures for 'capability' and 'misconduct', needed to establish a clear division between the two.

Variation among LEAs was marked. Analysis of documentation showed quite considerable differences between them. Despite having to make a distinction between procedures for 'capability' and 'misconduct', one LEA still placed both into a single document entitled 'Disciplinary Procedures', with the capability procedures forming an appendix to the disciplinary procedures. Reference was made throughout the document to 'disciplinary action' and 'breaches of discipline', while the formal meetings to set targets, review progress or consider dismissal were called 'Disciplinary Hearings'. Other LEAs made the distinction quite explicit in their document, saying, for example:

> Poor performance arises from a lack of competence in that the employee is willing to improve but needs help to do so. In this case the school's *capability procedure* should be invoked. Where there is an element of wilful refusal to perform to an acceptable standard, the head teacher may have to have recourse to the school's *disciplinary and appeals procedures* and issue appropriate warnings [our italics].

The scope and limitations of the procedures were clarified in other ways. Several LEAs made it clear that their capability procedures should not be used for newly qualified teachers, or for those returning to the profession after a career break, who should have a different programme of induction and support. A number emphasised that management of performance of *all* staff was an important task for head teachers. Some stated that a low rating from an OFSTED inspection could not be used exclusively to initiate the capability procedure, but might be used as corroborative evidence if there was already concern about that teacher's performance.

There were differences, also, between the LEAs studied in the recommended time scales for stages of the procedures. All allowed for the possibility of a final fast track period of four weeks, as they were required to do, but outside these 'extreme cases' the times set for both informal and formal improvement periods varied, as did the general approach to time scales. One set seven weeks as the recommended time for the informal stage, with a formal stage of 13 weeks, followed by a further 13 weeks if necessary.

Another authority was not specific about the informal stage, but recommended two periods of five to seven weeks for the formal stage, with the possibility of a further five to seven weeks before going to the governors' panel. Other LEAs said a time must be set for both informal and formal stages, but did not specify how long it should be. The amount of notice of meetings which must be given to teachers varied from between five to ten working days, with one LEA stating explicitly that, at each meeting, the date of the next meeting should be set.

One personnel officer in a small local authority also had responsibility for other employees. He said that the procedures for dealing with teachers were much more detailed than those for other local authority workers, a circumstance he attributed to the 'high accountability' model operating in education:

> The pressure [comes] from society in general but also from politicians to make teachers increasingly accountable . . . That is linked to the profile of teachers within our society. The electorate is not bothered when a librarian is not competent, but is when a teacher is not competent.
>
> (personnel officer)

Several LEAs included with their procedures detailed guidelines on target setting, support and monitoring and the conduct of meetings. One authority produced a model performance pro forma, with sections on time scales, targets, success criteria, details of monitoring and support and of the people responsible for providing them. It also produced seven model letters for each stage: from the invitations to the stage one meeting to actual notice of dismissal. This was the same LEA whose procedures were praised and used widely by the head teachers interviewed in Study 1 of the Teaching Competence Project and reported above.

Use of the procedures

The most common response to questions about the purpose of LEA procedures was that they were intended to raise the standard of teaching and help teachers improve, rather than act as a disciplinary tool. Despite this aim, officers were aware that often by the time the procedures were used it was already too late:

> The main stated aim is to produce an improvement in performance, and I would hope that anyone going into the process actually does believe that.
>
> (personnel officer)

> One of the difficulties has been a reluctance to move on to formal procedures, and often the decision comes at a time when someone has decided that it is an irretrievable situation. This has given the positive end of using the capability procedure a bad name because people think that, if they are put on the procedure, people want to get rid of them, whereas if it is used earlier it should be seen as a support mechanism.
>
> (personnel officer)

The importance of early identification of problems and early action was a recurring theme among LEA officers, as it had been among heads and union officers. They felt that often problems were not only left to fester but that heads then wanted the whole matter cleared up and the teacher disposed of quickly. For this reason, several interviewees stressed the importance of the informal stage of the procedures:

> When we begin the informal process, it is very much about helping individual members of staff. It is quite a lengthy process and often it works. We have actually helped a teacher become a better teacher and therefore have not needed to go down the formal competence route.
>
> (adviser)

Personnel officers said that all head teachers would be given copies of the LEA procedures, but their confidence that it would be used effectively varied considerably. One doubted whether all heads would be able to put their hands on it. Another said it was not always used at the appropriate stage. Some felt that heads were more likely to use the procedures now than they had been in the past, though not because poor performance was increasing, rather because of their own insecurity and dependency:

> Occasionally, a head will ring us up and say, 'I have done this. Is it right?' And we have to say, 'Have you read the procedure?' and they say, 'What procedure?' and we say 'The one that's in the personnel manual'.
>
> (personnel officer)

> This is a very paternalistic LEA. The heads, particularly the primary heads will not do anything unless they have consulted with the LEA. Immediately they have a problem, they will ask what the LEA's policy is in this respect, ask for advice and to be taken through this process.
>
> (personnel officer)

Capability procedures were seen as just one part of the help they gave to heads in tackling poor performance, to be supplemented by several other forms of support.

Training and support for head teachers

In the national survey only a third of head teachers said they had received any training on dealing with incompetence, yet most LEAs were said by their officers to offer training to head teachers, though this was usually as part of another course. Some LEAs included information about capability procedures in courses on personnel issues, employment law or staff development. Others covered it in induction courses for new heads and on schemes which prepare people for head-ship. LEA officers believed that heads and governors are often not particularly interested in the subject until a problem actually arises in their own school. There was general agreement that, although training was important, it was hard for any head to be adequately prepared beforehand and the most valuable help was that given during a case.

Personnel officers and advisers offered a range of support to the various parties involved in cases of alleged incompetence. The first request for help usually came to the personnel officer from the head, or sometimes from the chair of governors, but the information might also come from an adviser:

> One of our own advisers will come back from a school and say they've seen a not very good teacher and have brought this to the head teacher's attention. I then contact the head.
>
> (personnel officer)

It could well be that one of our own colleagues, an adviser, says. 'Look, there's a problem here', because they've been in doing something else, but usually it's either the head or the chair of governors.

(personnel officer)

Many officers emphasised that they had to act very carefully to avoid any conflict of interest, so the same person could not advise or support the head, the teacher and the governors. Whoever contacted them first might then gain their exclusive use:

In Personnel we cannot wear different hats . . . As soon as a head teacher gets in contact with me to say 'I've got a problem', I will then provide advice . . . Immediately I have done that, I then cannot take on another role. So if then subsequently it goes to a governing body panel and a panel member phones me up, I am debarred from giving them advice . . . If the individual teacher phones me up, I am debarred from giving them advice.

(personnel officer)

Most officers said they were first asked for help during the informal stage, while others did not become involved until just before the meeting which inaugurated formal procedures, or, occasionally, even later. Several mentioned that primary heads were more likely to ask for help earlier than their secondary colleagues, and the reason given for this was that they were less likely to have wide experience of dealing with cases of alleged incompetence. Some authorities had written into their procedures that there should be consultation with advisory and personnel staff at certain stages, particularly if the case might end in dismissal.

The role of the personnel officer

The LEA which had devolved most of its education budget to schools gave personnel advice only to those who had bought into its 'personnel service' package. Most other personnel officers said they would make certain checks on hearing from a head teacher. They would ascertain that the case really was one of capability, and not ill-health or misconduct. They would find out if heads had evidence to support their claims, and whether the informal stages had been carried out before advising on entry to the formal procedures, advise on the procedures, and then investigate, often after discussion with their adviser colleagues, whether the case was strong. They had to perform a careful check, and some were fearful of the possible consequences of wrong advice:

If we're involved at an early stage, it's the question of actually going through things with the head and saying, 'Well, you're right. There is an issue here which needs to be addressed. Let's address it'. Or we say, 'No, we think you're jumping the gun a little bit here. You need to do a little bit more before you actually get there'. There may be cases where a head has a bit of a downer on a teacher and say they're not doing this and this and you say, 'Well, is everybody else in the school doing this and this? Are the same expectations being applied to other staff?'

(personnel officer)

We want to make sure that schools are getting it right, so that we don't end up in a tribunal, that we don't end up having to pay thousands of pounds, and that's certainly a possibility under 'capability'.

(personnel officer)

This concern that, through misapplying or ignoring the procedures, schools could waste time, fail to deal with the problem satisfactorily or even be sued for wrongful dismissal, was a very common one. Some LEAs had written into their capability procedures that, if they gave advice which was ignored, any subsequent compensation which had to be paid to a teacher would come from the school's own budget. Advice could include the actual conduct of meetings and one said:

We would always recommend to a head to have someone with him as a witness and to take notes . . . A lot of heads are very nervous about dealing with union reps, so [we attend] for reassurance and procedural structure.

(personnel officer)

The overall impression given by most personnel officers was of head teachers expecting, asking for and duly receiving the advice and support they needed to guide them through the capability procedures.

The role of the adviser

While the personnel officers gave advice to the head and sometimes the governors, the role of the advisory staff was more complex. They might, for example, give a second and 'expert' opinion about the ability of the teacher, advise the head on how to proceed, help to draw up targets, and advise or monitor the teacher's subsequent behaviour. They also ensured that support was brought in from other relevant sources, either to fill in the gaps in their own expertise or to avoid any possible conflicts of interest that would result from combining support and judgement.

Personnel officers from different LEAs gave similar descriptions of the work they did, but, from the descriptions advisers gave of their role in general, and their actions in specific cases, it became evident that the level of support available from the advisory service varied considerably in different LEAs. In one LEA the adviser described how she had helped heads set targets, and, realising that this was an area where several heads needed support, had developed her own form and framework of guidance for heads to use. Then, after the heads had set the targets, she would ask several very specific questions, partly to reassure them:

> I have then talked to them about the targets they have come up with and gone through some of the issues to do with fairness. Are the targets similar to what you would expect for other people in the school? Are they reasonable about what is expected of a teacher? . . . I think heads and deputies feel so isolated and vulnerable, so anything that gives them the security that they are being reasonable helps – I think they need that reassurance.
>
> (adviser)

The adviser would then discuss with the head the support that should be given and meet the teacher to ensure the seriousness of the allegations was fully understood:

> In some cases, it has not been spelt out to them, the head has not been up front with them. In other cases, it has been said but the teacher hasn't heard it. I see my role as supporting the teacher to reach the targets, so there's a whole layer of other support that I don't get involved in. I would try to explain where they could get some of that other support, so if there are issues to do with challenging the targets, they need to do that directly with the head and I would recommend very strongly that they have the union support with that. If they're challenging the process or challenging the targets, that has to be through that route. Once their targets have been agreed I will actually work with them to meet them, not to challenge whether they're appropriate. It's not a cosy support – I am not there as the friend/shoulder to cry on, but I would talk to them about where they might be able to get that from.
>
> (adviser)

This adviser spoke of making about 20 observational visits, writing a running commentary as feedback to the teacher on the good and bad points of the lesson, and then talking these through with the teacher. Such advice could be time-consuming and individualised in nature, though schools might have to pay for it. One LEA provided a package of support, usually for a term, which cost the school £600. The form of it was standardised. After an initial visit and report of recommendations, the adviser would give a demonstration lesson for the teacher, help with planning the next lesson and arrange for them to teach together. Support would gradually be withdrawn and during the term four or five observational visits would be made.

Variation in the support advisers provided for schools was explained by the different positions they held. Senior advisers, for example, would not monitor or advise during the informal stage, and might only become involved in difficult cases as they neared the meeting of the governors' panel. Some LEAs were able to offer more support to their heads and teachers than others, but officers in individual LEAs did not always seem to be aware of this variation. Teacher union officers had sometimes been critical of the support and training their members received to help them improve, but only one adviser expressed the wish to be able to visit struggling teachers more often, others believing that sufficient help was already available.

Successful strategies in dealing with cases of incompetence

Local authority officers see 'success' both in similar and different terms compared with the views expressed by other groups. Their view is often parochial, more to do with internal LEA processes than classroom behaviour. There was much more mention of the existence of good written procedures, close liaison between LEA personnel and advisory departments, positive relationships with the teachers' associations and the willingness of head teachers to contact the LEA for help. Tackling problems early featured yet again.

With regard to their own practice, some mentioned helping to clarify the situation by exploring the evidence objectively, remaining neutral, preventing emotional overtones from dominating, playing the honest broker. Not all personnel officers described their role in these disinterested terms, however. One saw himself as more partisan, aligning with the head teacher as a kind of co-prosecutor, even providing a dress rehearsal for the confrontation with the union yet to come, so that the head would be better equipped to cope when the case for the teacher's defence was eventually put:

> I always play devil's advocate. I will go to the school and we will look at the case to date and I will play the teacher association representative and rip the case apart. So the key to that process is to equip the head teacher before the problem-solving interview, so that they have got a fair case to present to the individual in terms of failings, clearly identifying them, in terms of a process whereby there will be objective, clear, attainable targets to set.
>
> (personnel officer)

Advisers were more likely to be working directly with teachers to improve their teaching, even adopting an advocacy role with them on occasion. They were more likely to focus on the needs of the teachers, helping them become clear about what was needed, or stressing the need for a positive attitude.

Teachers who do or do not improve

The factors which officers identified as being important, in cases in which the teachers had improved, fell into four categories, similar to what other groups had experienced. First, factors to do with the teachers themselves, their attitude and basic ability. Second, the nature of the problems they had, with some short-comings being harder to remedy than others. Third, the nature and quality of the support the teachers received. Fourth, and crucially, there was the stage at which the problem was identified and tackled.

Advisers and personnel officers spoke of the importance of teachers recognising that they had a problem. They said that teachers who improve *want* to improve. They listen to advice and try to carry it out. They are prepared to change the way they work and take advantage of the support they are offered. While officers regarded the will to improve as a necessary condition for success, it was not, on its own, a sufficient one. There were teachers who were industrious, did not shirk their responsibilities, but achieved little in return for their efforts. Certain kinds of personality trait, which had caused problems in the first place, could also make it difficult for them to improve:

> [They are] hard working, but misdirected – quite conscientious, working hard. That's often the most frustrating thing for the head, the fact that they are working very long hours to very little effect.
>
> (personnel officer)

> I have to say that in 99.9 per cent of cases where the teacher doesn't improve, they are teachers who shouldn't have been in the profession in the first place and I feel after my initial visit that we're going to be flogging a dead horse. They are not receptive to change. They want to do everything from the front of the class. They have poor classroom management and they blame everyone else for their shortcomings. They blame the children, the system. They become bitter.
>
> (adviser)

Outcomes of incompetence cases

Officers confirmed what most others had said: that a minority would improve, most would leave the profession and it was extremely rare for cases to end in dismissal. In all but one LEA there had been no recent cases of dismissal on grounds of capability. One adviser said this was because incompetent teachers 'jump before they are pushed'. Most officers shared the pessimism of other constituencies, reporting that only a minority of teachers had reached an acceptable level of performance. Despite stating that the main aim of the procedures was to help a teacher to improve, personnel officers usually made it plain that they did not expect this to happen very often, and some commented specifically on this self-contradiction:

> The procedure states that the overriding aim is to 'provide an opportunity for the employee with appropriate counselling, support and training, to achieve

the required standard of performance'. I have to say that it's unlikely that we would go down these procedures if it was felt that the person concerned really had much of a chance of getting better. Though there have been one or two cases where people have managed to get back on line.

(personnel officer)

There was a noticeable difference between personnel officers, normally brought in at later stages, who tended to be pessimistic, and the more optimistic views of advisers, who usually became involved at the informal stage. One or two personnel officers reported 'about a quarter' improving, quite close to the head teacher national survey finding, but most referred only to 'a few' who improve. By contrast, some advisers felt that 'about half' would recover, nearer to the estimate made by union officers. These sharply differing beliefs and experiences are illustrated by the two quotations below, the first from a personnel officer, the second from an adviser:

Out of all the cases I have dealt with, I have never had a situation where a teacher has had a competence procedure applied to them, and they have improved, and the head teacher has decided to drop the competence procedure. That has never happened in my experience.

(personnel officer)

The fact that so few move to formal competence is very encouraging. In one case a teacher was a nightmare to start with, and she is actually now a very successful teacher. She had a lot of support from the head and from me. She got good grades from OFSTED, her planning is good, her organisation is good, her management of the support staff is good.

(adviser)

There was some concern that teachers who did reach an acceptable standard might not sustain the improvement once their support or monitoring was withdrawn, or that they tended to hover just above the dividing line between competence and incompetence:

[Two teachers I worked with] . . . were unusual in that they were actually able to produce good lessons when I was there. So they knew what they were meant to be doing, they just weren't doing it all the time.

(adviser)

One of the difficult things is that, although the teachers that have improved have reached a satisfactory level, they haven't ever gone beyond that.

(adviser)

The majority of teachers who came to the attention of LEA officers because of their poor performance, left the school, confirming what had been noted in our other studies. Some officers spoke of early or ill health retirement as an avoidance of responsibility of the LEA and school. Others felt more indulgent, supporting collusion with the union to secure an ill health retirement, believing that the experience of formal capability procedures was stressful, so teachers might become ill because of it and be absent from school:

> Those who have the possibility of early retirement don't try very hard to improve. They're aiming to get a deal. That causes a lot of bitterness in schools, when really poor teachers are seen to leave with what amounts to a golden handshake.
>
> (adviser)

> Most people recognise the high stress levels within the profession anyway. It is not surprising if someone is put under additional pressure, with their competence being challenged and potentially their future and their income at risk, that there is going to be stress. If the union were satisfied that the head had good grounds for concern, and if it was potentially going to lead to dismissal, the union advice would be go off sick for three months and then apply for ill health retirement, because the case against you is justified.
>
> (personnel officer)

Several officers expressed concern about teachers, found to be incompetent, returning in another authority or as a supply teacher. Speaking of a teacher he had encountered, who was regarded as having particularly unsatisfactory relationships with pupils, one personnel officer said, 'The best outcome would be that he should be sacked and not teaching'. Other officers shared the concern about agreed incompetents carrying on elsewhere and most did not support the view that those who had failed in one school could be a success elsewhere, although data from our interviews with other groups showed that this may happen in some cases:

> The teacher [found to be incompetent] resigned and is working, doing supply. It doesn't seem right really. These people are often in their forties and fifties and they can't suddenly say, 'OK. Well, I'll give up teaching and turn my hand to x', because they don't have anything else to turn their hand to. But if you're thinking of the point of view of the children, then it seems wrong that people get out of the final stage, the dismissal, and then do damage somewhere else. It's hard to balance your feelings about them as individuals and your feelings for the children.
>
> (adviser)

Time scales

Personnel officers were asked how long cases usually took to be resolved, in their experience, while advisers were asked about the timing of a specific case they had handled. Both groups gave their opinions about the time that needed to be taken, and on the government plans for a speedier process. The shortest time mentioned for a specific case was a teacher who had left only six or seven weeks after joining the school, while the longest was two years, which included the informal as well as the formal stage.

Several advisers and personnel officers expressed frustration, not so much at the length of time the *official* formal procedures took, but at delays during or before the informal process began, especially when the head had failed to make it clear to the teacher that procedures were under way, or when what officers saw as deliberate delaying tactics had been introduced:

> The frustration comes when two years have been spent going through the procedure without calling it 'the procedure'. Then they have to go back to square one and start it off as a formal process. That is where a lot of the problem comes, by not addressing it at the appropriate time.
>
> (personnel officer)

> Under the old procedure . . . a variety of obstacles used to be presented, such as sickness periods, maybe a dispute over target setting. Then by the time the hearing has been convened and there has been one adjournment, time is slipping.
>
> (personnel officer)

Just as was the case with other groups, both advisers and personnel officers said they were very aware of the difficult task of balancing the need to be fair to teachers and give them a realistic chance to improve, with the imperative to provide children with a good education:

> It's difficult because you're trying to be fair to everybody and at the same time you've got at the back of your mind, 'Well, what's happening to the children in the classroom?'
>
> (personnel officer)

> [One case I dealt with was] too long in terms of the impact on children. In terms of giving the professional a chance to move forward, [it was] probably about right.
>
> (adviser)

Of the interviewees who gave an opinion on the necessary time scale, two terms was generally considered adequate for the formal part of the process. Several officers, not only those from personnel departments, mentioned the need to comply with employment law. Like head teachers they were also anxious about their own position in the case of four week fast track dismissals, and a number were sceptical about the effectiveness of management in some schools:

We are constrained by employment law, and if we do end up in an industrial tribunal we will have to demonstrate that we have acted fairly, that the person has been performing at less than an acceptable level, that lots of measures have been taken to redress that situation and that those measures have not produced the desired result. If you can't demonstrate that, it won't be a fair dismissal.

(adviser)

If we take the fast tracking four week rule as it was written, you could be led into unfair dismissal very easily. To identify incompetence in employment terms, you must give reasonable opportunity to improve and in the context of teaching, it is rare for one single period of four weeks to be enough to be reasonable. The four week period may be reasonable if it comes after the informal stuff and a lot of work has been done already.

(personnel officer)

I don't accept the original allegation that the *procedures* were getting in the way of the dismissal of bad teachers. What delays dismissal of bad teachers is where the school doesn't initiate procedures early enough, where they have been tolerating poor performance over a period of time, and then want it done quickly.

(personnel officer)

SUMMARY

Interviews with 20 officers from personnel and advisory departments of 11 local education authorities (LEAs) have been reported in this chapter. A number of the issues emerging are listed below.

- Despite being based on a framework of model procedures produced by the Advisory, Conciliation and Arbitration Service, there were differences between the capability procedures produced by the LEAs. There was supposed to be separation between disciplinary and capability procedures, but one LEA's procedures formed a section of the disciplinary procedures. Other major differences were the length of time allowed for formal and informal improvement periods, and the amount of detailed advice included for head teachers.
- Changes in the role of the LEA since Local Management of Schools have meant that officers are less able to take the initiative in dealing with cases of poor performance. Some officers expressed concern that they have responsibility for raising standards, but not the power to require schools to take certain actions.

- Officers reported that most head teachers who wished to take action over a poorly performing teacher asked the personnel department for help in using the LEA's capability procedures and advisers for assistance in setting up support and monitoring for the teacher.
- There were variations between LEAs in the amount of support they provided to help teachers improve their practice.
- LEA officers reported a slight increase in the number of cases of alleged incompetence. They did not believe this was due to greater incompetence among teachers, although the introduction of and changes to the national curriculum and an increase in administrative tasks had caused problems. Higher expectations of teachers, a closer level of monitoring by head teachers, and fewer opportunities to move incompetent teachers into areas where they can do less harm, were also thought to have contributed to the slight rise.
- Officers believed some cases were not tackled as soon or as vigorously as they should be. The importance was stressed of heads identifying poor performance early, and dealing with it swiftly, in accordance with agreed procedures.
- LEA officers accepted that two terms could be a reasonable period for teachers to improve, but felt that only in extreme cases would four weeks be acceptable, and then it would indicate previous management failure. They were concerned about possible breaches of employment law leading to industrial tribunals. Officers were also well aware of the tension between fair treatment of employees and the need to provide children with a good education.
- Where teachers' performance improved, the following contributory factors were identified:

  - the teacher acknowledges there is a problem
  - the teacher wants to improve and is receptive to advice
  - the problems are not too severe
  - the problem is tackled early
  - the targets set are clear and achievable
  - appropriate support and close monitoring are arranged.

- Some officers saw early retirements as evasion of responsibility, others considered the pressure from capability procedures might cause illness. Many complained that teachers found to be incompetent were free to teach elsewhere.

Chapter 8

Chairs of school governors

The responsibilities of school governors have increased dramatically during the last decade. Since the end of the 1980s they have effectively become the employers of the school's teaching staff with responsibility over the school's budget, though the function of governors is not to run the school on a day-to-day basis. That is the responsibility of the head and the staff employed in the school. School governance is the principal means whereby a mixture of professional and lay people can, on behalf of the whole community, oversee policy and practice, support, advise, and initiate action, where necessary. In theory, at any rate, the governing body, and certainly the person who chairs it, should become closely involved in any allegations of incompetence in the school.

It was part of Study 4 of the Teaching Competence Project to find out more about the views and experiences of chairs of governing bodies who had themselves been involved in an incompetence case. In Chapters 8, 9 and 10 we describe the views and experiences of three groups, school governors, parents and children, who are involved in incompetence cases mainly as lay people, though some would be regarded as 'clients'. The first of these groups, governors, consists of a mixture of professional and lay people.

Since the 1988 Education Act there has been a significant shift, in terms of power and control over several issues, away from the local education authority and towards the school governing body. In practice, it is the governing body that is responsible for appointing and dismissing staff, but in most schools in the maintained sector teachers have their contracts with a local education authority.

Greater independence from the LEA has bestowed certain freedoms, but also formidable responsibilities on school governors, as many as three quarters of whom may be lay people: parents, members of the community, local politicians or their nominees, the remaining quarter being the head and teachers. Wragg and Partington (1995) have described some of the pitfalls governors may encounter when teachers are not deemed to be performing satisfactorily at their job:

> All staff of course can be dismissed on disciplinary grounds. Poor teaching (difficult but not impossible to prove), failure to carry out reasonable instructions, inefficiency, and poor time keeping are examples of possible grounds.

Every governing body however *must* have a code of practice agreed by the full governing body (not a sub-committee) and all staff must be informed of its existence . . . *The most common reason for a dismissal action to go wrong is because governors had not drawn up a reasonable policy and stuck to it.*

(p. 48)

By law, governors must also ensure that the school has in place a set of grievance procedures, to deal with issues brought to them by any member of the school staff and, in the case of local authority schools, the chief education officer also has to be consulted. Society appears to expect a professional role from governors, yet they are not paid, and relatively few have had personnel experience.

SAMPLE

Following a small number of pilot interviews, 200 questionnaires were sent out to a stratified random sample of primary and secondary schools located in 13 local education authorities (LEAs) in England. These LEAs consisted of new unitary authorities as well as long established rural and urban ones and included London boroughs. Within these LEAs a random sample of 2:1 primary to secondary schools was chosen, to reflect the greater numbers of primary schools. The questionnaires were designed to elicit the views and experiences of the chair of governors on the issue of alleged incompetence. In total, 74 completed questionnaires were returned.

Of the 74 respondents, two thirds were from the primary sector and one third from the secondary sector, which was representative of the sample of schools to which the questionnaires had been sent. Two thirds were from men and one third from women respondents. Over half of the governors had less than three years experience as a chair of governors, just over a quarter had between three and ten years of experience, with the longest serving governor having been a chair for over 20 years. Over half had served on a governing body for between 5 and 15 years, with a fifth having been involved for over 15 years.

Table 8.1 shows the nature of the sample of governors who replied, illustrating that the chairs were mainly co-opted or LEA appointed. Some 42 per cent of them had a child at the school.

PERCEPTIONS OF INCOMPETENCE

Definitions

Chairs of governors, like other constituencies we have studied, were asked how they would define the term 'incompetence' in relation to teaching. Some

Table 8.1 Breakdown of sample of chairs of governing bodies showing their background
(74 respondents)

Institution	Number	Percentage
Primary sector	47	63
Secondary sector	27	37
Sex of respondents	*Number*	*Percentage*
Female	26	35
Male	47	64
Missing data	1	1
Type of governor	*Number*	*Percentage*
LEA appointee	30	41
Co-opted governor	25	34
Parent governor	13	18
Church governor	4	5
Other	2	3

definitions were vague, others more precisely expressed. Responses ranged from those who saw incompetence principally as a failure to impart knowledge effectively and thus to enable pupils to learn, to those who were much more specific about why this was the case. The most common reason given by governor respondents was a 'lack of discipline', especially when teachers were no longer able to control the class's behaviour effectively and no longer commanded the respect of their pupils. Discipline and weak class management have been a recurrent theme so far in this project, frequently cited by other groups: heads, fellow teachers, parents, union and local education authority officers.

Personal relationships were also considered to be important by some governors, mainly those between the teacher and the pupil, rather than between teachers and other adults. A number also mentioned inadequate planning, lack of subject knowledge, not differentiating between children of different abilities, and poor examination results. Many used terms like 'failure' and 'inability'. One chair of governors summarised the sort of cluster of factors that others had mentioned individually:

> Inability to carry out the requirements of the job, poor communication skills and a lack of classroom control. Ineffectual teaching, poor pupil outcomes, alienation of pupils/parents. Failure to set standards, mark and assess work. Poor management/organisation of the work. Inadequate delivery of the curriculum, lack of professional commitment.

Incompetence was seen by many as recurrent, a pattern that occurred over a period of time, rather than as isolated acts. Such governors sometimes used words like 'persistent' or 'regular', often stressing at the same time the teacher's failure to respond to help and advice. Only one chair of governors confessed to having 'no idea' what incompetence involved. In general, chairs of governors defined incompetence from the point of view of pupils, rather than teachers, so pupil learning and poor discipline were stressed, with only a few references in their responses of the need to help, monitor, retrain or support teachers before they would eventually label them to be incompetent:

> More than a lack of achieving good exam results I feel it means a teacher who fails to reach the children, who 'turns the children off'. A teacher who loses control is also incompetent, if this is a regular occurrence since this affects all the class – those who wish to learn included. Once a teacher has been trained to try other ways to achieve results and, with careful help and monitoring, still fails, this is incompetence.

Analysis of the actual cases of alleged incompetence that governors described later in the questionnaire showed empirical evidence to support these definitions. Many seemed to have based their definitions on their own experiences of dealing with incompetence. Discipline problems were the most common element in the cases they reported. Table 8.2 shows, in rank order, the six most common features mentioned by those who had encountered allegations of incompetence, and poor discipline was in first place. The list contains almost exactly the same elements identified by head teachers, teachers and other groups. The degree of consistency in this aspect of our findings is notable.

Table 8.2 Rank order of the six most common features of incompetence encountered by chairs of governors

1 Poor discipline
2 Lack of planning and preparation
3 Problems with pupils' progress
4 Poor personal relationships with children
5 Low expectations of pupils
6 Inability to respond to change

Another finding consistent with other groups like head teachers was the level of improvement, as just under a quarter of the teachers concerned were said to have improved to a degree that was acceptable to the school. Similar findings to those of other groups were reported about outcomes: most teachers retired or left, dismissal was rare.

INVOLVEMENT OF CHAIRS OF GOVERNORS

A third of respondents stated that they had never been informed of a problem identified in a teacher's performance. Just over a third had been informed of one or two cases and the remainder knew of three or more. Between a quarter and a third said they were currently involved in such a case, with one chair being involved in two cases at the time. In total, 50 chairs of governors in our survey had been or were involved with a total of 147 cases of alleged incompetence.

How chairs of governors were informed of cases of incompetence

It is not always easy for the chair of governors to find out about allegations of incompetence. Although heads were the most common source of information, governors heard stories from parents, teachers, even pupils themselves. In the majority of cases respondents reported that a problem with a teacher's perform-ance had come to their attention through an informal conversation with the head teacher. For this to occur in a formal context was uncommon, as only about a third first heard formally, compared with about two thirds hearing informally.

Informal conversations with fellow governors and parents were also more common than formal settings, and of the nine cases where information came from pupils, only two were said to be in formal circumstances. There were only four cases of other staff in the school making comments, one of which was formal. Fifteen chairs reported becoming aware that there was a problem through their own informal or formal routine monitoring process. On four occasions it had been the presence of a team of inspectors from the Office for Standards in Education (OFSTED) that had brought matters to the school's attention.

The role played by the chair of governors

The 50 chairs of governors who had been involved in an incompetence case were asked to describe their own role. They had become involved in various ways, although the main emphasis seemed to be on discussing the case with the head teacher and on some occasions actively supporting people:

> I was informed that a teacher was losing control of their class and students were disenchanted. I supported the head's view that we start the disciplinary process. It became obvious no progress was being made but, before moving to the next stage, the teacher resigned – the inspector had been involved.

Many governors discussed the case only with the head teacher, and some chairs believed they had to support the head unquestioningly, while others saw their role as more investigative, wishing to check the case for themselves:

> I try to satisfy myself that the allegations have validity by discussing it with the head and other senior staff. I then monitor the steps being taken to see if the individual can improve his/her performance.

Most chairs of governors said that the school used procedures on offer from the local education authority, although in 11 cases they reported that their procedures had been developed in-house. Four said the school had improvised procedures as the case progressed, not advisable perhaps, given the possibilities of an unfair dismissal charge being laid one day. This figure (8 per cent) was lower, however, than the 17 per cent of heads who said they had improvised in our national survey.

Governors were asked whether they felt that they were kept adequately informed of matters concerning teachers' performance. The majority felt that they were, but a small number wanted more involvement:

> The whole group of us governors feel the need to be more involved. It's almost as though the head is putting a protective covering around his staff. We never know where our roles and responsibilities as governors begin and end.

> Yes [I do have sufficient information], but only if I ask questions; through my own observations and if it seems unavoidable that governors have to be involved.

Timing was important and some governors were aggrieved at not being informed of a problem in good time. Some felt they had been compromised or rendered impotent by being kept in the dark too long:

> When we were given the dossier of evidence it was already really thick . . . the Titanic was already sinking. If we'd known earlier, perhaps it could have been dealt with differently . . . We should have the knowledge of the problem at the same time that the head knows. The governors need to know, even if it's on an informal basis of telling us that there is a problem and this is what the head is doing.
>
> (chair of governors and also chair of personnel committee)

This governor expressed a clear first-hand view as to why there were problems about governors being informed fully and in good time. He saw a fundamental weakness in the very structure of a system which placed lay people in the role of professional executive officers, without the information, support, or authority to fulfil such a role:

> There is a major weakness in the governors' structure. Governors are supposedly responsible for activities within the school: budgets, discipline, redundancies, etc. And if governors get it wrong, they can be removed with a big black cloud over them. But there should be rights for governors too: the right to know which teachers are achieving what, and to have access to personnel files. We're given the responsibilities but not all the tools. It seems to be concerned with issues of confidentiality. Because governors are

volunteers, we are not required to sign any confidentiality agreements. So there is fear that we might go and tell someone else. This means that bits of information which are vital are withheld – mostly around personnel issues. Governors must be allowed to know what is going on. Apparently there is another teacher with a problem, but the head has not given the governors the name of the teacher concerned. I feel this is wrong. We're either governors or we're not . . . A manager in industry couldn't not tell his or her board about an issue like that. There needs to be a more formalised approach to governorship. At the present it's a bit hit and miss. A more formal approach would give governors more authority and status.

Natural justice decrees that those against whom there are allegations should be able to present a case without feeling that it has already been prejudged by the body that hears it. Should the teacher not improve at the informal stage, the case may go before the governors' personnel committee, who are supposed to have an open mind and not have prejudged the issue. Parent governors are in an especially difficult position, as they may hear about complaints from other parents, or from their own children, but not know what is being done about them. Hence the dilemma: some chairs feel that all governors should be in the know, but if they are, then a non 'contaminated' sub-committee of governors, fresh to the evidence, may be hard to assemble.

Governors with business or personnel expertise do not necessarily welcome additional responsibilities. One head teacher interviewed during this research reported that his chair of governors, though experienced in industry, had none the less told him he was 'on his own' when it came to an incompetence case. Some chairs of governors expressed wariness about becoming overwhelmed with more and more chores and responsibilities and this was another especially sensitive issue for parent governors. Parent governors in particular were apprehensive that if they were given detailed information about teachers, they would be put in a difficult position:

> I feel there's so much already on governors' shoulders. And only a few governors have any proper experience of schools. I know that some governors who are business people say that as schools are now run like businesses, they should have access to that sort of information. But as a parent governor, I would hate to have information about the teacher my child is going to have next year.

The needs of parent governors were often stressed. Parent governors have a more pressing interest in the quality of teaching and the competence of teachers in their school, because their own children attend it. Allegations of incompetence are of concern to them, but many experience the stresses of responsibility if they try to do the job of governor properly, and this is even more important when a parent governor takes on the chairmanship. This parent was forthright about the present load:

It's not what I envisaged when I became a parent governor. There's a lot of responsibility put on governors. Heads seem reluctant to let go of full control because we're not teachers and we're not in the education system, but we're supposed to take responsibilities and make decisions. The budget and stuff – I find that just impossible. And because it's all on a voluntary basis, you can't get the people you need. You need a mix of people on governing bodies but it's difficult to achieve in practice. We've got two LEA rep vacancies at the moment and we can't fill them. We need someone with financial know-how to help with the budgeting, but it just takes ages to fill vacancies. No one wants to do it when they realise the time it takes and the responsibilities.

Other people's help and involvement

The chairs were asked who else had been involved in the events. The head teacher was most often involved, as would be expected, followed by, in order of frequency, the LEA advisory service, the deputy head or senior management team, the LEA personnel department and the teacher unions. According to LEA officers, as reported in Chapter 7, advisers and personnel officers were likely to receive requests for help from the chair of governors, though many governors were not particularly interested in the issue of incompetence until a problem arose in their own school.

The most common theme, when chairs were asked about the help they actually received, or would have liked, was that they were lay people who needed precise information and guidance, making comments like: 'I think that as a "non-professional" I have to be guided by the experts, e.g. the head and LEA adviser', and '[We need] proper guidance from outside agencies'.

One of the governors interviewed expressed concern that the LEA did not undertake any monitoring of teachers' performance, adding that she thought it was important to have an external agency carrying out evaluation on a *yearly* basis, so that governors could identify areas where teachers needed training. She pointed out that some of the teachers at her school had been there throughout their teaching career and claimed they had received no significant professional development.

Constraints

Most (58 per cent) of those who had dealt with incompetence cases felt that there were constraints on them. While acknowledging the need for proper procedures to be followed, a number felt that time was a constraining factor, because the process had been drawn out over so long a period. A few spoke of the problem of lacking insider professional knowledge, or of the strain of keeping confidences in their community:

You had to be very careful about what you said. I suggested in my meeting with the teacher that perhaps it might be helpful to her to see a doctor.

Personnel told me off and said I should never say anything like that. And I was really only trying to help, to be supportive.

Need for confidentiality makes it difficult or impossible to discuss cases with other governors. Under [the] former head teacher this meant that incompetence was revealed to me but not acted on in most cases, or action [was] very delayed.

Chairs of governors were well aware of the devastating effect the process could have on everyone involved, not only the head and the teacher concerned, but also the other staff. This was especially noticed in small schools, where teachers' duties could not always be changed around, as they might in a larger school:

Governors have their hands tied. If we ever did need to take a formal dismissal procedure, the process looks very destructive to both school and teacher.

It is all very difficult, especially in a small school, where personnel cannot easily be redeployed in ways to suit their strengths while avoiding their weaknesses. What [can we] do about seriously borderline teachers who can or will not improve?

There was a particularly grievous situation for governors dealing with a member of staff who, perhaps even after a lengthy support process, had failed to improve, or who had improved, but not enough to reach a satisfactory level of competence. This could become especially problematic when the teacher was well liked:

There is a big problem if the teacher has a lovely personality and has been willing and trying to improve but is just incapable of doing so.

In some cases, the process itself was scrutinised and was deemed to be too long or too subjective, given the absence of an objective, working definition of incompetence. As lay people governors felt lost in the uncertainties:

I think incompetence in teaching is a very difficult area – a teacher may well be incompetent in *one* area but very competent in others. Some parents are too influenced by rumour, etc. Not all teachers can be excellent – where do you draw the line?

GOVERNOR EXPERTISE AND VIEWS ON TRAINING

The confusing role that governors have to play, in theory given the power to run a school, but often lacking the necessary expertise, can be seen as a major *constraint* or as a *challenge*. Relatively few governors have any background working in education or in personnel. None the less, in answer to a question asking whether they felt they possessed the relevant expertise, just over half the respondents stated outright that they thought that they did possess sufficient knowledge to carry out their role, mainly because of their own previous experiences and employment history. Others felt happy as a chair of governors only because they believed that they received the necessary support and advice from either the head teacher or the LEA. The prevailing mood was one of positive optimism.

The question about possessing sufficient expertise was answered mainly in the affirmative, albeit with qualifications, but some respondents were more negative, as these two contrasting responses reveal:

> Yes. I am not a professional educationalist, nor expert in personnel law. Therefore I am dependent on good professional advice and I need to have confidence in those giving it. I do have associated experience through my own employment and managerial experience which, combined with professional advice, provides the right knowledge and expertise.

> No. How could I – I really strongly feel that the LEA should take a *much* more active role where either it or the governors identify areas of weak teaching. It is beyond lay governors, many of whom are also parents, which adds another layer of complexity to the relationships.

The need for training was raised by a number of the governors. Chairs of governors were asked specifically whether they had ever received any governor training and also whether this training had included any advice on how to deal with cases of alleged incompetence. The vast majority, with only four exceptions, had received some general training, but only twelve of these had received training which included advice on how to deal with incompetence. Those that had, described the type of training they had received. It usually consisted of either short sessions run by the LEA, or within-school staff training. Unfortunately the emphasis seemed to be more on avoidance and identification, when what some governors really wanted to know was how to deal with the problem once it had occurred:

> Training focused quite a lot on avoiding recruiting poor teachers in the first place and on how governors/heads could identify poor teachers within the school. (It) also focused on dealing with incompetence/capability of the head.

Sixteen governors stated that they would not want any specific training in the matter of incompetence, but the majority of governors said that they did.

Perceptions of governors by teachers and heads

Governors have been already been mentioned in Chapters 3 and 4, when the views and experiences of heads and teachers were reported. Chairs of governors usually get to know head teachers better than any individual member of staff and will meet with them more regularly. Some of the teachers alleged to be incompetent were resentful of what they saw as collusion between the chair of governors and the head. A few teachers did think the governing body had been sympathetic, but more often they spoke of governors being automatically on the side of the head, or coming under pressure from the LEA.

Personal circumstances and different personalities are bound to affect how a particular case is handled, who supports whom and for what reasons. Head teachers were usually more positive about the role played by their governors than were the teachers alleged to be incompetent. Some heads mentioned the importance of good relationships with their governors. The accused teachers, not surprisingly perhaps, were in general more critical. Whereas the heads involved usually saw governors as an asset, or at least as neutral, the teachers under scrutiny did mention, on occasion, that more support from their governing body would have been helpful, as would a more actively critical role of the process.

PROPOSALS FOR REFORM

One third of chairs of governing bodies were unaware of the government proposals, described in Chapter 6, that were current at the time. This was surprising, particularly as governing bodies have the legal responsibility for the appointment and dismissal of staff. Even some of those who said they did know of the proposals confessed that they had little detailed knowledge of them and their implications for schools. Several chairs of governors who stated that they were aware of the government's proposals for dismissals within two terms and a four week fast track, still said they were not yet sure what the implications might be. Those who considered themselves reasonably familiar with what was being proposed were generally positive, although some commented that fresh measures would have to be applied with caution, to ensure that there was not any room for victimisation of staff. The main reason given by governors in favour of what was being proposed was the need to protect children's quality of education and make sure that they had the best teaching available.

One governor, having carefully considered the different aspects of the proposals, pointed out some of the pitfalls:

> I understand the reasons behind the proposals, and the urgency, but deplore the 'numbering' of 'incompetent' teachers by the head of OFSTED, and the attendant media hype. I feel there is a difference between being 'incompetent' and needing extra training and guidance from, say, an experienced

head, and the proposed training for heads and potential heads could be valuable in this direction. Where a teacher's performance falls rapidly and comes within this category, there could be outside factors, domestic, psychological, and one would hope help and counselling would be available before the ultimate dismissal. We are dealing with human beings, after all, but priority must be given to the best education for our children.

Some governors believed the problems of incompetent teachers had been overplayed, while others were wary about governors straying into professional fields, and being given further responsibilities. They feared that this would make them more dependent on professional advice, and thus less able to exercise their own common sense judgement, excavating the very gap between professionals and lay people that governing bodies were meant to bridge:

[There has been] over-reaction to unsubstantiated allegations made by [the head of] OFSTED. Teachers need good career improvement support and training, improved pay structure and improved status in the community. More respect from some parents, not constantly being undermined by trendy quangos, think tanks and ministers.

It is a pity [in government proposals] that more accent is not placed on positive achievements in teaching rather than constantly assaulting teacher morale by concentrating on the negative!

What is noticeable about these responses from chairs of governing bodies is that most are able to think broadly across the issues involved and express understanding of them from the point of view of pupils, parents and teachers. The dilemma of being a quasi-professional, however, still remains and governors themselves were not always in a position to know how to resolve it, though they described it very clearly.

SUMMARY

Many of the points raised in this paper by chairs of governors are similar to those raised by other parties involved in the process such as teacher unions, local education authorities, head teachers and teachers. This chapter has discussed the following findings from governors' experiences of dealing with incompetent teachers:

- In definitions of incompetence, a lack of classroom discipline was the most frequently mentioned characteristic; in actual reported cases of incompetence, poor classroom discipline was also the most common feature.

- Incompetence was defined as a recurrent problem rather than an isolated event.
- Chairs of governors reported that in most cases it was initially the head teacher who, informally, made them aware of a case of alleged incompetence.
- Most chairs perceived their role as discussing the case with head teachers and supporting them in the course of action adopted.
- In most schools the capability procedures produced by the LEA were applied in cases of alleged incompetence.
- Although the majority felt adequately informed over matters concerning a teacher's performance, some chairs of governors felt they were not advised of the matter early enough.
- Governors often felt constrained by the process, by aspects such as time, or a lack of professional knowledge.
- One of their concerns was about being expected to possess expert knowledge instead of exercising common-sense judgements, excavating the very gap between professional and lay constituencies that they were supposed to bridge.
- Chairs of governors did, in general, feel that they had sufficient expertise to carry out their role, albeit with some expressing a number of reservations.
- Although governors had received general training, there was little in-depth training specifically on dealing with incompetence, something from which many thought that they would have derived benefit.
- About a third of the chairs of governors said they were unaware of government proposals on capability procedures. Of the majority who did know about them, most were positive, although there were reservations about 'protecting' teaching staff, while at the same time safeguarding children's education.

Chapter 9

The views and experiences of parents

There was evidence from the data gathered in various strands of the research that parental complaints about a particular teacher might act as the trigger for a head teacher to raise issues of competence with the teacher concerned. Parents were often a source of such information, according to both head teachers and teachers. It was important, therefore, to talk to parents about their views of teachers and teaching, and to explore the matters that some might raise.

Parents, like pupils, are often left out of research that focuses principally on teachers and teaching, yet the competence of their children's teachers is an issue on which many have strong views that frequently go unheard, so interviews with a sample of parents became a part of Study 4 of the Teaching Competence Project. In the case of both parents and pupils we decided it would be unethical to ask about a named teacher we had encountered in one of our other studies, so more general questions were asked about competence and incompetence. When parents did talk about a particular teacher or incident, no attempt was made to find out which school or teacher was involved. Anonymity was especially important if these groups were to feel free to talk honestly, though the weakness of anonymity is that we cannot check what people said against other evidence.

SAMPLE

Studies of parents can easily concentrate on those who are especially active or articulate. Obtaining names of parents selected by a particular school might have produced a list of those most likely to be parent governors, to have attended school functions, or to be favourably disposed to the school, and omitted parents who were less well known. Finding 'ordinary' parents, whatever that might mean, is not easy. There are 8,000,000 children in primary and secondary schools and their parents come from all social groups.

In order to avoid interviewing only parents from a professional background, or those attending their child's school, the research team sought out a mixture of parents in various locations. These included school playgrounds, but also town centres, shopping areas and health centres, so as to find adults likely to have children of school age. Potential interviewees were stopped randomly by the researchers and asked, first, if they had children who were currently of school age or had been at school within the last five years, and second, whether they would be willing to spend a few minutes answering some questions relating to their children's education. No specific data were collected relating to the socio-economic/ethnic origin of parents interviewed. Interviews were undertaken with an opportunity sample of 100 parents in four different geographical areas.

The interview schedule used was designed to take only a few minutes to complete. It contained a mixture of closed and open questions. Data were gathered on the number of children each parent had, their sex and age, and whether their children were being or had been educated in the state maintained or independent sector. The age group and sex of the interviewees were also recorded. Despite our attempt to obtain as balanced a sample as possible, 85 per cent of respondents were women. Even when couples were approached it was frequently the mothers who answered the questions, and they, rather than fathers, are more likely to collect their children from school or be found in shopping areas and health centres, the main locations for the interviews.

It is not surprising that 58 per cent of the sample were in the age band 31–40 as we were specifically seeking parents with children of school age. We sought the current employment status of interviewees, in order to discover whether they had an 'insider' knowledge of schools, but 83 per cent of the parents interviewed had no adult knowledge of schools, other than as parents, while only six per cent were teachers or ex-teachers and four per cent had been teaching support staff. Nearly two thirds (62 per cent) had experienced the primary phase only as parents, while the others knew of both primary and secondary. Nearly nine out of ten (88 per cent) were involved in the state sector.

Parents were interviewed in an even-handed way, in that we asked them what qualities they believed 'made a good teacher' and then discussed their construct of 'a bad teacher'. The remainder of the interview was devoted to questions relating to whether interviewees had ever been unhappy about any aspect of the teaching their own child had received. If the answer was in the affirmative, they were asked what aspect of teaching had concerned them, and whether they had taken any action to resolve the matter.

PARENTS' CONSTRUCTS OF GOOD AND BAD TEACHERS

Some interviewees were clearly taken aback by the questions asking them 'What do you think makes a good teacher?' and 'What do you think makes a bad teacher?' and had to think for some time before coming up with a response. This was in contrast with the findings from the pupil study, which will be reported in Chapter 10, where children showed no hesitancy when asked to describe characteristics thought to be effective or ineffective. Children are in daily direct contact with teaching, whereas most of their parents rarely need to reflect on it, despite all the attention given to the topic by government and the media. It may be that some of those interviewed who were hesitant believed there was an expected 'right answer' to questions about competence. Most parents used natural everyday conversational language in their responses, rather than the professional terminology of other groups studied in this research.

Parents' replies to our question about what 'good' teachers did or had, ranged from the very minimalist answer, sometimes a single word, even after prompting, to a more comprehensive list of attributes. Some responses, like the need for patience, which recurred a number of times, seemed to reflect the parent's perspective on their own relationships with children:

Patience

Must like kids.

Good discipline. Someone who takes an interest in children.

They must be prepared to explain to the child if he doesn't understand something. They need to push the children academically. And they have to be good listeners. I suppose patience is one of the most important things.

[A good teacher] has good communications skills, gets on well with the children, is able to exercise discipline and control the class, must know their stuff, is able to motivate a class.

Similarly the answers to the question 'What makes a bad teacher?' produced a wide range in the amount of detail offered:

Can't control the class.

A teacher who shouts all the time.

Someone who's just in the job for the money.

Just pumps out the curriculum. There's more to it than that.

Someone who doesn't listen, makes the children feel nervous of asking a question. Doesn't create the right environment.

Short-tempered and impatient. Doesn't make each child feel valued. Doesn't know their subject, or how to make it interesting. Doesn't bother to take the time to talk to parents.

A 'good' teacher

Analysis of the data relating to parents' constructs of good teachers revealed the perhaps surprising finding, given the emphasis on school league tables and standards in education, that the parents in this sample seemed more concerned that their children should be happy and safe at school than they were about their progress and levels of attainment. Table 9.1 sets out the analysis of the responses to the question 'What do you think makes a good teacher?', showing the five most frequent answers. The unit of analysis in this table is the number of times a particular type of feature was mentioned. It does *not* represent the number of parents making the comment. Thus if a parent identified two qualities that fell within one particular category, such as 'good tempered' and 'caring', both of which were coded as 'personal characteristics', then these have been counted as two comments, not as one.

Parents are able to empathise with teachers, often commenting that they do not know how teachers cope with 30 or more children, when they themselves sometimes have difficulty with two. Within the major category 'personal characteristics', nearly half (35) of the 71 comments referred to the 'patience' that good teachers display. As one parent put it: 'Good teachers have bags of patience. I don't know how they do it. I couldn't do their job.'

Other qualities mentioned in this category were: being good tempered; displaying a sense of humour; able to command respect, having charisma; and being a 'caring person'. The category 'relationships with pupils' links closely with the type of attributes listed under 'personal characteristics' but the comments made by parents focused on the way in which a good teacher is thought to interact with pupils. 'An understanding of children and their needs' accounted for 21 of the 67 comments in this category, while 15 related to how good teachers make the time to listen to what children have to say. Parents believe that good teachers enhance children's self-esteem, treat them fairly and do not show favouritism.

Only 15 per cent of the total number of comments were related to teaching methods and style. Of these 37 comments, 17 parents said that good teachers explain clearly, while 16 referred to interesting and stimulating lessons. Lay people like parents do not use terms such as 'differentiation' and only four

Table 9.1 Most common responses by parents to the question 'What do you think makes a good teacher?'

Categories of features of good teachers	Number of times mentioned	Percentage of number of mentions n = 254
1 Personal characteristics	71	28
2 Good relationship with pupils	67	26
3 Effective teaching methods/style	37	15
4 Classroom discipline	32	13
5 Good subject knowledge	17	7

parents, in response to this question, mentioned the need to match the level of tasks to children's individual abilities and needs. Few parents nominated 'subject knowledge' as a category, this accounting for only seven per cent of the total number of responses.

A 'bad' teacher

In answer to the question 'What do you think makes a bad teacher?' some simply said 'the opposite of what I've just said a good teacher is', but others supplemented this or responded with features unrelated to their definition of a good teacher. Table 9.2 lists the six most common categories. Although some elements are the obverse of their 'good' teacher preferences, the rank order is not identical in the two tables. Parents discussing 'bad' teachers were more likely to refer to the quality of 'classroom discipline' than when they were discussing 'good' teachers.

Issues such as 'planning and preparation' and 'monitoring and assessment', aspects of teaching which receive prominence when professional people talk about teaching, were hardly referred to by parents in either the 'good' or 'bad' context. Equally, however, professional respondents to questions about teaching tend not to use a term like 'shouting', though parents and children have no such inhibitions. Some of the differences between professional and lay people may be genuine differences in perception, others may simply be the result of differences in language register.

There were also differences *within* some of these categories as to the types of feature that were mentioned. For example, a number of those referring to classroom management issues said that bad teachers 'shouted' at the class. A *lack* of shouting was not mentioned in descriptions of good teachers. In addition, within the 'personal characteristics' category for bad teachers were terms such as 'bossy' and 'untidy in appearance'. In general, parents had less to say about bad teachers (201 items were mentioned in contrast with 254 features of good teachers). Indeed, some parents said they had never encountered a bad teacher.

Table 9.2 Most common responses by parents to the question 'What do you think makes a bad teacher?'

Categories of features of bad teachers	Number of mentions	Percentage of number of mentions n = 201
1 Poor relationship with pupils	64	32
2 Lack of classroom discipline	43	21
3 Personal characteristics	37	18
4 Poor teaching methods/style	23	11
5 = Lack of subject knowledge and understanding	10	5
5 = Lack of commitment to job/in it for the money	10	5

The relatively infrequent mention by parents of such elements as 'children's progress' seems surprising, but when people are given the opportunity to express themselves freely in interview, without prompting, they do not always describe matters that might seem important from the outside. Sometimes this may be because it is not as vital an issue as others may think, but it can also be because something seems self-evident to them, so they do not refer to it specifically.

Parents seemed generally more concerned about their children's relationship with the teacher and whether they were happy and safe at school, features which are often more highly regarded at the primary stage of education. Nearly 40 per cent of the parents interviewed had children at secondary school, but only about one per cent of the total sample spontaneously mentioned children's progress in their responses. These findings appear to corroborate an unpublished OFSTED report based on the confidential responses of a quarter of a million parents who received questionnaires as part of the OFSTED inspection process at their children's schools. According to a press report (*Times Educational Supplement*, October 1998), analysis of the parent data gathered by OFSTED had revealed that dissatisfaction with standards of achievement is uncommon.

PARENTS' ACCOUNTS OF AREAS OF CONCERN AND ACTION TAKEN

In answer to the question 'Have you ever been unhappy about any aspect of the teaching your child has received?', fewer than half (46 per cent) said they had at some time been concerned about an aspect of their child's education. About a third said they had made a complaint to their child's school. As would be expected, parents with experience of both primary and secondary education were more likely to report a concern over an aspect of the teaching their children had received, since they have more years of experience of schools as parents. In some cases they also had more children. One of the interviewees in this category had six children, one still in primary, the others in the final years of secondary school or recent school leavers, giving a total of 'child education years' of something like 65 years. In comparison, another interviewee had one child who, at the time of the interview, was in only her second term in a Reception class. Consequently 39 per cent of primary only parents said they had ever felt unhappy, compared with 58 per cent of those with both primary and secondary age children.

Parents' areas of concern

The 33 per cent of parents who said they had ever complained about some aspect of the teaching their children had received were asked about the nature of their complaint. Many parents felt reluctant to complain for a variety of reasons. Some were apprehensive about going into school, others did not want to be seen as carping. The reasons parents actually gave for not complaining included: the

Table 9.3 Aspects of teaching which had been the subject of parental complaints

Nature of complaint	Number of cases (n = 33)
1 Level of task not matched to child's ability	7
2 Bullying	6
3 Discipline/class management issues	5
4 Child unhappy/nervous in relationship with teacher	3

child had asked them not to; they felt nothing would be done if they did complain; the child was about to move up to the next class or leave the school. Table 9.3 shows what was most likely to concern the relatively few parents who did make a complaint.

It is interesting that while eleven parents mentioned that, on some occasion, they had felt unhappy about the level of discipline in their child's class, fewer than half of these, five, had actually made a complaint to the school. Three of these complaints were made in primary, the remaining two at secondary schools. On other matters there was less reluctance to complain. Of the nine parents who felt that the 'level of task being set was not matched to their child's ability', seven actually lodged a complaint. There was a similar reaction in the case of 'bullying', with six of the eight parents feeling this to be a problem and deciding to complain about it.

Although the overall numbers of complaints are low, it seems clear that the nature and quality of a child's classroom work or social well-being are more likely to provoke action from aggrieved parents than other aspects of school life. Three of the complaints about inappropriate work were made by parents who felt the reading book sent home with their child was too easy, and all the complaints related to work being at too low a level.

Parents often become more actively involved in their child's education in primary schools, when sharing books at home, or undertaking maths and science tasks with their child. They gain more awareness of the type and level of tasks their child is given. It is perhaps not surprising, therefore, that six of the seven parental complaints in this category took place when the child was in the primary phase.

Bullying of their child by other children, though often taking place in the playground, rather than in the classroom, was the second most common area parents seemed likely to complain to the school about. Once again, there was a noticeable primary/secondary difference. No complaints were reported by parents of children in the secondary phase, though bullying is not unknown in this sector. Parents of secondary school children sometimes feel it is up to the children at this stage to resolve the problem themselves. It may be that older students do not tell their parents, or, for fear of reprisal, insist that their parents take no action. It may simply be that, as secondary school parents have far less direct contact with a school than primary school parents, any action taken by these parents is necessarily on a more formal level, which perhaps discourages complaint unless the situation is considered very serious.

How parents became aware of the problem and what action they took

The 33 parents who had complained to the school about an aspect of their child's education were also asked how they had initially become aware of the problem. In just over half (17) of the cases the children themselves had been a direct source of information, while in over a third (12) of cases parents reported that they themselves had recognised there was a problem through observation of their child at home. Seven had noticed that there was 'something wrong' when they were in school, either as visitors or as parent helpers.

In about two thirds (21) of the cases parents had then raised their concern directly with the class or subject teacher. In six of these instances, when the problem was not resolved to their satisfaction, they involved others, a more senior figure in the school or a governor. Four parents (three of whom were primary children's parents) went to the head teacher. In twelve of the 33 cases, parents bypassed the teacher completely from the beginning and took their complaint straight to a higher authority.

Certain areas of concern were more likely to be taken directly to the head teacher than others, often because they were school management issues, rather than a particular teacher's incompetence. Of the six complaints made directly to the head teacher, four related to bullying, perceived by the parents as more than just the class teacher's responsibility. Of the other two, one complained that the class teacher shouted at the pupils and the other said she believed that the teacher was 'picking on' her child. Of the four cases involving line managers and deputy heads, two related to classroom discipline problems and two to the quality of teaching and learning.

Parents were also asked *how* they had made their complaint to the school. Primary school parents were much more likely than secondary school parents to raise their concerns by calling informally into the school, accounting for 17 of the 19 cases in this category. Parents are more likely to be physically present in schools in the primary sector: taking their children to and from school, helping in classrooms, attending class assemblies and other school events. This easy access to school might account for the fact that only one primary parent waited until the parents' evening to discuss worries. For secondary parents, the more typical route was for contact to be made initially by letter or telephone in order to seek an appointment with the teacher concerned, or with the head of department or head teacher.

Outcome of complaints

Parents were asked whether they believed that action had been taken to address their concerns. Nineteen of these 33 parents did feel that action had been taken by the teacher or school. Nine parents reported that the matter had been resolved to their satisfaction, while ten were not entirely satisfied with what had been done, seven indicating that, while the situation had improved, they still had slight concerns, and three feeling that no real progress had been made. Only four of these ten still dissatisfied parents indicated that they intended to press for further action. More surprisingly, perhaps, was the sense of resignation that a minority of parents reported. Of the fourteen parents who reported that no action at all had been taken to address their complaint, only five said they had contemplated complaining again.

Merely counting numbers of respondents in different categories can mask the real despair and frustration that some parents experience when their concerns are not accepted or acted on by their child's school. Lay people can feel a sense of impotence when confronted by a professional person, as they lack professional expertise, yet feel unhappy if they have to defer. Some parents reported that they had intuitive feelings about their own child's progress and welfare, but they did not have the breadth of knowledge and experience of the professional.

One parent who stated that her child had not been 'stretched as much academically as I think she could cope with' tackled the class teacher about her child's reading because she felt the child 'wasn't enthusiastic about books and wasn't learning to read'. Like most of the primary parents in this study, she raised the matter with the teacher informally one day, but was unhappy with the response to her concerns. According to the parent, 'the teacher said it was really her [the teacher's] business what scheme my daughter was on'. So far as this parent was aware, no action was taken and she remained uneasy with the situation. She decided not to make any further complaint because she thought it would be pointless. Instead she attempted to help her child more at home: '[I didn't take any further action] with the school, but privately I tried to encourage her myself.'

Some of the parents who had complained that their child was the victim of bullying felt that the issue had been badly handled. One parent explained that the teacher had brought all the children concerned, including her son, into the classroom, talked to them together and asked what had happened. She felt that the teacher 'had tried to make it appear insignificant'. When asked whether the matter had been resolved to her satisfaction she replied, 'Not yet' and said that she would press the school for further action if the situation did not improve. She believed, however, that not all parents were prepared to take positive action: 'This is the problem. There are other parents in the same position but they don't want to rock the boat.' She said she would like the school to arrange for 'an outside body to come in and make children aware of how damaging bullying is – physically and psychologically', but appeared to think this was unlikely. She did not know whether the school had any policy in place to deal with bullying.

In another case, a parent, an ex-teacher herself, reported that her child had complained at home that the geography teacher was unable to keep control of the class. The parent described the situation as 'a young teacher with insufficient support from other staff and telephoned the teacher's head of department to discuss the matter. However, there was no apparent improvement in the teacher's classroom management and the eventual outcome was that her daughter became disillusioned with geography and dropped the subject.

It is not always easy to determine whether teachers and schools deal more effectively with some types of issues than others. No significant patterns emerge from the data, and it may be the case that problems and their outcomes are personal and individual, rather then generic, very much determined by the circumstances and the particular children, parents and teachers involved.

While 33 of the 100 parents having a concern serious enough to warrant a complaint to their child's school can be seen as a minority, albeit a sizeable one, in only nine of these cases had the matter been resolved to the parent's complete satisfaction. It was interesting that none of the cases of classroom discipline problems was fully resolved. This seems to confirm the views of other parties interviewed in this research – heads, LEA staff and teacher association officers – that it is more difficult for a teacher to overcome difficulties when poor discipline is the problem than in other areas.

SUMMARY

Interviews were undertaken with a sample of 100 parents to elicit their constructs about teachers and teaching and to investigate what matters parents are most likely to complain to schools about. The following points emerged:

- Parents in this survey were more concerned that their children were content and relaxed in school than they were about levels of academic achievement.
- When asked to describe a 'good' teacher, parents referred in particular to qualities such as patience and a caring attitude, and believed that good teachers were interested in and listened to pupils. Professional attributes such as effective teaching methods, good classroom discipline and subject knowledge accounted for only about a third of the total number of features mentioned.
- Fewer than half of the parents interviewed said they had at some time felt concerned about the teacher or teaching their child/children had received.
- Only 33 of the 46 parents who reported being concerned at some time had complained to the school. Comments they made suggested a range of reasons: the child did not want them to, the parents felt nothing would be done, the child would soon be leaving the class/school.
- Lack of differentiation (matching task to individual pupil), bullying and classroom discipline issues were the most frequently mentioned subjects of complaint.
- Parents became aware of problems with their children through a number of routes. The most common source of information was the child telling the

parent about a problem. Some parents had noticed at home that the child seemed unhappy or worried; a few parents had become concerned when in the school themselves, either as visitor or helper.

- The majority of parents had raised their concerns directly with the class teacher. In primary schools this was usually informal, no more than the parent 'calling in and having a word'. In secondary schools, a more formal approach was taken, usually with a meeting being arranged.

- In cases related to bullying or where the parent was raising a specific concern about the teacher, parents were more likely to bypass the teacher and see either a line manager or the head.

- In fewer than two thirds of cases where complaints were made did parents feel that any action had been taken by the school in response to their concern, and fewer than half of these parents reported that the matter had been resolved to their satisfaction. Where no action had been taken at all, few parents had contemplated making a further complaint.

- Some parents expressed a sense of impotence when confronted by professionals, feeling able to identify their child's problem intuitively, but unable to back their judgement with professional expertise and thus frustrated when this produced no satisfactory outcome.

Chapter 10

The views and experiences of pupils

Children in school observe 1,000 hours a year or more of teachers at work. They may be less mature than adults, but they witness teaching at first hand every single school day. As was pointed out at the beginning of this book, children as young as three and four already have a good idea of which adults are likely to explain something to them more clearly than others. Yet research into teaching often neglects to study their views and experiences. Other studies in the Teaching Competence Project, reported in previous chapters, have shown that complaints from pupils, directly or through their teachers and parents, often form one source of information for those, such as head teachers, who deal with allegations of incompetence.

Study 3 of this research focused on pupils' perceptions of teaching, concentrating on their notions of a good and bad teacher and what they do if they are unhappy with an aspect of their schooling. As was the case with parent informants, there were ethical matters to consider, so we did not ask children directly about their own teacher or about any teacher studied in another part of this research. The approach was a mixture of general questions, about what they saw as 'good' or 'bad' teaching and specific questions about how they would react to poor teaching.

There are quite legitimate reservations about children as informants. They often have limited experience, especially in the early years, and may have seen few teachers at work. There would be some danger, therefore, in making the assumption that there is some correlation between children's perceptions of good teachers and bad teachers and their actual competence. They may be trapped in short-term expectations, not always appreciative of longer-term benefits. Adults sometimes esteem in retrospect a teacher they did not value so highly when they were at school. The reverse of this can also occur, when teachers who are popular at the time do not seem to have made any sustained impact. Furthermore, children may be reluctant to express their true opinions to adults, even when assured that their responses are anonymous, or they may say what they think adults expect them to say. None the less, despite these reservations, we decided the pupils' point of view was too valuable to overlook.

SAMPLE

It was decided to focus on pupils at the end of each major phase of schooling, so interviews or questionnaires were used with (a) 6–7 year old pupils in Year 2, at the end of the infant school Key Stage 1 phase, (b) 10–12 year olds in Years 6 and 7 at the end of their primary or middle school education and of the Key Stage 2 phase, (c) 13–14 year old Year 9 pupils at the end of Key Stage 3 and (d) 15–16 year old Year 11 pupils at the end of the Key Stage 4 phase. Seven schools were visited, with the views of a total of 519 pupils being collected, fairly evenly divided between the primary and secondary phases of schooling. The breakdown according to the age group of the pupils is shown in Table 10.1.

The 46 Year 2 pupils were interviewed in groups of two by a researcher. Six and seven year old children do not always have the necessary reading and writing competence to cope with a questionnaire, so it was decided to interview children, so that the interviewer was able to read the questions and write down the responses. The pupils were interviewed in pairs to make it less intimidating. These interviews were relatively short, focused specifically on what the pupils thought was a good and bad teacher, which kinds of problem, if any, they had experienced in school and what they would do if they were facing problems. Their time in school was inevitably more limited than that of older pupils, and their responses were often less detailed. Consequently their answers have been analysed qualitatively and separately from the responses of older pupils, which were elicited by questionnaire and then analysed.

The bulk of the sample, consisting of 473 pupils, were given questionnaires by the researchers and asked to complete them during supervised lessons. The pupils were told that their answers were anonymous. They were asked not to name any teachers, but rather to list particular attributes of good and bad teachers, and then invited to comment on these two groups and rate their different characteristics. They were also asked what they would do if they were experiencing problems: to whom they might address complaints, and what they might complain about. The numbers of questions asked were restricted for two reasons: the first because of the time it takes to complete such a questionnaire, and the second because of the

Table 10.1 Number of pupils in the sample

Year group	Number of pupils
Year 2 (6–7 year olds)	46
Years 6 and 7 (10–12 year olds)	204
Year 9 (13–14 year olds)	126
Year 11 (15–16 year olds)	143
Total primary/middle (Years 2,6,7)	250
Total secondary (Years 9 and 11)	269
Overall total	519

sensitive nature of the questions. The questionnaire was constructed so that it would elicit pupils' general views on competency in teaching, without giving the impression that we were focusing on any one teacher.

YOUNGER PUPILS AGED 7 – YEAR 2

A total of 46 Year 2 pupils were interviewed from three schools. There were 22 girls and 24 boys. The children were told that there were no 'right' or 'wrong' answers to the questions, but that the researcher was interested in what they thought about teaching and what happened in their school.

A 'good' teacher

The first question they were asked was what they thought made a good teacher. The main attributes these younger children valued was a teacher who let them have some autonomy over doing the curriculum subjects and topics that they liked. Some pupils enjoyed the opportunity to do more on their favoured subjects:

> Do lots of mathematics.

> They [good teachers] let us do what we wanted.

They also welcomed the opportunity to do more 'choosing', either at any time of the school day, or when they had finished their work as a reward. Quite a few of the children also mentioned types of extrinsic rewards and positive reinforcement, including the systematic implementation of rewards and privileges, such as extended play, stickers or stars: 'If you were star of the day they'd let you go out first.'

Children wanted a caring teacher who was nice and kind. They also wanted someone who was fair and was not unduly 'bossy', did not shout unnecessarily and was good humoured and funny, characteristics which were particularly welcomed. Despite the use of anonymity, children sometimes described a teacher in such personal terms that it appeared they were referring to one single person, rather than a whole genus: 'He's never bossy, never strict and always funny and he does sport.'

Like parents, children use natural everyday conversational language in their replies, rather than the professional jargon of practitioners and administrators. Few teachers ever use a word like 'shout', preferring instead the more measured 'reprimand', or 'take firm action'. So far as children are concerned, some of their teachers shout at them when they are cross, so they do not hesitate to say so. The mealy mouthed approach is alien to their discourse on teaching and learning.

Some children wanted their intellect to be stretched and therefore valued a teacher who gave them harder work, while others liked the idea of having easier work:

Gives you work you don't know. Gives you tests. Is nice. Gives you stickers when you've done good work.

Lets us choose all the time . . . gives us easy work.

A 'bad' teacher

The second question the pupils were asked related to their notions of what type of person a bad teacher was. The main attribute they disapproved of was a teacher who was unnecessarily strict and punished them too harshly for something that they may or may not have done. Associated with this were the notions of fairness and equity, which were mentioned in their responses about the attributes of a good teacher. They therefore also commented on teachers who shouted at them, did not let them have privileges and were too 'bossy':

If you do something a bit wrong and they shout at you really loud.

When they get really, really cross when you 'jog' something in your work and so they send you to the head teacher or outside.

Younger pupils, like the parents quoted in Chapter 9, valued caring teachers and wanted to feel safe and nurtured, so they did not like any suggestion that a teacher might not look after their welfare, be unkind, reprimand them without reason and not explain clearly or assist them when they needed help:

They always tell you off. Shout at you and screw up your work and throw it in the bin. When my sister fell over she was told to stop crying.

Give you impossible work, impossible words to read. If you're good, they think you're bad. They wouldn't say you've been good. Be bossy. Not remember your name. Wouldn't take you home if you were ill.

Quite a few children, as in the above example, mentioned teachers who set work that was too hard for them, unable to differentiate between pupils of different abilities: 'Tell us off. Doesn't let us catch up with the class. Doesn't help.'

One pupil neatly summarised the views expressed by many about a 'bad' teacher's lack of care and concern, poor social relationships, inability to differentiate, and insensitivity:

She won't be nice and give us treats. She won't give us good work. [She will] give you hard work. Won't look after us. Won't let us play. Won't give us time to finish our work.

Problems at school

The third question younger pupils were asked related to who they would tell if they were having a problem at school. The majority felt that they would go straight to their class teacher if they needed help, but their answer depended on the nature of the problem and where and when in the school it had occurred. Sometimes their problems were with friends or about difficulties with their work, not just complaints about their teacher. Fewer than a quarter of younger children mentioned their parents (the figure for older pupils was three quarters), which suggested that their experience to date in the school had meant that many could not, at that stage, envisage a problem which could not be resolved within the school.

The head teacher was also likely to be approached in about a quarter of cases (no difference between them and older pupils), which sometimes coincided with them telling their parents. This usually occurred if the problem was regarded as more serious, or seen as beyond their class teacher's jurisdiction. One pupil mentioned a specific reason why he might tell the head: '[I'd tell] my teacher, but if I had a bad teacher, I'd go to the head . . . Tell your mum.'

Another girl was worried in case, if she did tell the teacher, her problem might not be taken seriously, a judgement which seemed to be based on her personal experience: '[I'd tell] my best friend. I might tell the teacher, but they'd just say, "You'll live", and "Surely, it can't be that bad".'

Teachers who were not the pupil's specific class teacher were also mentioned by a few children, as were friends, 'dinner ladies' and the school secretary. These people were often selected if the problem took place outside classroom time, such as at lunchtime or playtime: '[I'd choose] the other teacher because she's a good shouter.'

In this case the ability to shout, normally regarded as a negative characteristic, was seen as positive when directed at other deviant pupils. Playgrounds are often seen as places to relax and play, but some children are wary of them. Social relations can go astray during rough and tumble play and this may explain why quite a number of children reported problems to teachers or other adults on duty at these times.

The final question these younger pupils were asked focused on what sort of problems they might experience inside school. The answers to this question showed that nearly half of the pupils were aware of problems that related to name calling, pushing, or being left out of games and activities. Some of the children mentioned that this would happen in the playground, which reinforces the responses to the previous question: 'If something happens in the playground where other children fight me, I tell the dinner lady.'

Fewer than a fifth of the Year 2 pupils cited problems such as falling down, or hurting themselves. Other problems took place inside the classroom and involved being unable to do their work properly, because of interference from others, or occasions where they might have broken a classroom rule:

You might answer back and get into trouble. Being rude . . . Calling people names. I talk too much and that's a problem . . . Bullying in the playground.

OLDER PUPILS AGED 10 TO 16 – YEARS 6, 7, 9 AND 11

The older pupils' views from Years 6, 7, 9 and 11 were elicited by the use of supervised questionnaires. A total of 473 questionnaires were completed, evenly split between the sexes (231 boys, 242 girls). Older pupils have greater experience of school and are also more literate and most are able to cope with questionnaires. The first part of the questionnaire focused on the pupils' views, on what is important in a 'good' teacher, and this information was sought through their reactions to a series of statements. Pupils were asked to state, on a four point scale, whether they thought the particular attribute of teachers was 'very important', 'quite important', 'not very important', or 'not at all important'. All the pupils who completed the questionnaires were given clear instructions and a researcher or teacher was always available to answer any queries they might have.

Important attributes of a teacher

The sample of 10 to 16 year old pupils was asked about a number of different teacher characteristics and Table 10.2 shows the rank order of those elements considered to be 'very important' by pupils in their responses on the four point scale. The items were all taken from previous research we have conducted into pupils' views of teaching (Wragg 1993) and from features mentioned in interviews with other groups of informants.

Table 10.2 shows that pupils hold highest in their esteem those aspects of teaching that enable them to learn. The ability to explain clearly, good exam preparation, treating all pupils fairly, control of the class, and matching tasks to the level of pupils' ability are the five most highly regarded qualities, all of these esteemed by at least three quarters of respondents. Dress, classroom displays and punctuality, though often well regarded by teachers and heads, are seen as superficial, with only a quarter or fewer of pupils mentioning them as being very important. Reprimands produce a varying response, with a scolding for poor behaviour much more acceptable (39 per cent) than one for inadequate work (14 per cent).

Complaints

In previous chapters we described how head teachers and fellow teachers found out that there might be a problem with a teacher in their school. Although many heads said, in the national survey reported in Chapter 3, that they became aware through their own monitoring or complaints from other teaching staff, there were

Table 10.2 Important attributes of a teacher (percentage of older pupils (n = 473) saying, in each case, 'very important' on a four point scale)

Teacher characteristics		Percentage saying 'very important'
1 =	Explains clearly	91
1 =	Good exam preparation	91
3	Treats all pupils fairly	88
4	Can keep control	83
5	Matches task to ability	77
6	Subject knowledge	74
7	Interesting lessons	61
8	Punctual for lessons	59
9	Good relation with pupils	57
10	Marks work regularly	50
11	Makes useful comments on work	44
12	Tells off for bad behaviour	39
13	Praises good work	36
14	Praises good behaviour	34
15	Sets homework	29
16	Doesn't keep you waiting	27
17	Dresses smartly	17
18	Tells off for bad work	14
19	Displays your work	11

also numerous cases where pupils, either directly or through their parents or teachers, had made complaints to the head teacher. In Study 3, therefore, we asked pupils who would be the most likely recipients of their complaints, if they were having a problem, and what types of problem they might complain about. Table 10.3 shows the seven most common recipients of pupils' complaints.

Informal channels of complaint are more common than formal ones, with over three quarters of pupils saying they would tell their parents and nearly half telling a friend.

Pupils may turn to parents first for a variety of reasons, including the need for advice, immediate response, the perceived greater likelihood of parents gaining a hearing on their behalf, though pupils are often reluctant to let their parents contact the school. They might simply want to keep the emotional temperature lower than it might be if they got into face to face argument with their teacher. Friends are not necessarily any more empowered than pupils themselves, but they are in a position to empathise and may even attend the same school or lessons.

Within the school structure, high status people, like head teachers, come lower than more immediate teachers. Heads of a school year group are in a middle management position and are the most favoured of the in-school professionals among older pupils, partly because their role is often one of pastoral care, and partly because they combine immediacy and status, but not at the highest level. Their own class teacher, another teacher in the school, and the head teacher,

Table 10.3 Most common likely recipients of complaints from pupils (n = 473): percentages who nominated each category

Recipients	Percentage naming
1 Parents	76
2 Friends	45
3 Head of year	32
4 Another teacher	23
5 Head teacher	21
6 The class teacher	20
7 Deputy head	10

were chosen by similar numbers of pupils, with a fifth to a quarter opting for each one. The least likely person was the deputy head, selected in less than 10 per cent of cases.

Complaining to officialdom, however, is not always straightforward. The comments below suggest that some respondents see teachers as combining in formidable and impenetrable professional solidarity:

> I wouldn't know who to go to really. Teachers are all friends with each other and it could get me into trouble with the teacher concerned.

> It's hard to complain about a teacher, because the one you complain to is not there, so it's the teacher's word versus yours, and the teacher wins 99 per cent of the time, but they know they're in the wrong.

Actual reasons for complaint were varied. Most were about fundamental professional skills, such as the inability to control pupils' behaviour, arouse interest, or teach a syllabus successfully, or poor personal relationships and qualities. Over half the pupils said they would complain if they thought teachers behaved in an unfair manner, did not explain clearly, set too much homework, or if the work was too difficult. Poor classroom discipline, inadequate exam preparation, boring lessons and 'shouting' also aroused ire, as did absence from school, lack of punctuality and infrequent marking of work. Pupils were least likely to complain if they thought the teacher was giving them too little homework, re-emphasising the point they had made earlier. Table 10.4 shows the percentage of pupils citing each reason.

What makes a good teacher?

Each pupil was asked to try and write down at least three actions illustrating what they thought a good teacher actually did. Since this gave respondents a free choice the responses were initially analysed qualitatively and then quantified.

Table 10.4 Complaints by pupils (n = 473): percentages in each category

Reason for complaint	Percentage citing
1 Not treated fairly	65
2 = Unclear explanations	51
2 = Too much homework	51
2 = Work too hard	51
5 Curriculum not covered	40
6 Can't control the class	39
7 Subject knowledge	37
8 = Teacher who shouts	36
8 = Boring lessons	36
10 Poor exam results	35
11 Not punctual	30
12 Work too easy	25
13 Often away	23
14 Work not marked regularly	21
15 Too little homework	13

Table 10.5 Attributes of a 'good' teacher

1   Helps when pupils are stuck
2   Explains clearly
3   Can control the class
4   Has a sense of humour
5   Is friendly/has a good relationship with the pupils
6   Interesting and enjoyable lessons
7   Listens to children

Over 40 characteristics were identified, although some of these were only mentioned by a few pupils. Some major factors could be detected, showing that the most highly valued teachers were likely to demonstrate pupil-centred, supportive behaviour: helping those in difficulty, explaining concepts clearly, having a sense of humour, but being in charge none the less. Seven characteristics were mentioned by 100 pupils or more, that is by a quarter or more of the sample. Table 10.5 lists these in order of frequency. These characteristics, elicited from their own freehand responses, corroborate many of the features mentioned as being 'very important' by pupils in Table 10.2, where they were responding to attitude statements assembled by the researchers.

Most of the children made unambiguous statements about what they valued and the large numbers of children mentioning the same set of characteristics suggests that there was a degree of consensus over the type of teacher pupils liked. One 14 year old girl was very clear about the type of teacher she wanted:

Makes the lessons fun, but educational at the same time. Can control the class well but not harshly. Doesn't punish all the class for one person's mistake. Explains the lesson clearly and is willing to listen to questions.

The same combination of qualities occurred numerous times. Pupils often liked similar clusters of characteristics, and these were again expressed not in the language of professional discourse (e.g. 'differentiation'), but in natural conversation: 'A good teacher treats pupils equally. Explains work clearly. Listens to your opinion. Gives work to your ability.'

One 14 year old boy summarised neatly the delicate combination of friendliness and control:

Someone who you can have a joke with. Someone who can control the class. Someone who is good tempered. Someone who doesn't tell you off all the time.

Other respondents echoed the same theme of balance between the firm and the friendly, seeing it as an essentially human blend of mastery of the relevant knowledge, combined with an intimate understanding of the needs of those in the process of acquiring it:

Needs to have discipline. Needs to know what he/she is doing. Should be responsible/honest/organised. Should get on well with the students.

They're kind. They are helpful. They know what they're talking about and aren't just reading what they have written earlier.

What makes a bad teacher?

To some extent the image of a 'bad' teacher, as one would expect, is the obverse of what is seen as 'good'; not the precise mirror image, but reflecting near enough the opposite of what was said above. Instances of ineffective teaching were elicited and analysed in a similar manner to what was described earlier. The most negative attributes to emerge were a teacher who was perceived as too strict and who shouted too frequently. The next two least favoured characteristics, mentioned by over hundred pupils, were teachers who did not explain clearly and did not help pupils when they were 'stuck':

A bad teacher is a teacher that never listens to you. A bad teacher is a teacher that is never happy. A bad teacher is a teacher that shouts at you for no reason.

Very strict, unkind. Doesn't explain anything. Sets impossible work.

It was the disrespect of someone who appeared not to listen to them that irked a number of pupils. Other obverse characteristics of what was seen in 'good' teachers included: teachers who could not control the class, bad tempered teachers, those who were unfair to pupils, those who did not make their lessons enjoyable and teachers who had poor relationships with pupils. Each of these features was mentioned by at least 50 pupils:

> No sense of humour – is always 100 per cent work. Has favourites in the class – ignores others. Is never willing to help. Sets work which is too hard and never explains.

> Tells you off all the time for nothing. Too strict with you. Doing it for the money and doesn't care about the children.

DIFFERENCES BETWEEN BOYS AND GIRLS AND PUPILS OF DIFFERENT AGES

The literature on pupils' views of teachers is astonishingly consistent (Wragg 1993). Studies as early as the 1930s have shown that the ability to explain clearly is frequently the most highly esteemed professional skill in the eyes of children. Other features consistently found include several of those we have identified in the present study: fairness in the use of rewards and punishments, interest in individuals, enthusiasm for the subject being taught, a sense of humour. What is less well researched is the differences between sub-groups, like boys and girls, and younger and older pupils, so we studied these separately.

Despite the near universal quality among different age groups and between boys and girls on several characteristics, there were certain aspects where significant differences should be noted. Many of the characteristics mentioned by groups of pupils were similar, though taking slightly different forms. Older and younger children wanted fair-minded teachers who could explain things to them, were 'in charge', though not unduly strict, and who had a good sense of humour. As pupils grew older they became more aware of a teacher who was able to control the class and who would prepare them well for examinations.

At all ages pupils seemed to value differentiation, albeit articulating it differently. Many said they valued caring teachers who allowed them a degree of autonomy, although there was a shift in how they were meant to achieve this as the pupils got older. Younger pupils liked the privilege of choosing, as well as winning extrinsic rewards such as stars and stickers, while older pupils, particularly the 16 year olds in Year 11, focused more on the adult notion of mutual respect and a desire to be seen as young grown ups rather than as children:

> Shows discipline from day one. Treats students with respect (and gets the) same in return. Understands society and talks openly about issues. Has a

personality of being confident, but also knows when to cross the line with work.

Helps to give a better understanding. Can control the class. Likes to have a laugh. Treats us like adults.

Chi-square tests were performed on all measures taken of the 473 pupils aged 11 to 16, with boys and girls compared, as well as younger pupils at the end of the primary phase (Years 6 and 7) with older secondary pupils (Years 9 and 11). The following significant differences emerged, with one, two and three asterisks indicating the 0.05, 0.01 and 0.001 levels of significance respectively (i.e. likely to happen by chance one in 20, one in 100, and one in 1,000 times):

Boys and girls

Girls were more likely than boys to value:

Good class control***
Teachers who listened***
Teachers who didn't shout**
Interesting lessons**
Clear explanations*
Girls were also more likely than boys to complain to a friend*

Boys were more likely than girls to value:

Teachers who were caring and kind**

Some of these differences seem a little surprising. Traditional masculine stereotyping would not predict that boys would value teachers who were 'caring and kind' more than girls. On the other hand, some of the differences observed are more in line with what one might expect: for example, that girls, traditionally regarded as industrious in their attitude to schooling, might favour good class control, as it established the conditions within which they could work more effectively.

Younger (Years 6 and 7) and older (Years 9 and 11) pupils

Younger pupils were more likely than older pupils to value:

Good display of their work***
Teachers who were caring and kind***
Interesting lessons***

Teachers who were good tempered**
Teachers who didn't shout*
Teachers who were fair*

Older pupils were more likely than younger pupils to value:

Teachers who dressed well***
Good class control***
Good subject knowledge***
Friendly teachers***

Older pupils were also more likely than younger pupils to complain to a friend***

The attachment of greater value to display of their work from younger pupils might reflect the greater incidence of wall display of children's work in primary schools. The higher value placed on teachers' subject knowledge and class control by older pupils are also to be expected, as they are at a stage when they are taking important public examinations. The concern by older pupils about their teachers' dress sense might reflect adolescents' own growing interest in fashion and clothing at that stage of their development. Similarly their greater emphasis on teachers being friendly may reflect their need to be treated as adults.

SUMMARY

- A sample of 519 pupils aged 7 to 16 was studied. There were 255 boys and 264 girls, with 250 pupils in the primary and 269 in the secondary phase of education.
- The 46 infant age pupils (7 year olds) were interviewed, while the 473 pupils aged 11 to 16 completed questionnaires.
- Pupils were asked what characteristics they expected in teachers; what they saw as the key features of teachers they regarded as especially good or bad; who they would complain to and about what if they were dissatisfied.
- The youngest primary age pupils liked teachers who set interesting work, let them choose what they wanted to do on some occasions, and were fair in their award of extrinsic rewards, such as stars and stickers.
- Secondary pupils also appreciated clear explanations, good exam preparation, fairness and friendliness, effective class control, skilful differentiation and the matching of activity to ability, good subject knowledge and interesting lessons.
- The oldest pupils, aged 16, expressed similar views, but with the added observation that mutual respect was valued and they welcomed being treated as young adults.

- Girls were more likely than boys to value good class control, teachers who listened and did not shout, interesting lessons and clear explanations; while boys were more likely than girls to value teachers who were caring and kind.
- 'Human' qualities, such as care and concern, interest in their pupils and a sense of humour, were also welcomed.
- Pupils were most likely to complain about unfairness, unclear explanations, too much or too difficult work being set in class or for homework, poor coverage of the curriculum and weak class control.
- Complaints were most likely to be through informal channels, such as parents and friends, but in school it was the head of year group or another teacher who was most likely to be the recipient of complaints, rather than the head or deputy.
- Several significant differences emerged between the preferences of boys and girls and between younger and older children. Boys preferred teachers who were caring and kind, girls esteemed those who had good control. Older pupils were more impressed than younger pupils by subject knowledge, class control and dress sense.

Chapter 11

Implications and consequences

The absence of detailed research findings in a field can be both a blessing and a curse. During the Teaching Competence Project we carried out the largest systematic study of its kind ever undertaken in the United Kingdom into allegations of incompetence in the teaching profession, with hundreds of responses from head teachers, teachers, governors, parents, pupils, teacher union and local authority officers. The advantage of working in a field where there has been little research is that one can try to establish some fresh baseline information, which may be limited, but can be illuminating. The disadvantage is that there is little else with which to compare the data, or on which to hang the findings, and fundamental first-time research projects often contain more flaws than replications or research which investigates a field where there are numerous previous studies on which to build.

There are many ways of interpreting what we found during the research. Sometimes informants contradicted each other in what they described, though there was often corroboration from different constituencies of several of the main observations. Personal views colour the extent to which people will view the findings as good news (for example, many teachers were thought to have improved), or bad news (many of the heads and teachers involved became severely stressed). Pessimists will feel that those who lack competence have simply blighted the education of the children they failed to teach effectively. Optimists would say that, since the overwhelming majority of teachers are regarded as competent when inspected, the problem is over a small minority of incompetents.

Few would argue that there is no problem when incompetence has been alleged, even if one is only talking about a single case. Every professional practitioner ought to be competent, so it is grievous if even one is thought not to be effective, especially when judgements about cases are contested. Discussion needs to focus on the nature of any perceived problem, whether or not it is a serious problem, the origins of the allegation, the impact it has made, what can be done in the circumstances, how similar difficulties might be avoided in future.

In this final chapter some of the main findings will be brought together, to see how they reinforce or contradict each other. There will be an analysis of a number of the theoretical issues and practical implications of what has been found. We also report a small number of interviews with school inspectors and subject specialists, undertaken after the main data collection had been completed, to elucidate some of the issues. As often happens, this research partially answers some questions, while posing yet more.

SIGNIFICANT FINDINGS

There are numerous conclusions of one kind or another, some tentative, others more firmly supported, that have been described in the various chapters of this book. There is no point in merely revisiting them all, because they have in any case been summarised at the end of each chapter. It is worth considering, however, some of the main ones that can be derived from the national survey of head teachers and the hundreds of interviews and questionnaires completed with heads, teachers, governors, officers of teacher unions and LEAs, parents and pupils. Caution must, of course, be exercised, as not all of these were drawn from stratified random samples, though several of the major studies were. Here are 20 overall, if tentative conclusions that emerged from different sources.

1. Most cases of alleged incompetence originated from complaints

Head teachers reported that complaints from fellow teachers were their most common first sources of information, followed by their own formal or informal monitoring and complaints from parents and pupils. Parents said they were most likely to complain about work not being matched to their child's ability, poor classroom discipline, or some aspect of relationships between teacher and pupil or between pupils, as in the case of bullying.

2. The most commonly identified problems concerned clusters of the same set of features

Teachers' expectation of their pupils (usually too low, but sometimes too high), inadequate preparation and planning, lack of pupil progress, classroom discipline (usually too lax, but occasionally too strict), and negative relationships with others were commonly cited by several groups as the most likely features of cases they had experienced. The great majority of cases involved a combination of several characteristics, rather than just a single one.

3. There was a high degree of emotional stress for those involved

Many head teachers, teachers alleged to be incompetent, and those fellow teachers working alongside them, stated that the events had caused them great stress. Heads were torn between their duty to children, which came first, and their responsibilities as the senior manager of someone not performing well.

Teachers alleged to be incompetent saw their lives blighted by the accusation and often felt their health and personal problems had not been understood. The different parties described the impact on themselves and their family in almost identical terms, using words like 'hell' and 'isolation'.

4. Perceptions of events could differ with different groups and individuals

Some teachers, seen as 'lazy' or 'incompetent' by their heads or colleagues, regarded themselves as misjudged or misused victims, bullied by those in authority, or as dissenting from the head's ideology, especially when the head was new to the school. Head teachers sometimes expressed frustration that teachers thought to be incompetent by colleagues, pupils and parents, tried to deny there was a problem. In other cases, however, there was general agreement about poor performance between the various people concerned, including the teacher alleged to be incompetent.

5. Most of the teachers alleged to be incompetent were in mid or late career

About three quarters, in some samples more, of all the cases in the various samples were teachers over the age of 40 with 15 or more years of experience. There were very few cases of young or newly qualified teachers. Many were experiencing some of the problems often associated with middle age, such as ill health, stress in work and home, broken marriages and relationships, elderly relatives, or difficult adolescent children. Considerable caution needs to be exercised here, however, since about two thirds of the teaching profession was in any case over the age of 40 during the period when the research was carried out.

6. Willingness to face up to the problems was a key requirement for success

Head teachers, union and LEA officers were among groups which believed that denial of the existence of a problem was the biggest single obstacle to improvement. Some teachers alleged to be incompetent stated that they were not in denial, but rather that their particular problems, or their philosophy and practice, were not fully understood or supported by those in authority.

7. Support was critical if teachers were to succeed

Some teachers alleged to be incompetent felt they had no chance of keeping their job because the head or their colleagues wanted them to fail. Union officers believed that if the school wanted teachers to succeed there was a high likelihood that they would. Head teachers, when asked to explain why some teachers did improve, pointed to in-house support: assigning a mentor, sending the teacher on a course, encouraging lesson observation of fellow practitioners thought to be competent, in the same or another school. These approaches were not always successful, however.

8. About a quarter of teachers improved

Head teachers reported that about a quarter of cases improved, while three quarters did not. Union officers and local authority advisers believed that, with appropriate support and early identification, about half of the teachers were likely to improve what they did. Having a positive attitude and responding to advice and support were seen as key elements.

9. Each case was unique

While there were, on the surface, certain common features, each of the hundreds of cases studied was unique. Some teachers might, for example, appear to have a shared or generic problem, such as 'failure to adapt to change', but one could be a secondary teacher resisting the philosophy of a new head, another a primary teacher lacking the relevant subject knowledge in a field like science or technology, while a third person might simply have become overwhelmed by the detail of a rapidly changing curriculum, alongside other personal problems.

10. The context was important

One teacher studied was regarded as a failure in her first school, but as a success when she moved to another school. Heads in schools with few social problems felt that some teachers might have great difficulties in schools in which it was more difficult to teach. There were teachers in primary schools who were competent in certain subjects, but regarded as incompetent in one particular key subject, like mathematics.

11. Heads used a wide variety of coping strategies

'Damage limitation' was one of several coping strategies used by head teachers, such as reducing the teacher's programme, removing some of the more difficult pupils, assigning the teacher to different classes. Others included: confront the teacher with each allegation from parents, pupils or colleagues (some heads used the term 'break' the teacher); bring in an external authority, such as a LEA adviser; assign a mentor from among the staff; involve other senior managers, such as the deputy head (there was a particular problem, as happened in some schools, when the teacher alleged to be incompetent was the deputy head or another senior person).

12. Agreed procedures were not always followed

About one in six head teachers said they did not follow an agreed procedure. This was a cause of dismay to local authority officers. Accused teachers and union officers felt especially aggrieved when this happened and unions usually insisted that the whole process should start again.

13. Earlier action, before escalation, was often advocated

Many heads, when looking back on events, said they wished they had taken action earlier. Union officers and LEA respondents believed that early intervention was a key element of success. Teachers alleged to be incompetent often said they only realised at a late stage how serious their predicament was, because they had not been given a clear indication there was something wrong. The transition between the informal and formal stages of the process often proved the most difficult to manage.

14. Lay people often had some apprehensions about making or dealing with complaints

Only a third of parents interviewed had made a complaint about their child's schooling, mostly in an informal manner, but a number were reluctant to complain, often because their children had urged them not to make a fuss. Children sometimes stated that teachers would probably show professional solidarity with each other, so they talked instead to parents or friends. Parents felt they lacked the professional expertise to put their view across and, when their complaints had not been addressed, few were willing to take the matter further, unless it was an issue like bullying. Some governors also felt excluded, though others said they were well informed, or did not wish to become more involved.

15. Most allegations led to the teacher leaving the school

Over three quarters of teachers alleged to be incompetent left their post, mostly taking early retirement if they were in their fifties (an option which was virtually eliminated in March 1997), retiring through ill-health, or simply leaving their post or the profession. Only a few took a teaching post elsewhere, but when they did, this often caused concern or resentment from heads, fellow teachers and LEA officers, the last of whom felt powerless to stop something over which they had once had control. On the other hand, some teachers said they had got a post elsewhere and done so well they had been given senior posts in their new school.

16. Few teachers were dismissed

Only about three per cent of teachers were actually dismissed from their post and another three per cent made redundant. Persuasion to retire or leave was a much more likely policy from both head teachers and union officers. An 'exit with dignity' was the phrase often used by different groups to describe what they sought when there was sympathy for the teacher concerned.

17. The role of union officers and fellow teachers was not always as is commonly assumed

There is a popular assumption in the public mind, often reinforced by press accounts, that union officers and fellow teachers band together to protect the incompetent. This was not in evidence in this research. Indeed, although many teachers expressed gratitude for their union's help and for that of their colleagues, some teachers accused their colleagues and their union of not defending them strongly enough against allegations, of colluding with head teachers. A few actually went instead to other organisations that take on advocacy of a teacher's case. Union officers often said that their first duty was to the children and did admit to brokering deals in some cases, making their own personal judgement that the teacher was indeed not performing well. Fellow teachers were often more critical of colleagues said to be incompetent than were other groups studied.

18. There was a shared belief that cases had taken too long

Head teachers reported that about half the cases had taken between one and three years and most felt this was too long, only one per cent saying it was too short. The likelihood of the teacher concerned going on sick leave was often stated as one of the reasons for the prolonged nature of the process. Even teachers alleged to be incompetent believed, in many cases, that events appeared to have dragged on and a shorter time scale would have caused them less distress, though their main concern was that proper procedures should be followed, or about the injustice, as they saw it, of the original allegations, which needed time to refute.

19. Many wanted a shorter process but were concerned about 'fast-track' proposals

Some period between one and two terms was felt by many groups to be better than a more long drawn out process. Head teachers, governors, LEA and teacher union officers were all worried about any 'fast track' dismissal procedure of four weeks that left them looking vulnerable in the eyes of an industrial tribunal. They were aware that to seek dismissal in a very short time would make it appear that the school had not acted soon enough.

20. A change of head teacher was often critical, yet few had been trained to recognise and deal with incompetence

Many cases were said to have arisen when there was change of head teacher. New heads spoke of 'inheriting' a problem, while accused teachers felt aggrieved that they did not satisfy the new head, when the previous head had not complained. Only one third of head teachers said they had had any training in identifying and dealing with professional incompetence. The overwhelming majority of the rest said they wanted training.

REFLECTIONS ON THE PROCESSES OBSERVED

A study of this kind inevitably raises several consequent issues: about human competence, power and authority in society and in institutions, the nature of teaching as a job, the rights of pupils and teachers. These can be both practical and theoretical in nature. For example, the use or misuse of power and authority raises theoretical issues, in that one can analyse the concepts involved, or speculate about meanings, manifestations and effects, but it is also an intensely practical matter when one considers how power and authority are actually used in schools and classrooms, or what practices might need to change.

Human competence

One of the reasons why there was often a substantial emotional overlay to the cases of alleged incompetence studied during this research is because any attack on professional competence is seen as an attack on the person. Accountability became a key term in discussions about public services during the last two decades of the twentieth century. There are many forms of accountability that can be deployed, and in the United Kingdom what might be termed a 'low trust, high accountability' model was in operation. Close scrutiny of education by press and politicians in particular led to an extension of the bureaucracy associated with teaching, the more frequent imposition of models and procedures from the centre.

The curriculum, national tests, financial formulae, even the forms of school reports and records of attendance, or the shape of a literacy hour, were all determined by the government and passed down to schools. Many teachers, despite the rapidity and frequency of change, coped well, but others were unable to accommodate what was happening so successfully. Numerous informants in this research cited the changing style of governance in education and the greater demands as possible reasons for some teachers becoming incompetent.

'Competence' is a notion capable of several interpretations. 'Functional competence' involves being able to operate at a level judged by society, employers or peers as appropriate to the demands of the job. But functional competence, like 'literacy', is not a stable concept, for it depends very much on circumstances. In the nineteenth century, for example, it was not thought to be important if a primary teacher knew little science and technology. Nowadays these are regarded as two key subjects in the curriculum and those lacking the knowledge, or the necessary skills to teach them, are seen as incompetent. As in other fields, like medicine, the entry fee to the profession has gone up.

Employment is also an important part of people's lives. The nature of work may well have changed, but it is difficult to separate the person from the job: an allegedly incompetent teacher becomes an incompetent person. Most people, especially in the middle years of life, have significant financial and personal commitments to members of their family and community, so any threat to their livelihood is seen as an attack on their own wellbeing and that of the members of their family. For this reason many heads commented on the torment they felt when pressing a teacher to leave a post, realising the likely economic and personal consequences, even though they knew they had to put the welfare of children first.

Power and authority

In theory, many elements of power and authority in English education have been devolved to local level. The introduction of a competitive business type of model in the 1988 Education Act meant that school governors effectively became teachers' employers, the head teacher being responsible for the daily running of the school and for giving them professional advice, acting as their chief executive. This theoretical model of power, however, does not always withstand scrutiny. All these parties must act within the conditions and terms of employment law. If they dismiss an employee for incompetence, they must face the consequences, should the teacher sue for unfair dismissal. That is why head teachers, governors and LEA officers were so concerned about the up-to-date accuracy of their knowledge, and indeed about their own position, should they fall foul of the law. Many head teachers felt shrouded in a web of legislation, highly accountable to their governors and to the wider society, apprehensive about teacher unions, unable to act as quickly or as freely as they would like, so they expressed a sense of impotence rather than potency.

By contrast, many accused teachers saw themselves, and sometimes their union, as lacking power, seeing the outcome of their case as a foregone conclusion. It was one of many ironies in this research that heads in turn frequently saw unions as powerful forces against whom they had to be wary. For accused teachers the perspective was often quite different: head teachers were in authority, able to make decisions over their lives, so they felt resigned to their fate, believing there was nothing that an individual teacher could do. This had the effect of paralysing some and galvanising others. Consequently power could shift, depending on the determination with which a particular teacher was prepared to pursue the case and the degree of support available. Some heads said they were aware that a teacher might marshall the rest of the staff against them, if they pressed the case too hard.

Power is, therefore, much more fluid and elusive than it may appear. Some governors felt they lacked it, or did not want it, but governors as a group were seen by some teachers as society's uncritical endorsement of the head teacher's authority over them. Yet head teachers sometimes felt they had so little direct power that one head teacher union officer expressed envy of heads in independent schools who could dismiss teachers much more readily. Parents and pupils often saw themselves as impotent, but several heads and teachers regarded them as a powerful source of complaint which exerted pressure on the school.

Power relationships, in this context, therefore, sometimes appear to be diffuse. One party or another may seize control over events to advantage, only in turn to see it wrested away on another occasion. Sometimes it is only in retrospect that one can make a judgement about where true power over outcomes lay, or who appeared to be controlling what happened at any particular point. The participants themselves, their judgement frequently coloured by their own experiences and role, are not always in the best state or place to see the position clearly.

Expediency and pragmatism

Even where there are carefully worked out procedures and conventions, pragmatic considerations sometimes take over. Head teachers have to run a school and teachers and pupils have to work in one. Difficult decisions must be made setting the impact of one kind of decision against that of another. Most frequently, when head teachers decided to pursue the case, despite some of the difficulties, they found there were critical events along the way that caused them to rethink, like the teacher's performance improving, the union becoming involved, the teacher being away ill, further complaints from parents, pupils or fellow teachers. The process is not a simple linear one with a clearly defined path.

Instead events are more like a branching program, a series of successive options to take one route or another, so that progress is erratic at times, especially when the unexpected occurs. In such circumstances each decision makes an impact, the consequences of which cannot always be clear. For example, if the head teacher has made an error at any stage of the proceedings, like failing to give a written warning, the union is likely to insist that the process loops back on itself to an earlier stage, possibly even to the beginning, so that the correct process can be followed. Similarly, if a teacher appears to be making progress, then the formal proceedings may be relaxed or terminated; but if there is a further decline they may be reinstated, and if the teacher then goes off on sick leave, the whole process may lapse once more into uncertainty.

Written procedures often assume that events will follow a clear linear path – informal advice, then oral warning, followed by written warning, next a final chance to improve with structured support, followed by threat of dismissal, assessment and actual dismissal. Analysis of hundreds of cases in this research shows that the process may appear to be following the written procedures, but not so smoothly as is assumed. More usually it takes unique pathways, via a succession of small feedback loops, each influencing what happens next.

Consequently the parties concerned have to accommodate each other for the sake of expediency. This may lead to compromise, where people agree to waive some of their demands or expectations in order to reach a solution thought to minimise harm or disruption. An example of this occurs when a union brokers a retirement deal, to the satisfaction, or sometimes to the wrath of the member. The assumption is that excessive time and costly litigation can be avoided by compromise and negotiation. Another example is when a teacher's duties are reduced, which minimises the negative effect on classes and allows the teacher time for retraining or observing other teachers. Head teachers are often key players in these cases of trade-off and accommodation, deciding almost on a daily basis when to concede and when to insist.

The vocabulary of the process is difficult here. 'Compromise' is a word that can be seen as an honourable and intelligent appraisal of what is best, or as a feeble collapse of principle. It is difficult to dry-clean such words as 'compromise', 'expediency' and 'pragmatic' of their various connotations. In the end it is the individual circumstances that determine whether an assessment of the events that took place should be positive or negative. A sensible negotiated settlement in one context will be a more acceptable 'compromise' than an abandonment of scruples or judgement in another.

The rights and responsibilities of pupils and teachers

One of the most tormenting issues that all participants faced during incompetence procedures was the clash of rights and responsibilities of the different groups concerned. There was no ambiguity among any of the groups studied about the rights of children to receive a decent education. Heads said it was their first duty, as did union officers. Teachers accused of incompetence, aware of their responsibility to do their job effectively, often said that they felt guilty if their classes' education was disrupted in any way, though a few blamed the pupils for indiscipline in lessons or for their failure to learn.

What was more problematic, even given the overwhelming consensus about the primacy of pupils' rights, was that teachers have rights which may, in some cases, clash with those of pupils. For example, natural justice decrees that anyone accused of incompetence must be given a clear indication of their shortcomings and a chance to improve. But in order to improve they must be given the opportunity to carry on teaching, albeit under more controlled conditions, which means that, if the allegation of incompetence is correct and they then fail to improve, more children will be in receipt of substandard education.

Head teachers, in particular, felt torn. They all stated that children's interests came first, but they then had a legal responsibility, acting for the employer, to ensure that failing teachers were given every chance to succeed. It was not an easy balance to strike. Even when heads had given teachers support, several talked in interview of their sense of personal failure if the teacher failed to improve. It was a dilemma that caused many of them considerable inner turmoil and stress, especially when they were not able to discuss the case with anyone.

THE CONTEXT OF TEACHING

At the beginning of this book we described the complex nature of classroom competence: how teaching consisted of thousand of acts even in a single day, with little time to make decisions, or appraise the effectiveness of what was being done. Most teachers in this study found themselves accused of incompetence in the second half of their career. If they have engaged in a thousand or more interpersonal transactions in a single day, as is reported in the literature described at the beginning of this account, then after 20 years they may have repeated favoured patterns of interaction some three or four million times. If their teaching style is no longer effective, it is not easy to unscramble forms of classroom control, verbal habits, types of question, methods of explaining, that have been repeated on such a vast scale.

To be effective, retraining must penetrate deeply laid down structures. This cannot be done lightly or speedily, nor can it usually be achieved against the wishes of the teacher concerned. The way people teach is often the way they are, so those who are carefully organised and structured in their own thinking may well behave in the same manner in their classroom teaching. Exhortations, instructions, threats, or detached and discrete single ideas and suggestions may make little impact on styles of teaching that have taken years to lay down and perhaps a similar period to decline.

Furthermore, teaching can take place in highly specific contexts, like a physical education class in which seven year olds are learning to swim, or a maths lesson with 14 year olds preparing for a public examination. The solutions to incompetence can be as disparate, therefore, as the causes of it. The most likely ingredients for success were programmes of support that first of all engaged the teacher, not always easy when there was resentment, and secondly addressed the elements of teaching that were judged to be failing. There can be no omni-purpose programme of remediation that successfully makes all teachers better at their job, irrespective of the context in which they teach.

Specific issues in different contexts

In order to illuminate some of these vital context issues we interviewed a small number of experienced teacher trainers, working in university departments of education, who all had considerable experience of classroom observation in quite specific subject areas and with different age groups. They were asked about matters that they thought were particularly important in their subject and also about general issues, such as classroom management. It became apparent that the characteristics of one subject or age group might demand slightly different, or even a higher order of skill in particular aspects of teaching compared with another. Although some differences were slight, others were rather more fundamental.

Classroom management

Issues of classroom management were mentioned by early years, science, RE, music, drama and PE specialists. Classroom management is a *threshold factor*, in that absence of order and poor control of anti-social behaviour usually prevent teachers from deploying other skills, like communicating knowledge and establishing positive relationships. The early years specialist believed that high quality class management skills were absolutely vital with 4–7 year olds, particularly in Reception classes where children were new to the school environment and had to learn not only to obey instructions and manage resources, but to successfully develop relationships with other pupils:

> I think it is actually really quite difficult to motivate thirty new four year olds, and I think the classroom management in the very early years, say in Reception class, is getting children to become a pupil, to learn to be a pupil, and an awful lot of work on socialisation takes place in the early years and Key Stage 1, probably more so, I think, than in the later stages.

A secondary science specialist talked of the need for careful organisation of resources, especially when laboratory safety was involved:

> There's the whole realm of health and safety, specialised equipment and a specialised teaching room, and the whole of the nature of practical work, [and there are also] non-health and safety issues to do with practical work, so children's manual dexterity and ability to read instruments and this sort of thing which can have a knock-on effect on class management if the skills aren't in place, or if the teacher doesn't organise the class management such that the skills can be exercised properly.

Interestingly, a primary science specialist believed that teachers' concerns about health and safety could sometimes militate against science being taught effectively in primary schools:

> Teachers do it badly because they're afraid of it. They're afraid in terms of risk, for instance, in teaching electricity. A lot of teachers don't give children practical activities to do because they think it's unsafe. They think that electricity's dangerous so they don't do it. They're not aware, a lot of teachers, that a dry cell is not dangerous at all, so they will avoid these things or demonstrate, so the notion that science is about tackling a problem, getting stuck, asking what might happen here doesn't happen in classrooms very often.

This science specialist also argued that incompetent science teachers needed to make their lessons more interesting, but worried too much about coping with class management in case there might be noise and mess in the classroom:

There are two things that many teachers are frightened of in relation to class management. One is noise and one is mess. Effective science involves doing things which are interesting and exciting and novel and unexpected, and children get excited and they make more noise . . . I've also seen student teachers get into a great deal of trouble for doing experiments with mixing oil and water, for instance, and they spilled a bit and the oil and water has gone over the floor and then people walk in it and then the cleaners complain.

Drama lessons usually take place in a hall or a gymnasium and this, a drama specialist believed, demands greater skill, because of movement in a large space: 'Drama is more difficult because it's managing space and people in space, it's different from in the classroom.'

Music teachers need to be capable of managing varying sizes of groups and music is a subject which has traditionally been seen as one where there might be instances of disorderly behaviour if the class is badly managed. A music specialist explained that teachers will frequently use pairs, small groups and whole class teaching, depending on the activity being undertaken, but also, unlike most other teachers, they need to be able to manage very large numbers, such as choirs of over 100 children.

Classroom management is not just about managing resources or keeping the children under apparent control. In PE, although a group of children may seem 'busy, happy and good', this does not mean that quality learning is taking place. According to a PE specialist interviewed:

> In PE there's a lot of just keeping children active. There's a lot of activity in PE, but it's not related to learning, and I think that's a big issue for the subject. If you just try and keep children active, you're not actually planning specific objectives, you're not monitoring the objectives, you're not providing individual and whole group feedback as necessary, you're not differentiating it, and differentiating in relation to all aspects of equal opportunities, the gender aspect, the disability aspect.

A specialist in religious education believed special management skills were required of teachers in his subject area, talking about the need to foster and facilitate within a group of children a willingness to listen to and value each other's opinions, when values and beliefs were being discussed:

> Because discussion is an important part of the climate of RE, then class management is crucial because I've seen discussion lessons which have failed because they've simply been an exchange of prejudiced monologues. I've seen discussions which have failed because really loud-mouthed verbal bullies have dominated the scene and the teacher has actually rewarded them, perhaps because she or he was frightened that if they shook the verbal

bully up, they'd have an awful embarrassing silence to cope with. So I've seen people actually intimidated in discussion and the RE specific end of this, which again is perhaps different from a discussion in geography or history, is that, very often, in a predominantly secular climate, which is the climate of most schools, the 'religious' children have been intimidated into silence. And if you sat at the back of the class you would conclude that there were no religious children present in the room at all and that is simply not the case. They don't want to voice it where they think the majority might go for them.

Planning and preparation

Most specialists felt that poor planning and preparation was a generic feature of incompetence but the secondary science specialist highlighted that planning in science often required more forward thinking than in other subjects:

> [Incompetence] is not getting your act together over getting equipment together, co-ordinating equipment and resources, and particularly in biology, organisms. Just to give you an example: if you want to do factors affecting growth or photosynthesis, and you haven't got the plants planted and the seedlings may be needed to be raised 10 days ago or something. It's planning and preparation. Unless you're highly organised, it can come unstuck with nonchalant ease.

The PE specialist drew comparisons between primary and secondary teachers:

> For primary, their planning is not always as in depth enough to extend pupils. In secondary, their planning would be good but their actual implementation of it wouldn't match the planning. They don't necessarily extend the children, even though they might plan for it in secondary.

The point made by the PE specialist about the mismatch between planning and practice in lessons was also discussed by one of the English specialists, but she felt that a lack of formalised planning or written 'lesson plans' did not necessarily imply an incompetence on the part of the teacher:

> I think there are extremely competent teachers who, for all sorts of reasons, their ways of planning aren't conventional documented ways, they kind of plan in their heads. They actually think a lot about what they're going to do, but don't write it down . . . I think the planning and preparation is something that with novice teachers, certainly, is an issue, but for experienced ones it takes many different forms.

Subject knowledge

Some subject specialists were able to identify particular aspects of their curriculum in which teachers were more likely to have inadequate subject knowledge. The music specialist believed that many music teachers lack knowledge of the conventional classical repertoire and are less good at teaching 'composing' because their training did not include this, as it has only been part of the music curriculum since the introduction of the national curriculum in the 1988 Education Act. One of the English specialists believed that grammar is often not well taught. She pointed out that 'you've got actually one and a half generations now of teachers who didn't do grammar themselves at school'. With drama, she felt subject knowledge was an issue with teachers who were not themselves drama specialists. She felt that 'they have a limited repertoire of ideas and an even poorer sense of what continuity and progression might look like'.

The RE specialist emphasised that a lack of subject knowledge not only resulted in children receiving only a partial curriculum, but also had wider repercussions:

> Teachers who do not know themselves sufficient about the subject they're teaching will stereotype, for example, Sikh men – they all have beards and turbans . . . and they will produce caricatures of religion rather than descriptors of it . . . Teaching world religions badly can actually generate racism.

Science teachers explained how teachers' own lack of subject knowledge could lead to them fostering misconceptions about science in their pupils' minds. As the Leverhulme Primary Project found (Wragg 1993), many primary teachers, required to teach science when the national curriculum was introduced, had not studied science themselves beyond the age of 13. The primary science specialist claimed this led to a dependence on 'Bright Ideas' types of books, where one-off activities were often selected, with no real understanding by the teacher of the scientific concepts involved or how they would fit into a coherent programme of learning. Furthermore, when children asked questions, teachers were unable to answer them because of their own lack of knowledge.

The secondary science specialist said there had been a growing problem with subject knowledge in recent years, especially since the combination of separate sciences into a combined science exam at GCSE:

> Science is a broad church and graduates I deal with are becoming more and more specialised, so, for example in biology, you can have graduates in molecular genetics who know very little about ecology. Science is a very broad subject because of the nature of the national curriculum, so we have to spend a lot of time gearing up graduates in their non-degree science for Key Stages 3 and 4 and A Level. And even within their own so-called specialism, there are huge areas that they may not know about above their own A Level.

The art specialist felt that teachers in his area often had poor subject knowledge but that it was less likely to be identified than in other subjects. He believed the reason lay in a cultural ignorance among other teachers and, in particular, senior management in schools about art as a subject and how it should be taught:

> Some art teachers are doing, I think, relatively poor work with pupils, but pupils think they're wonderful and other members of staff think they're great. So what's going on? I think, that because my subject is low profile compared with science or English or maths or modern languages, people aren't aware of some of the inadequacies of teaching the subject. Say if you've some teacher who gets on with kids or appears to have a certain flamboyant style, somehow those people in school think that's all you need to teach art, because like 'It's self-expression, isn't it?'

Some specific examples were given of a lack of appropriateness relating to actual material processes. One teacher did not even know the difference between chalks and pastels after four years at art college and other teachers had been using charcoal with children on kitchen paper, off which, the art specialist explained, charcoal just slides.

The PE specialist believed that teachers with a lack of subject knowledge would sometimes use a problem-solving approach to an activity to avoid direct teaching:

> I often see the gymnastics lesson where the teacher doesn't teach anything. Instead they use an open-ended, problem solving approach to gymnastics and I believe it's because their subject knowledge is so limited, they're scared to actually teach anything formal.

Monitoring and assessment

Many of the specialists talked about poor monitoring and assessment within their subject area but this was not just confined to those they would identify as 'incompetent'. The PE specialist said that, although PE teachers are usually good at giving feedback in relation to particular skills, they are not as effective at giving feedback in relation to a whole unit of work:

> They have a scheme of work and they deliver it regardless of how the pupils respond, and then they evaluate at the end in a way which may not be related to the original objectives of the unit of work. Assessment is one of the major problems in PE.

Similarities could be identified here with the comments made by the drama specialist who believed that the freedom and lack of structure in drama, which empowered the effective drama teacher, manifested itself in poor monitoring and assessment by non-specialists: 'Some of them [non-specialists] haven't really got any clue how to assess [drama].'

The music specialist explained that the successful music teacher is very alert and ready to stop children during an activity to give them feedback and discuss with them and other pupils how they can improve their work, whether it be composing or performing. He described the incompetent music teacher who 'tells the pupils that something's "excellent" when it really isn't excellent and what they mean is "I'm so glad we got through that and you behaved yourselves".'

The maths specialist believed that high quality listening skills were vital in mathematics to make accurate diagnostic assessments about a child's cognitive processes in a culture where children are now encouraged to develop their methods for approaching problems:

> What is difficult is being able to listen and follow a child's reasoning, which might not be your own. That is particularly difficult with mathematics when most of the generation of teachers at the moment have been brought up to be competent at *standard* ways of doing things. To follow and track somebody else's way of thinking isn't easy.

ASSESSMENT, TRAINING AND SUPPORT

Although teachers' competence is supposed to be appraised on a regular cycle, many schools have given staff appraisal a low profile, because of other pressures. In this research it became clear that most early indications of possible problems over a teacher originated from complaints or informal monitoring. Formal monitoring by the head accounted for about 40 per cent of the cases and a much lower 15 per cent of incompetence allegations began with an official school inspection by OFSTED. It was not possible, nor was it the central purpose in this research, to do a thorough study of the inspection process, so interviews were conducted with an opportunity sample of ten school inspectors to shed light on their identification of problems.

School inspections

The ten inspectors interviewed had between one and a half and six years of inspection experience since the establishment of OFSTED in 1992, the majority having been an inspector for at least four years. Their experience within education included time as a class teacher, deputy head teacher, head teacher, local authority adviser, through to university lecturer. Some of the interviewees had only carried out a few inspections, whereas the majority had done at least 15, with a maximum of 55 by one of them.

OFSTED uses a list of criteria to make judgements about teaching quality, with a seven point grading scale ranging from 'excellent' to 'poor'. One inspector pointed out some of the difficulties of interpretation:

> What it is not able to do, obviously, is to show you exactly what it is, where the actual border is and, therefore, what your tolerance should be. And, of course, it is very difficult to interpret it in different circumstances, so that when you're making judgements about discipline and competence, you clearly are going to make allowance for the teacher who is struggling with an inner city group.

All but one of the inspectors had at sometime encountered a teacher considered to be incompetent. The most common recurrent theme they mentioned was the issue of classroom management, not only organisational skills, but also an ability to control the behaviour of their classes and command the respect of their pupils.

In the cases where inspectors had identified a teacher who was performing poorly, the operational definition of which was that they had been graded either 6 or 7 on the seven point scale, the procedure used was very similar. The registered inspectors were told, as was the teacher involved and the head teacher. One inspector summarised the procedure:

> First of all I report back to my Registered Inspector who then takes it up with the head, at which point I then go and see the head and explain my reasons for failing him, at which point the head then talks to the member of staff.

A mixture of reactions from the teachers was reported, with most appearing to accept the inspector's judgement, often because they were already aware that they were having problems and wanted help to try and improve. Some teachers were hostile and one inspector explained the difficulty he had had when approaching a teacher about perceived problems:

> Well, he agreed with it in its essence, in the sense of 'Yes, it wasn't [very good]' . . . When I referred [my interpretation of the inspection framework] back to him he agreed with it, but his justification was that the framework didn't apply to these children, and it was stupid, and what the hell was I doing there anyway!

The head teachers were also informed of the inspectors' observations and the majority of them said that they were either already aware of the situation or had had suspicions. Heads gave different explanations for the ways in which they had dealt with the problem prior to the inspection. In one case it was said to be a recruitment issue and there had been difficulty finding someone else to take the job. Another head said he had not been in post for very long, while others listed a series of difficulties within their school, of which the recruitment of high calibre staff was one. Some of the heads had already tried to take steps to support or alleviate the problem and in other cases they were intending to do so after the inspection.

Inspectors were asked whether they felt that the teacher's problems might have been caused or exacerbated by circumstances within the school. There was an approximate 50:50 split as to whether this was likely to have been the case, as the two quotations below indicate. The first describes a case where the blame seemed to lie mainly with the teacher, the second suggests that environmental factors in the school, including the performance of the head teacher, were more significant, especially as the job was not the one that the teacher had envisaged when accepting the post:

> I'm saying it was him, and I think they [the school] did all they could to support him. There was a good atmosphere. They had been able to pick up that he was struggling. It wasn't as if there was a 'you mustn't fail here' [attitude]. 'Failure' wasn't used. That word wasn't used. It was 'struggling'. They were trying to support him both as a department and as a school.

> It was certainly exacerbated because this teacher came to that school with a good track record. She was a very experienced teacher and, as I say, she'd come with an evidence base of 'satisfactory' at least performance and probably 'good', and she was appointed as a mathematics co-ordinator. Well, of course, when she arrived in the school, she actually found that her job description was totally different to the one that she'd been appointed to, so I felt that that was poor management anyway. She was given this very, very challenging group of youngsters – it was [a school for children with behaviour problems] anyway – but they were even worse than the norm, and she found herself teaching probably only about 20 per cent timetable which was maths. On her timetable she was given what I would have considered were total either childminding or 'fill-in' lessons, so, I mean, that's soul destroying. Things like social skills – go out and play petanque or something like that – which was appalling. So when I was saying this to the head, as I say, it came as a surprise for him that this teacher wasn't performing as he expected, but this head's knowledge of what was going on in his school was just staggering in its ineptitude. He didn't have a clue. His deputy did, but he kept his deputy in the dark as well.

Unlike the expectation of local authority advisers, the role of OFSTED in schools is not to advise and follow up visits, but to give an objective assessment of performance, an external appraisal of strengths and weaknesses. Although some of the inspectors would have liked to have been able to offer advice to teachers performing poorly, if they did so it had to be done informally, as officially they were there to highlight areas of development. One OFSTED inspector gave a powerful justification of the detachment of inspection from advice:

An OFSTED inspector is purely there as an independent observer and judge of competence and standards and has no role to play in what actually happens as a result of his or her report. One thing I'm not allowed to do, and I wouldn't want to do and certainly don't do, is flash around my card with my name on it saying to a head teacher 'This is an incompetent teacher, I'll come and help you do some in-service training'. We're not allowed to do that, we shouldn't do that, quite rightly we shouldn't, so I think the answer to that is absolutely plain and straight . . . It seems to irritate people because they say the terrible thing about OFSTED is that they criticise but don't do anything about it. But that's the whole point of an independent inspectorate. You need to have a system that has people who can make independent judgements. This is as an advocate for children.

You then need to have a system that takes up these suggestions and provides the support. That's, if you like, the problem. The government, particularly the last government in setting up OFSTED, totally failed to set up a parallel system, probably run by local authorities shall we say, that would pick up the advisory tab, and I'm as critical of that as some people appear to be critical of OFSTED for not doing that job, and the obvious analogy is the 'good old days' when local authority advisers were supposed to be inspectors, but they were also responsible for what they were inspecting. We all know that that was a complete nonsense. No local authority adviser was going to be objective when he or she had for the last four years been advising a department on how to get better.

You get all sorts of wonderful cases I've heard about, where advisers went back to the schools as inspectors, having lost this responsibility for accountability, and were highly critical of things that they themselves had done, whereas they hadn't been critical of them when they had been advisers. I feel very strongly that it is right that OFSTED should have no role in improving the qualities of a teacher, because as soon as you do that, it would lose its independence. What one can do is try and provide some helpful advice to people around that teacher, maybe the head or the head of department, as to exactly what it is that you've seen that the person is doing wrong, what strengths they have, if any, to build on, because the only way to improve anyone's performance in any area is by building on strengths as well as going at the weaknesses, so you can provide some information, you can informally provide some advice, but that's as far as you should go.

Inspectors made a range of suggestions about overcoming poor performance. These included confidence building and the improving the self-esteem of those whose self-image had been dented by professional or personal stresses; being positive and building on existing strengths of weaker teachers; ensuring that they have a framework and a learning model to help them move forward; and also assessing whether they actually have the ability or the desire to change. Within the school, they believed, management teams needed to accept there was a problem, because in some poorly run schools they did not. What is more the school needed to capitalise on its in-house expertise, monitor teachers' performance and run effective subject and practical professional development programmes.

In-house monitoring, appraisal and support

What inspectors suggested fitted closely with what other groups and individuals had proposed. Head teachers believed that positive actions, like providing a mentor, and offering opportunities to observe others or attend courses, were valuable ingredients of success. Others advocated firmer action with those who seemed merely to be resisting the very idea of changing what they did.

It is much more likely that incompetence will be identified in the first instance by those inside the school, however, rather than by people outside it, so the onus lies particularly on senior people in the school to initiate an intelligent response. These include head teachers, deputies, senior teachers who are heads of depart-ment or curriculum co-ordinators, as well as experienced fellow practitioners who might be respected by the teacher concerned. One of the findings in the Leverhulme Appraisal Project (Wragg et al. 1996), which studied over 1,100 teachers and appraisers, was that teachers were more likely to change what they did in the classroom if they respected their appraiser.

'Support' can be a psychologically empty concept, unless it has real substance. Modelling oneself on what are thought to be successful practitioners, for example, may work with those whose problem is that they cannot think up ideas, but may fail with teachers who do have ideas but lack self-confidence. Being made to watch someone else can sometimes be taken as a further attack on confidence which may already be frail. The most effective kinds of further training and support seemed to be those that were tailored to individuals, struc-tured in such a way that the direction intended and the reasons for it were clear, and strongly allied to a belief that success was possible. In most cases the support of the teacher concerned also had to be won, for no external person can change the hundreds of interpersonal transactions that take place in a classroom every single day.

The specific issue of a dignified exit, for those over 50 who seek it, was clouded by the virtual closure of the early retirement option in March 1997. Many professions have now become stressful for those in middle age, so there is a prob-lem for society as a whole over people who appear to have burned out. Where other forms of support have failed, it does seem an omission that some form of phased or complete retirement before the age of 65 is not a feasible option. Partial retirement, for those in their fifties who would benefit from it, is a matter which needs further exploration.

Papalia and Olds (1998) have summarised some of the views and evidence on the notion of crisis in middle life, for it is certainly not an uncontested belief. Erikson (1985), in one of the best known formulations, sees it as the seventh stage of human development, during which there is a tension between 'generativity' and 'stagnation'. He sees 'generativity' as teaching the next generation and 'stagnation' as self-absorbed inactivity or lifelessness. Peck (1955) put forward a similar view of mental flexibility versus mental rigidity. Jung (1953) noted a period of introspection, when middle aged people gave up youth and had to contemplate mortality, which could lead to morose self-doubt.

By contrast, Vaillant (1977) followed a group of male Harvard students into middle age and, like Jung, noted a period of looking inward. However, although some of Vaillant's group became stressed by the demands of parenting, or disenchanted with their jobs, many saw the period from their late thirties to their fifties as the happiest period of their lives, often coping through altruism or humour. It is by no means inevitable that most middle aged people should decline in their job and personal life, even if some do so.

FAILING OR SUCCEEDING?

We began this account with a question mark in the title of the book, knowing the issues were not always straightforward. Although the research we conducted provided a great deal of information and suggested numerous possibilities for improving practice, we never expected that it would answer all the possible questions that could be put. There are many reasons for this, not the least of which remains the difficulty of picking out objective 'truth' through a miasma of emotion.

Objectivity in an emotionally charged climate

One factor became very clear from many different groups and individuals during the research. Such was the emotional strength of people's reactions, not just accused teachers, but fellow practitioners and heads, that a degree of objectivity was desperately sought. Teachers wanted a neutral 'friend in residence' who did not take sides, but just offered honest counsel and support. Heads sought an external evaluator who could pronounce more coolly on the evidence and give intelligent, but objective advice to all the parties involved. In the case of heads who were facing an incompetence allegation for the first time, what they wanted was an expert mentor who could offer advice and help on the basis of first-hand personal experience. Such people were often not available outside the head teacher unions.

There is a distinct lack of people with the relevant professional, legal and counselling expertise. In many cases both heads and teachers felt a sense of isolation which a number expressed graphically. It was as if they were entangled in a lethal web of stress, intense emotion, conflict, ignorance often, and loneliness. Without objective guidance the combined pressures often became intolerable, threatening the mental and physical health of those involved, whether accuser or accused. The provision of a mentor support scheme does seem to be a priority, especially if it prevented minor problems from escalating into major ones.

Failing teachers?

It is not easy to confront possible failure. The very word is often taboo in education, for it can condition events, especially where self-confidence is low. As we pointed out at the beginning of this book, most of our previous research has been into teachers in primary and secondary schools who are regarded as competent in their work, and in some cases we have studied teachers who were regarded as experts, so this research into the minority that are alleged to be incompetent has been different.

There is no doubt that some of the teachers studied were failing to reach the standards which society rightly expects. Many agreed themselves with the judgements of those who felt they were falling short of what was required. A number of these wanted to do something about it, others simply wished to quit the profession with a dignified exit. The consequences of incompetence were often dire: ineffective teaching and class control, complaints, strained relationships, manoeuvres of one kind or another, ill health, the termination of a career. The price of failure could be high for all concerned, not least for the teacher, but also for the pupils, the head, the teacher's colleagues and the whole community, especially in a small primary school.

There is also little doubt that some teachers were being failed through inaccurate judgements, lack of support, open hostility even. These may well have been in a minority, but there was sometimes ambiguity, differences of opinion about a person's proficiency, lack of advice and support. There were teachers who did badly in one context, but better in another, or who felt that their desperate personal circumstances or illness were not understood. Equally there were heads who felt that nothing they tried was working, or that the teacher was determined to resist any attempt to modify practices for the better, merely blaming children, circumstances, changes, or external forces. The best news is that a quarter of teachers were thought to have improved, but the depressing finding was that many did not and eventually left the profession.

So to some extent the story told in this research may be seen as an account of failure, sometimes by individual teachers, sometimes by those around them. But this has to be set in the overall context in which teaching and learning take place. The story we have tried to tell is located in settings in which most teachers are far more successful than many of those we have described here. In any profession there will be some people judged to be failing. One can either ignore this or try to analyse it so that future practice can be improved.

Despite the contested nature of some of the allegations, many messages from these research findings are clear. Teachers need to be selected with great care, both at the initial training stage and when appointed to vacant posts in school. They should be supported in their work, but also monitored so that possible problems are identified early, rather than at a point when it is too late to improve. Most early warnings came from complaints, often emanating from colleagues as well as from children and parents, so the informal stage of the process must be handled skilfully, as must any transition from informality to formality, since this was shown to be a difficult phase. Training is important here, for few heads and even fewer teachers said they had received any proper preparation for what was involved. The context of teaching is especially important, so this will need to be scrutinised to see what might be done, not just to make teaching easier, as this can simply throw more responsibility on to fellow teachers, but to assist teachers struggling with changes, unusually difficult classes, or negative personal relationships, to manage their teaching more effectively.

In the intensely subjective and sometimes highly charged emotional atmosphere in which allegations may be made or denied there is also a desperate need for objectivity, for people who are detached from the immediate issues, but aware of the circumstances and able to offer expert and effective advice: mentors for teachers and heads, external appraisers, advisers or counsellors. It does not require all of these, as too many disinterested people may actually confuse matters, but perhaps one or two key players who can lubricate the process, help to improve what the teacher is doing, even heal the wounds. That is why it is also important that procedures are well known and are followed, since many of the people we interviewed said they had not been. Failure to follow agreed procedures, or indeed ignorance of them, can lead to frustration, aggravation and possibly litigation. There are dozens of other important conclusions that can be drawn from the many findings in this research, depending on people's own particular role or circumstances, for the issues are very much ones that need to be dealt with sensitively at an individual level.

Bibliography

Assessment of Competence Steering Group (1989) 'Understanding Competence: A Development Paper', Unit for the Development of Adult Continuing Education.

Biddle, B.J. and Ellena, W.J. (1964) *Contemporary Research on Teacher Effectiveness*, New York: Holt, Rinehart and Winston.

Boyce, A.C. (1915) 'Methods of Measuring Teachers' Efficiency', in *14th Year-book, National Society for the Study of Education*, Part 2, Chicago: University of Chicago Press.

Bridges, E.M. (1986) *The Incompetent Teacher: The Challenge and the Response*, London: Falmer Press.

—— (1992) *The Incompetent Teacher: Managerial Responses*, London: Falmer Press.

Brophy, J. (1981) 'Teacher Praise: A Functional Analysis', *Review of Educational Research*, 51: 5–32.

Cameron-Jones, M. (1988) 'Quality and Competence in Teaching', in R. Ellis (ed.) *Professional Competence and Quality Assurance in the Caring Professions*, London: Chapman and Hall.

Cohen, L. and Manion, L. (1981) *Perspectives on Classrooms and Schools*, London: Holt, Rinehart & Winston.

Darling-Hammond, L. (1986) 'A Proposal for Evaluation in the Teaching Profession', *Elementary School Journal*, 86: 531–51.

Delamont, S. (1976) *Interaction in the Classroom*, London: Methuen.

DES (1991) *The Education (School Teacher Appraisal) Regulations 1991, (S.I. No. 1511)*, London: HMSO.

Deutsch, M. (1960) 'Minority Group and Class Status as Related to Social and Personality Factors in Scholastic Achievement', *Society for Applied Anthropology Monograph*, 2.

DfEE (1996) *Educational Statistics for the UK 1996*, London: DfEE.

Digilio, A. (12.8.84) 'When Tenure is Tyranny', *The Washington Post Review*, 1, 12–14.

Doyle, W. (1978) 'Paradigms for Research into Teacher Effectiveness', in L.S. Shulman (ed.) *Review of Research in Education*, 5, Itasca, Illinois: Peacock.

Dunkin, M.J. and Biddle, B.J. (1974) *The Study of Teaching*, New York: Holt, Rinehart & Winston.

Erikson, E.H. (1985) *The Life Cycle Completed*, New York: Norton.

Fidler, B. and Atton, T. (1999) *Poorly Performing Staff in Schools and How to Manage Them*, London: Routledge.

Gage, N.L. (1978) *The Scientific Basis of the Art of Teaching*, New York: Teachers College Press.

—— (1985) *Hard Gains in the Soft Sciences*, Bloomington, Ind.: Phi Delta Kappa.

Giaconia, R.M. and Hedges, L.V. (1985) 'Synthesis of Teaching Effectiveness Research', in T. Husen and T.N. Postlethwaite (eds) *International Encyclopaedia of Education*, 9: 5101–20, Oxford: Pergamon.

Glass, G.V. (1978) 'Integrating Findings: the Meta-analysis of Research', in L.S. Schulman (ed.) *Review of Research in Education*, 5, Itasca, Illinois: Peacock.

GMC (June 1998) *Performance procedures: a guide to the new arrangements*, London: GMC.

Guetzkow, H., Kelly, E.L. and McKeachie, W.J. (1954) 'An Experimental Comparison of Recitation, Discussion and Tutorial Methods in College Teaching', *Journal of Educational Psychology*, 45: 193–209.

Haertel, E.H. (1991) 'New Forms of Teacher Assessment', *Review of Research in Education*, 17: 3–29.

Jackson, P.W. (1962) 'The Way Teaching is', *NEA Journal* (National Education Association), 54: 10–13.

Jung, C.G. (1953) 'The Stages of Life', in H. Read, M. Firdham and G. Adler (eds) *Collected Works (vol 2)*, Princeton, New Jersey: Princeton University Press.

King, L.A. (1925) 'Present Status of Teacher Rating', *American School Board Journal*, 70: 44–46.

Kulik, J.A., Kulik, C-L.C. and Cohen, P.A. (1979) 'A Meta-analysis of Outcome Studies of Keller's Personalized System of Instruction', *American Psychology*, 34: 307–18.

Lavely, C. (April 1992) 'Actual Incidence of Incompetent Teachers', *Educational Research Quarterly*, 15, 2: 11–14.

OECD Center for Educational Research and Innovation (1994) *Quality in Teaching*, Paris: OECD.

Office for the Supervision of Solicitors (September 1996) *Can we Help?*, Leamington Spa: Office for the Supervision of Solicitors.

—— (September 1996) *What to Do if you are Dissatisfied with your Solicitor*, Leamington Spa: Office for the Supervision of Solicitors.

—— (1997) *Annual Report 1996/97: The First Year*, Leamington Spa: Office for the Supervision of Solicitors.

Papalia, D.E. and Olds, S.W. (1998) *Human Development*, Boston: McGraw Hill.

Peck, R.C. (1955) 'Psychological Developments in the Second Half of Life', in J.E. Anderson (ed.) *Psychological Aspects of Aging*, Washington DC: American Psychological Association.

Potter, E. and Smellie, D. (1995) *Managing Staff Problems Fairly: a Guide for Schools*, Kingston upon Thames: Croner Publications Ltd.

Ramsay, P. and Oliver, D. (Dec. 1995) 'Capacities and Behaviour of Quality Classroom Teachers', *School Effectiveness and School Improvement Journal*, 6, 4: 332–66.

Rich, R.W. (1933) *The Training of Teachers in England and Wales during the Nineteenth Century*, Cambridge: Cambridge University Press.

Rowe, M.B. (1972) 'Wait-time and Rewards as Instructional Variables', Paper presented at the National Association for Research in Science Teaching, Chicago, April.

Ryle, G. (1949) *The Concept of Mind*, London: Hutchinson.

Stallings, J.A. and Mohlman, G.G. (1985) 'Observation Techniques' in T. Husen and T. N. Postlethwaite (eds) *International Encyclopaedia of Education*, 6: 3640–5, Oxford: Pergamon.

Teacher Training Agency (1995) *Head Teacher's Leadership and Management Programme: (HEADLAMP): Procedures*, London: HMSO.

Teacher Training Agency (June 1997) *Career Entry Profile for Newly Qualified Teachers*, London: Teacher Training Agency.

The General Council of the Bar (April 1997) *Complaints against Barristers: What the Bar Council can Do*, London: The General Council of the Bar.

Times Educational Supplement, (1998) 'Standards are not Parents' Top Priority', in *Times Educational Supplement*, 9.10.98.

UKCC (June 1992) *Code of Professional Conduct*, London: UKCC.

—— (March 1998) *Complaints about Professional Conduct*, London: UKCC.

Vaillant, G.E. (1977) *Adaptation to Life*, Boston: Little, Brown.

Waintroob, A.R. (May 1995) 'Remediating and Dismissing the Incompetent Teacher', *School Administrator*, 52, 5: 20–24.

Wragg, E.C. (1984) (ed.) *Classroom Teaching Skills*, London: Croom Helm.

—— (1993) *Primary Teaching Skills*, London: Routledge.

—— (1999) *An Introduction to Classroom Observation* (2nd edition), London: Routledge.

Wragg, E.C. and Partington, J.A. (1995) *The School Governors' Handbook* (3rd edition), London: Routledge.

Wragg, E.C., Wikeley, F.J., Wragg, C.M. and Haynes, G.S. (1996) *Teacher Appraisal Observed*, London: Routledge.

Index